T0294656

DONALD SELDIN

DONALD SELDIN

THE MAESTRO OF MEDICINE

Raymond S. Greenberg

The University of Texas Health Press

Permission has been granted to reprint from *The Collected Works of W. B. Yeats,
Volume I: The Poems, Revised* by W. B. Yeats, edited by Richard J. Finneran. Reprinted
with the permission of Scribner, a division of Simon & Schuster, Inc. All rights
reserved. "The Young Man's Song" and "Vacillation," copyright © 1933 by The
Macmillan Company. Copyright renewed 1961 by Bertha Georgie Yeats. "Politics,"
"Under Ben Bulben," "An Acre of Grass," and "Man and the Echo," copyright 1940
by Georgie Yeats, renewed 1968 by Bertha Georgie Yeats, Michael Butler Yeats, and
Anne Yeats.

Requests for permission to reproduce material from this work should be sent to:
    Permissions
    University of Texas Press
    P.O. Box 7819
    Austin, TX 78713-7819
    utpress.utexas.edu/rp-form

♾ The paper used in this book meets the minimum requirements of ANSI/NISO
Z39.48-1992 (R1997) (Permanence of Paper).

Library of Congress Cataloging-in-Publication Data

Names: Greenberg, Raymond S., author. Title: Donald Seldin : the maestro of
medicine / Raymond S. Greenberg.
Description: First edition. | Austin : University of Texas Health Press, 2020. | Includes
bibliographical references and index.
Identifiers: LCCN 2019052087 (print) | LCCN 2019052088 (ebook)
    ISBN 978-1-4773-2075-4 (cloth)
    ISBN 978-1-4773-2076-1 (library ebook)
    ISBN 978-1-4773-2077-8 (nonlibrary ebook)
Subjects: LCSH: Seldin, Donald W., 1920-2018. | Medical teaching personnel—
Biography. | Internists—Biography. | University of Texas Southwestern Medical
Center at Dallas—History.
Classification: LCC R154.S45 G74 2020 (print) | LCC R154.S45 (ebook) | DDC
610.7306/9092 [B]—dc23
LC record available at https://lccn.loc.gov/2019052087
LC ebook record available at https://lccn.loc.gov/2019052088

doi:10.7560/320754

Dr. Seldin was a true maestro in the way he taught
clinical medicine.

—J. L. Goldstein and M. Brown, "Acceptance of the
Kober Medal," *Journal of Clinical Investigation*
110 (2002): S11–S13.

CONTENTS

ACKNOWLEDGMENTS

This project started out innocently enough with a telephone call from my colleague Dan Podolsky, president of the University of Texas South-western Medical Center. In answering the call, I assumed that he was reaching out to discuss some pressing academic or operational issue on campus. Little did I suspect that he was about to ask me to become involved in writing the life story of Donald Seldin. President Podolsky knew of my interest in medical history, and he was being charitable in thinking that I might be able to tackle a subject as complex as the iconic Dr. Seldin. I asked him for a little time to think it over.

My initial reaction was that I was not the right person to tell this story. With scores of devoted former trainees, colleagues, and friends who knew Donald Seldin for decades, it seemed logical to approach one of them to produce a biography. My personal contact with Dr. Seldin was limited and paled in comparison to the larger-than-life accounts of others. Preparing to give President Podolsky a polite but firm refusal, it began to dawn on me that there might be some merit in selecting an author who was not a Seldin disciple. Without the taint of years of interaction, either positive or negative, an outsider could try to paint a composite, and hopefully balanced, picture of Seldin from the memories of others. At least, that was my goal—others will have to judge whether it was achieved.

The research for this book was conducted primarily through private interviews with about forty individuals, including former students, resident physicians, and fellows, as well as faculty members and professional associates. Virtually everyone I approached graciously accepted the invitation to participate, and all interviewees were generous with their time and their candor. The circle of respondents grew larger as participants recommended others to include, and it became clear that the book would never get written if the interviews continued without limit. For those who shared their recollections with me, words cannot adequately express my appreciation. For those whom I did not get a chance to interview, please forgive any unintended slight.

One of the most important contributors to this book was Donald Seldin's widow, Ellen. A very strong and talented woman, she is deeply committed to ensuring that her late husband's remarkable life is portrayed accurately. She opened up her home and her life to me, providing me with memorabilia from Seldin's youth, family photographs, contacts, and memories. I cannot thank her enough for her confidence in me to try to put into words the story of such an amazing man. Similarly, Donald Seldin's former trainee and close personal friend David Hillis was kind enough to share with me and the readers photographs from his travels with Seldin.

Many colleagues at the University of Texas Southwestern Medical Center were helpful in undertaking this project. In addition to President Podolsky, Executive Vice President for Business Affairs Arnim Dontes was instrumental in the negotiations with the University of Texas Press. Vice Provost and Senior Associate Dean for Education Charles Ginsburg helped to schedule interviews and ensure access to archival material. Chuck's warm sense of humor and ability to get things done were immensely helpful. University archivist Chianta Dorsey did yeoman's work organizing Dr. Seldin's files and coordinating my access to them.

One of the surprising discoveries during this project related to Seldin's expert testimony before a military tribunal for a Nazi physician accused of atrocities. Over the following decades Seldin told and retold this story on many occasions. It was only late in his life that he encouraged his friend and fellow nephrologist Michael Emmett to locate the transcripts from the trial. Emmett was kind enough to share these files with me, providing an unexpected twist on the story about which Seldin apparently was unaware.

At the University of Texas Press, director David Hamrick is a tireless advocate for publishing in the health sciences, supporting this and other projects. UTP managing editor Robert Kimzey guided me throughout the development of this book and was a helpful adviser. In addition, once again, Jon Howard has proven to be a thorough and wise editor and I am grateful for his efforts.

At the University of Texas System, thanks go to Chancellors William McRaven and J. B. Milliken, as well as the Board of Regents for supporting my time to pursue scholarly interests. Trisha Melonçon ensured that all interview transcripts were accurate and coherent. She also scheduled those interviews, maintained digital files of images, and kept me organized. When the project seemed overwhelming, Trisha was a calming and patient friend and colleague.

Finally, I thank my wife, Leah, who has goodheartedly endured many absences while I worked on the manuscript. Her support and encouragement throughout more than three decades of married life are beyond measure.

Raymond S. Greenberg, MD, PhD
Sarasota, Florida

DONALD SELDIN

CHAPTER 1

WELCOME TO BIG D

On a cold January 8, 1951, Donald Wayne Seldin pulled his hulking Kaiser automobile to a stop at the corner of Maple and Oak Lawn Avenues in Dallas, Texas. The thirty-year-old Seldin was tall, lean, and handsome. Like many of his fellow World War II veterans, he was coming to Dallas for a new job opportunity. Unlike the other newcomers, however, Seldin had left a faculty position at an Ivy League university to build a program at a startup medical school. Accompanying Seldin were his wife, Muriel, and their toddler daughter, Leslie.

The city that greeted Seldin was enjoying an economic boom, belying its humble origins on the banks of the Trinity River a century earlier. Dallas was formally incorporated as a city in 1856, and the census four years later identified fewer than seven hundred residents, a mix of European immigrants and enslaved African Americans. In 1861, its citizens voted to secede from the Union, and many residents provided money and supplies to the Confederate army. Remote from the fighting of the Civil War, Dallas escaped the devastation many other Southern cities endured. During postwar Reconstruction, the prosperity of Dallas attracted many freed former slaves, stoking fears and hostility within the white community—a legacy that would last for much of the following century. Civic leaders were not blind to the racial tensions but were more focused on building economic power in Dallas. They managed to convince the Houston and Central Texas Railroad, and then a year later the Texas and Pacific Railroad, to run tracks through the city, making Dallas the key intersection of north-south and east-west railway lines in Texas.

With the completion of the railroad interchange in 1872, the population of Dallas more than doubled within just six months. The city grew as a transportation hub and as a center for trade in cotton, grain, and livestock. In 1890, it was the largest city in Texas, although it would be overtaken at the turn of the century by San Antonio; Houston became the most populous city in 1930. A merchant class arose in the early twentieth century, with stores such as the one founded by Herbert Marcus and his brother-in-law, Abraham Lincoln Neiman, catering to an increasingly fashion-conscious community. Dallas was on the map, but it was still considered part of the Wild West by elites on the East Coast. In 1914, the Federal Reserve Bank surprised the financial world by placing a regional bank in Dallas instead of Pittsburgh or Cincinnati, the presumed leading contenders. By the time of the Great Depression, Dallas was the principal banking center of the Southwest.

The discovery of oil, first in East Texas and later in West Texas, was a boon to the state's economy. While Houston became the refining and shipping epicenter of the oil industry, Dallas leveraged its banking strength to serve as the financial engine for oil companies, including what would later become Phillips Petroleum. Over the first three decades of the twentieth century, the population of Dallas quintupled to more than a quarter-million people.

The onset of World War II brought new manufacturing demands to Dallas. Between 1942 and 1945, the North American Aviation plant in Dallas produced 18,000 aircraft, including P-51 Mustang fighters, T-6 Texan trainers, and B-24 Liberator bombers. In 1942, the Ford Motor plant was converted from civilian to military production, rolling out Jeeps and trucks for the Armed Services. Love Field, a military training site built during World War I and later converted to a commercial airline hub (now operating as Dallas Love Field), was reestablished as a US Army Air Forces training base and the largest Air Transport Command base during World War II.

Through all of these changes, Dallas, popularly known as the "Big D," had maintained a certain swagger. When contrasting Dallas to its neighbor thirty miles west, the famous writer and humorist Will Rogers declared: "Fort Worth is where the West begins, and Dallas is where the East peters out." The promoters of Dallas had their eyes constantly on the cosmopolitan cities of the East Coast. For example, from the launch of the original Neiman Marcus flagship store in downtown Dallas in September 1907, the owners sought to rival the best shops on Fifth Avenue in New York. In addition, Dallas leaders wanted the city to be at the vanguard of emerging industries and technologies. This sentiment was captured at the Texas Centennial Exposition of 1936, where the banker (and later mayor) R. L. "Uncle Bob" Thornton pronounced of the host city: "Dallas doesn't give a damn about history; it only cares about the future."[1]

Donald Seldin arrived in Dallas at the beginning of 1951 equally focused on the future. The Brooklyn native had resigned his faculty position at one of the most prestigious medical schools in the country—Yale University—to join a fledgling institution—the Southwestern Medical School of the University of Texas, now known as UT Southwestern. The question immediately arises as to why a rising star at one of the most venerable medical schools in the country would want to start all over again at an unknown school in a medical wasteland.

For Seldin, the answer was quite straightforward: "Opportunities to have your own academic unit didn't come around all that often, especially in those days. After all, there weren't that many academically oriented medical schools in the country at that time." Seldin conceded that "the thing in Dallas was one of the more minor developments going on [in] the country. But I thought that it might be exciting." In the final analysis, he decided that "I couldn't and shouldn't turn down an opportunity to build something on my own. Besides, I was young and I didn't have to be in Dallas forever."[2]

Despite the exhausting automobile trip from New Haven, Connecticut, Seldin was anxious to see the campus. After searching in vain, he pulled into a gas station at the intersection of Maple and Oak Lawn Avenues. The attendant, likely unimpressed by the disoriented Yankee, pointed in the general direction of a railroad crossing down the road.

Seldin got back into his car and drove to the location indicated. After scouting out the area and seeing nothing that looked to him remotely like a medical school, Seldin assumed that he had misunderstood the Texan's directions and returned to the gas station. After reporting to the attendant that all he had seen were shacks and a tumbledown red-brick building with garbage strewn across the entrance, the attendant smiled and replied: "That's it. That's the medical school."[3]

Seldin swallowed hard and wondered how he could have been so naive as to accept a job offer sight unseen. He had never misjudged a situation so badly before. How could a city approaching a half-million residents, and with evident prosperity, have such a poor excuse for a medical school?

Seldin's knowledge of medical schools was based primarily on his experience at Yale as a student, resident physician, and faculty member. The heart of Yale's medical school was Sterling Hall. That palatial Renaissance Revival building featured imposing wings meeting at a central rotunda. In addition to housing an amphitheater and laboratories for five basic science departments, Sterling Hall was home to a vast medical library with more than 12,000 volumes. Directly across the street was the teaching hospital, New Haven Hospital. With five hundred beds, including a pavilion for private patients, as well as large wards for public patients, New Haven Hospital was a state-of-the-art facility with separate dedicated wings for surgery and obstetrics and pediatrics.

In contrast, the Southwestern Medical School was largely a series of prefabricated plywood barracks left moldering away since World War II. As described by John Chapman, who joined the faculty around this time, "since the buildings had no formal foundation, they leaned rather informally away from the prevailing winds. In one place or another one could see the rich earth of Texas between walls and floor. When the wind was strong that same rich earth made its way into the buildings."[4] Already well beyond their life expectancy, these huts were particularly dreadful on a cold winter day such as this one. Frigid air would flow freely through the numerous holes in the flooring and around the windows, many of which would not close tightly. The plumbing lines ran unprotected and unburied, so when the mercury fell, experiments often were cancelled due to iced pipes. One winter blizzard froze the gross anatomy laboratory, so dissections were postponed for a week while the cadavers thawed. At the other extreme, during the heat of a Dallas summer, the lack of air-conditioning could make the barracks sizzle like a griddle.

"It was a hell of a place," Seldin later recalled.[5] A lesser man would have turned his car around and headed straight back to New Haven. With a keenly developed sense of honor and duty, however, Seldin decided to stay. Perhaps he hoped that his initial impressions would prove inaccurate. Sadly, however, the more he saw of the medical school, the more he appreciated its challenges. Clinical teaching was performed largely by community physicians on a voluntary basis. The medical school's Department of Medicine, for example, had only three full-time faculty members: Charles Burnett, its recently appointed chairman; Thomas Farmer, a neurologist; and Seldin. Medical students were introduced to patient care in the adjacent busy public hospital, Parkland.

The original hospital was built on seventeen acres of parkland (thus the name), and by the time Seldin arrived in Dallas the hospital was nearly four decades old and showing its age. The first hospital in Texas to be built of brick, it was designed in the Colonial Revival style, with a stately two-story porch supported by limestone columns. Behind the gracious façade were four wings crammed with patients housed in large wards. Chock-full and outmoded, the hospital was in desperate need of replacement. According to Seldin, the medical students, who spent countless hours at Parkland Hospital, referred to it disparagingly as "the black hole of Calcutta."[6]

Jean Wilson, one of the early Southwestern medical students and later a distinguished faculty member, described the four large wings at Parkland Hospital, which were segregated by race and gender: "There were black men, white men, black women, and white women. There were a hundred patients or so in one ward. They varied from very sick people to people who were less sick and less debilitated." Wilson recalled how the patients supported each other: "The ones that were relatively healthy helped nurse the sick ones. Friendships broke out and people became very close to one another on those wards."[7]

The problems at the Southwestern Medical School were not confined to its facilities. There were tensions existing among the faculty and between the faculty and community physicians. The local private

practitioners were concerned that the faculty might compete for paying patients. Physicians in private practice also were hesitant to make
referrals to the faculty, fearing their patients might not be returned to
their practices after a consultation.

The early struggles of the Southwestern Medical School can be
traced, at least in part, to events in Dallas long before the school was created. At the turn of the twentieth century, the practice of medicine in
Dallas could be described as little more than frontier quackery. No medical degree was required to care for patients—one simply needed to pay
a $15 fee, appear before a board, and answer some questions correctly.
Those who had a diploma could register with the health officer, receive
some instruction on ethics, and then boast the title "specialist."[8] Given
this absence of educational standards, the knowledge base of most practitioners was woefully inadequate. For example, germ theory—developed decades earlier by Louis Pasteur in France and refined by Robert
Koch in Germany—remained contentious within the Dallas medical
community in 1900.[9] Not surprisingly, the quality of patient care was
abysmal. For example, hand-washing was not performed before surgery
or delivery, and operative mortality rates were frighteningly high.[10]

Around this time Dallas had almost 43,000 residents and 146
physicians. In August 1900, when a medical school was first proposed,
a meeting with local physicians revealed that only fifteen of fifty-five
attendees favored the idea. Despite such resistance, the University of
Dallas Medical Department opened three months later.[11] This academic-
sounding name was merely window dressing, as there was no parent
institution named the "University of Dallas." Nevertheless, within
two years, the first nineteen graduates completed their studies.[12] The
school's dean, Edward H. Cary, was concerned about the viability of a
freestanding school, so in 1903 a true university linkage was brokered
with Baylor University, a Baptist-affiliated institution whose main
campus was located nearly a hundred miles south in Waco. Although
the Baylor affiliation brought academic credibility, it did little else, as
the university made no financial commitments to the medical school
bearing its name.[13]

A handful of proprietary medical schools popped up in Dallas
around the same time, most of which died in their infancy. ("Proprietary" medical schools were for-profit diploma mills that were of lower

quality compared to those affiliated with a university.) By the end of World War I, the two other surviving medical schools were merged into Baylor, meaning only a single medical school remained in Dallas. Tensions with the local medical establishment flared again in 1920 when the former Baptist Memorial Sanitarium was renamed Baylor Hospital and its medical staff was limited to medical school faculty members. Virtually overnight, three-quarters of the hospital's physicians lost their admitting privileges. Even with a monopoly on Baylor Hospital, most of the teaching of medical students occurred at the public hospital (Parkland).[14]

In 1939, the former dean of the Baylor University College of Medicine, Edward Cary, organized the Southwestern Medical Foundation to provide financial support for medical research in Dallas. Cary was disappointed both in the paucity of research conducted by the Baylor faculty and the meager resources that the parent university provided to support the medical school. As a former president of the American Medical Association, Cary had firsthand knowledge of the nation's leading academic medical centers. He understood that building a top-tier academic medical school would require significant investment. Cary referred to Dallas as a "medical wilderness," and he enlisted a local patron named Karl Hoblitzelle, a wealthy theater owner, banker, and philanthropist, as a partner in creating a vision for a major medical center in Dallas. Under the leadership of Cary and Hoblitzelle, the Southwestern Medical Foundation proposed relocating the Baylor University College of Medicine to a thirty-five-acre tract of land that included Parkland Hospital. (In 1954, the hospital moved to 5201 Harry Hines Boulevard and the name was changed to Parkland Memorial Hospital to honor all those who died in defense of our nation.) At that site, they envisioned the development of a grand medical center complex. The foundation proposed that Baylor would be responsible for academic matters and that the foundation itself would control facilities in addition to the medical staff appointments at Parkland Hospital, which would become the designated teaching hospital. The medical school dean at that time, Walter Moursund, and the parent university in Waco resisted the move, fearing that the foundation's motives were to wrest away control from Baylor.[15]

This tug-of-war ended abruptly in 1943, when the MD Anderson

Foundation invited the financially strapped Baylor University College of Medicine to join the newly created Texas Medical Center in Houston. The inducement to relocate included a commitment of land plus a generous $1 million gift to build facilities and a similar amount of money to support research. The proposal was accepted by Baylor University on May 7, 1943, and a month later moving vans began delivering books, journals, and equipment to the new temporary home in Houston. The transfer occurred while many of the faculty were serving in Baylor's World War II medical unit—the 56th Evacuation Hospital —initially in North Africa and then in Italy.[16]

In the Lone Star State, Baylor's sudden retreat to Houston left Dallas without a medical school. Viewing medical education as an essential ingredient in the vitality of a great city, Cary, Hoblitzelle, and a group of Dallas business executives raised $1.7 million of private funding to establish a new school—the Southwestern Medical College. Some of Baylor University College of Medicine's full-time faculty members and many of the volunteer faculty accepted appointments at this new startup school, and they were joined by most of the student body who elected to remain in Dallas.[17] Less than half a year after Baylor's departure from Dallas, Southwestern Medical College was accredited as the sixty-eighth medical school in the United States. No doubt, the skids were greased for a quick accreditation because of Cary's strong connections at the American Medical Association.[18]

The military, in need of medical personnel, was more than happy to assist in constructing the new school. The United States Army's Eighth Service Command, headquartered in Dallas, assembled prefabricated wooden barracks to house classes and laboratories in nearly 3,000 square feet of temporary facilities.[19] With an annual operating budget of less than $300,000, the school opened its makeshift doors with eighteen full-time faculty members and two hundred students.[20] A third of the operating budget was provided by a ten-year commitment from the local Chamber of Commerce and a private nonprofit group of community leaders working as the Dallas Citizen's Council.[21] The first class to graduate, on March 20, 1944, had sixty-one students (fifty-nine males and two females), including thirty-eight Army and fifteen Navy officers.[22]

When World War II ended, so did the military's need for a pipeline of physicians, and the medical school partnership dissolved. In the absence of federal support, Southwestern Medical College needed to find another patron. Fortuitously, the University of Texas—which operated a single medical school in Galveston—was interested in opening a second school. The Southwestern Medical Foundation proposed a deal that was too good for the university to refuse: the foundation would donate the college's faculty, equipment, library, and funds if the new state school was established in Dallas. In 1949, the partnership was consummated, and the six-year-old private school was renamed as the Southwestern Medical School of the University of Texas.

By the time that Seldin arrived two years later, there was little evidence of any state support at the struggling school. Classes and laboratories continued to be taught in the decaying temporary facilities that the military had constructed eight years earlier. There were few full-time faculty members. At Yale, Seldin had felt crowded out by senior colleagues, but in Dallas he was housed in a department with only three faculty members. Despite its diminutive size, UT Southwestern was divided into camps already, and conflicting lines of authority fed their disputes. For example, Carl Moyer, chairman of surgery and a distinguished educator and researcher, was not the head of the surgical service at Parkland Hospital. Without control of the clinical service, Moyer found this situation untenable. Not long after Seldin arrived, Moyer left for St. Louis, where he was appointed chairman of the Department of Surgery at the prestigious Washington University School of Medicine.[23]

The founding chairman of the Southwestern Medical School's Department of Obstetrics and Gynecology, William Mengert, headed north to assume the chairmanship at the University of Illinois Medical Center in Chicago. The chairman of pediatrics in Dallas, Gilbert Forbes, returned to his alma mater, the University of Rochester School of Medicine and Dentistry, as a faculty member. The loss of these key leaders led medical school accreditors to put the school on probation.[24]

Although the exodus of senior colleagues from other departments was alarming, Seldin was really unprepared for an unexpected departure closer to home. In April 1951, three months after his arrival in

Dallas, Seldin went to Charles Burnett's office to share with him some exciting news. An abstract, based on research he conducted at Yale, was accepted for presentation the following month at the major academic medicine meeting held each year in Atlantic City. To have a paper presented at the American Society for Clinical Investigation meeting was a high honor. The thrill of that moment—a singular achievement for a young faculty member—did not last long. After congratulating Seldin on his selection, Burnett mentioned that he was offered the position of chairman of medicine at the University of North Carolina. In June 1951, only eight months after he himself had arrived in Dallas, Burnett departed for Tobacco Road. Adding insult to injury, Burnett took the only other full-time faculty member in the department, Thomas Farmer, with him to Chapel Hill. Burnett offered Seldin a job in North Carolina as well, but the thought of beginning again at another startup operation was not appealing. Besides, if Seldin wanted to move, he had a much more prestigious offer on the table from Harvard.[25]

Seldin declined both the North Carolina and Boston offers, and when he was asked to assume Burnett's former position in Dallas he rejected that idea as well. He could see no reason to become captain of a sinking ship. The safest course, in his opinion, was to return to Yale, where his mentor, John Peters, wanted Seldin to rejoin his all-star team of faculty at the nationally prominent metabolic unit (what Peters referred to as the "Chemical Division"). With the blessing of Paul Beeson, chairman of medicine at Yale, Peters sent Seldin a letter of offer, which Seldin accepted. Muriel and their daughter quickly returned to New Haven to search for an apartment. Now living as a bachelor, Seldin moved out of the family's apartment in Dallas and roomed with a friend and colleague from the private practice community named Sam Shelburne.[26]

While Seldin bided his time in Dallas, some unexpected events transpired at the Southwestern Medical School. After many years of debate, Dallas County, which owned Parkland Hospital, voted to issue bonds to build a badly needed replacement facility. Similarly, the state of Texas finally authorized funding to construct the inaugural permanent building for the medical school. Legend has it that Texas governor Allan Shivers was convinced to support the new facility following a hazardous visit to campus. A faculty member described the scene:

"Students, fellows and faculty were lined up in the shacks to welcome the governor and his entourage. The governor walked in through the back of one of the long shacks and as he got half-way down the edifice, a window simply dropped out of the wall. The governor continued walking and another hundred feet later, one of his feet went through the floor. We knew from the look on his face that he was going to help us."[27]

The future also looked brighter because a new politically savvy dean, George Aagaard, was recruited from the University of Minnesota. Only thirty-nine years old at the time, the prematurely balding Aagaard had a calm demeanor and the diplomatic skills needed to navigate the minefields of the Texas legislature and the UT System. With a trusted leader in place, plus the commitments for a new hospital and academic facilities, it appeared that the Southwestern Medical School-might be turning a corner.[28]

Aagaard approached Seldin again about assuming the position of chairman of medicine. Seldin faced a legitimate decision for the first time since arriving in Dallas: return as planned to the safety and security of Yale, or stay in Dallas and help shape the emerging school quite literally from the ground up. Not only did the two medical schools stand in stark contrast; the amenities of the two host cities could not have been more disparate. Michael Brown, who also hailed from the Northeast and was recruited by Seldin to Dallas two decades later, used the local restaurant scene as a barometer of the cultural milieu of Dallas: "The amazing thing is he [Seldin] came to a city [where] . . . you couldn't buy wine or liquor in restaurants, so there was no restaurant business. . . . We tried to find a Chinese restaurant . . . there wasn't a Chinese person in the place. And there were no Italian restaurants. How can you ever live in a city without an Italian restaurant? It was all barbecue."[29]

Seldin, a confirmed gourmand, was not dissuaded by the paucity of fine dining in Dallas. He saw his wine goblet as half-full rather than as half-empty; he decided to stay and try to fill it to the brim. Having placed his bet on Dallas, Seldin had to make a difficult telephone call to his wife and tell her not to sign a pending apartment lease in New Haven.

Muriel, also a native of New York, had attended the prestigious Julliard School, where she studied the piano. At Yale, she had befriended members of the Music School faculty. Paul Hindemith, the renowned German composer, was on the Yale faculty, and he attracted a steady stream of talented students to New Haven. So Muriel, with her striking good looks and musical talents to match, had her heart set on returning to New Haven. Inseparable since they first met in college and now married for eight years, the Seldins had built a strong partnership. Although the decision to remain in Dallas was not her preferred option, Muriel supported her husband's decision to stay there.

With Muriel now on board, Donald Seldin was prepared for the biggest challenge of his thirty-one years. He had overcome long odds before. It was time to draw on the strengths that had raised him from the mean streets of New York during the Great Depression to the top of his class at the Yale School of Medicine. If his was not exactly a rags-to-riches story, it was nevertheless a most remarkable journey.

CHAPTER 2

THE NICKEL EMPIRE

Coney Island, which during the early 1900s was the exclusive playground of the rich and famous, became accessible to all comers in 1920 when a new subway line connected it to New York City. Anyone possessing the five-cent transit fare could make the trip, and almost instantly Coney Island became known as the "Nickel Empire." On Sundays during the summer more than a million city-dwellers would flock to the beach, located on the southern underbelly of Brooklyn. This mass of humanity, swelled by the ranks of recent immigrant laborers, descended on the beach when it opened to the public in 1921. Packed like sardines on the nearly sixty acres of sand, or strolling along the recently completed eighty-foot-wide wooden boardwalk, these visitors, many of whom lived in crowded tenement buildings, soaked up the sun and entertainment.[1]

Typically, lunch was a ten-cent hot dog from Feltman's, while those looking for a bargain enjoyed half-priced frankfurters from the upstart competitor Nathan's. When the nourished crowd tired of the beach, there were many other diversions where they could spend their spare change. Just inland from the boardwalk and running parallel to it was the raucous and risqué four-block area known as the Bowery. The entertainments there catered to every taste, although some justifiably considered the steamy offerings to be completely devoid of any taste whatsoever. The central corridor was lined cheek-by-jowl with freak shows, gambling halls, penny arcades, brothels, saloons, and food vendors, all competing for attention. It is small wonder that Coney Island earned its richly deserved reputation as "Sodom by the Sea."[2]

Into this chaotic mix, Donald Wayne Seldin was born on October 24, 1920, just six months after the subway connected Coney Island to the rest of New York City. His father, Abraham, was a native of Bessarabia, a region in Eastern Europe ruled in various eras by the Ottomans, the Russians, and the Romanians. When he immigrated to the United States, Abraham already had graduated from high school. He was bookish by nature and was conversant in Latin, Greek, and Hebrew. In search of a profession in his new homeland, Abraham pursued a dental degree from a proprietary school and, upon graduation, opened a successful dental practice.[3]

Donald's mother, the former Laura Ueberal, was a native of Vienna and a teenage bride when she married Abraham in 1917. Laura was intelligent, but as was the custom for women of that period, she had no formal education beyond high school. Laura's focus was directed at raising Donald and his sister, Marion, who was five years younger.[4]

The family's fortunes, like so many others, took a devastatingly negative turn during the Great Depression. Many of Abraham's patients could no longer afford dental care, and as a result his practice fell on hard times. To make matters worse, Abraham had invested in financial instruments that collapsed when the stock market crashed. Suddenly, he had lost both his savings and a substantial part of his income. With so little to show for his efforts, Abraham questioned his decision to pursue a profession. He felt that he had bought into an illusory American dream, and his unhappiness spilled over into the family's domestic life. As time went on, and Abraham's spirits sank further and further, marital discord ensued. Although Donald was not close to his father, he admired Abraham's intellectual interests, ranging from great literature to societal concerns.[5]

This is not to say that young Donald complied with his father's wishes. For example, Abraham wanted Donald to learn Hebrew. This desire was based more on the perceived social, intellectual, and cultural value of Hebrew school than on any deep spiritual or religious motivation. His son, however, boycotted classes and distanced himself from any religious life. When Abraham invested his limited funds in violin lessons for his son, Donald again demonstrated his rebellious streak by refusing to practice. The younger Seldin was less interested in playing a string instrument than in the manly pursuits of football, baseball, and street life.[6]

Donald attended public schools—first elementary school at PS 188, followed by Seth Low Junior High School. He was bright enough to skip several grades and then matriculated at Brooklyn's famed James Madison High School. Students entered the front door of the six-story red-brick building under an inscribed quote from its namesake: "EDUCATION IS THE TRUE FOUNDATION OF CIVIL LIBERTY." Through that doorway came many bright young students who went on to great achievements. US senators Bernie Sanders (Vermont) and Chuck Schumer (New York) and the former US senator Norman Coleman (Minnesota) attended James Madison, as did US Supreme Court associate justice Ruth Bader Ginsburg. Its alumni also included multiple future Nobel Prize winners, placing it among the leading American high schools producing laureates. Of his own scholastic performance at James Madison, Seldin later confided that he became "moderately interested in academic work. I wouldn't say that I was distinguished. I graduated fairly high in the class, but I was by no means an outstanding student. I graduated very young, in 1936, when [I was] 16 years old."[7]

Nevertheless, the years spent at James Madison made an indelible impression on Donald Seldin. Decades later, he would regale a fellow James Madison alumnus and UT Southwestern trainee, Neil Kurtzman, with an impromptu and spirited, if not entirely on-key, performance of a school song, such as "Madison Forever," featuring the lines:

> O Madison, James Madison
> Early president of fame.
> Our school is highly honor'd
> With his great illustrious name.[8]

Another school song was "Going Back to Madison," which included such prosaic lyrics as:

> There's a place they think of, longing to be there.
> It's the one and only place that makes us gush,
> Situated and celebrated in old Flatbush.[9]

Yet a third Madison school song was "The King's Highway":

> Hey boy, what is all the noise about?
> Hear the lads and lasses gaily shout.
> Why are all the neighbors turning out
> Along the King's Highway?
> Why sir, surely if you had a son,
> Or daughter who had school begun,
> You would know the great James Madison High School
> On the King's Highway.[10]

As Kurtzman recounted: "I had forgotten every one of them, but he remembered them all. Not only did he sing them full voice in the middle of a conference, but they were delivered with the complete Brooklyn accent needed for their true actualization."[11]

While at James Madison, Seldin became immersed in subjects as diverse as political science and philosophy. He was attracted especially to the Romantic poets such as Keats, Shelly, Byron, and Wordsworth. Seldin's passion for poetry may have been born during his adolescence, but it remained a constant companion throughout his adult life. Seldin's absorption in poetry and other intellectual pursuits did not arise from the classroom or from the coaxing of any teacher but rather as part of a personal journey of self-discovery.

Donald became an avid reader, and he was a regular patron of the New York Public Library on Fifth Avenue, with its seventy-five glorious miles of bookshelves. Invariably, he would gravitate to the third floor Beaux-Arts reading room. There he could luxuriate over books in the soft glow of the light that filtered through the massive windows, enhanced by the eighteen elegant chandeliers that hung from the fresco-adorned ceiling.

For Seldin, the library was a tranquil retreat from the family tensions that continued to fester at home. In the serenity of the library, Seldin read widely and deeply, always at a measured pace and accompanied by extensive note-taking. One of the works that grabbed Seldin's attention was the magnum opus by the Harvard art historian and medievalist Arthur Kingsley Porter titled *Romanesque Sculpture of the Pilgrimage Roads.*[12] Nine of the ten volumes of this work were filled with

Porter's photographs of eleventh- and twelfth-century art that adorned the Christian pilgrimage routes in France, Italy, and Spain. Motivated by the aesthetic and not the spiritual elements of these journeys, Seldin promised himself that he would follow in Porter's footsteps one day on these ancient paths. Given his modest financial means, such a trip was more fantasy than reality. Within a decade, however, Seldin would fulfill his dream of traveling the Camino de Santiago leading to the legendary site of the remains of the apostle Saint James. More than a half-century later, he would repeat this pilgrimage still inspired by the readings of his youth.[13]

When he was not daydreaming in the public library about medieval sculpture, Donald could be found among the beautiful art books at the Weyhe Book Store and Gallery at 794 Lexington Avenue. The Weyhe (pronounced "VAY-ya") store was an architectural gem decorated with colorful handmade tiles. Its eclectic book collection occupied the first floor and the art gallery was housed on the second floor, featuring works by such luminaries as the mobile designer Alexander Calder, the writer and illustrator Rockwell Kent (who designed the ironwork for the doorway), and the Mexican muralist Diego Rivera.[14]

Between schoolwork, reading, and art appreciation, Donald managed to join the James Madison track team, where he ran the 100-yard dash. The speedster also played on the school's championship basketball team. In what little spare time that was left, Donald was expected to find after-school employment. This was no easy task during the Depression, when every job vacancy attracted hundreds of applicants. Nevertheless, Seldin worked as a delivery boy and briefly sold magazines door-to-door. He also applied for a position as a bellhop at the famous Grossinger's Resort Hotel in the Catskill Mountains. He was selected to work there for a couple of months during the summer without the benefit of a salary, but he made up for it in tips.[15]

At Grossinger's, Seldin also served as a ballroom dancing instructor at the resort's Arthur Murray studio. Graceful and light on his feet into his later years, Seldin enjoyed a good spin around the dance floor. One former trainee, John Warner, who later went on to become executive vice president for Health System Affairs at UT Southwestern, recalled Seldin displaying his dancing skills at departmental holiday parties: "He'd dance with all the people that were good dancers. He didn't dance with bad dancers. Just like everything else, it had to be worth his time."[16]

A jack-of-all-trades, Seldin also was one of the lucky few applicants selected to be an usher at New York's Paramount Theatre at 43rd Street and Broadway. With nearly four thousand seats, the Paramount was a massive entertainment palace that alternated movies with live performances, featuring headliners such as the heartthrob crooner Frank Sinatra and the singer Martha Raye, as well as comedians like Milton Berle and Eddie Cantor. One of the ushers' principal responsibilities at the Paramount was to encourage patrons to sit in the balcony, thus freeing up desirable seats in the orchestra section for more customers. The fifteen-year-old Seldin was star-struck by the performers, but more important, he brought home a much-needed paycheck. Unfortunately, the dynamic at home deteriorated further, leading to his parents' separation. Abraham moved out of the family home and secured an office and small apartment for himself. Laura and the two children remained together, with Seldin visiting his father's apartment about once a week.[17]

When it came to college admissions, Seldin chose to enroll at New York University (NYU), where he had obtained a scholarship and could save money by living at home. NYU had two campuses: the original location, established a century earlier, at Washington Square in crowded Lower Manhattan; and a second, spacious, architecturally inspired venue at University Heights in the Bronx. The downtown undergraduate program, which Seldin attended, was referred to as Washington Square College and primarily served subway commuters like himself. Students were admitted based on academic performance without regard to family background or finances, so when Seldin arrived most of the seven thousand students were the bright, aspiring children of poor immigrants. Surrounded by a very active arts community, Washington Square College could draw faculty from among the local literati. One such instructor was Thomas Wolfe, who taught there between 1924 and 1930 while he was working on his first novel, *Look Homeward, Angel.*

Wolfe was no longer at Washington Square College when Seldin arrived, but there were stimulating English classes on campus nevertheless. Seldin composed and saved many essays from his English courses, and these writings give some insight into the teenager's mature command of language and critical thinking. Insightful and presented in beautiful penmanship, these assignments always earned top marks. One such essay compared two literary accounts of the death of King Arthur and was graded as "a grand paper" by the professor. Seldin's analysis of John Steinbeck's *Of Mice and Men*, less than two months after the play opened on Broadway, earned the following comment: "You deal masterfully with the meaning and significance of the plot."

Seldin and his fellow students at Washington Square College studied in an art-infused environment. The philanthropist A. E. Gallatin, a descendant of a founder of NYU, established the Museum of Living Art at the NYU Main Building in 1927. This was the first museum in the United States to exhibit works by painters such as Picasso, Miró, and Mondrian, as well as many American abstract artists. Gallatin wanted fresh and individual work by living artists to be accessible to the students. Even the cafeteria was adorned with priceless works of art.[18] These artists were an inspiration to Seldin, and later in life his office featured a rug with a Miró design, and his personal art collection included Picasso ceramics.

To Donald Seldin, Washington Square College must have seemed a world away from his home in Coney Island. His professors included Sidney Hook, Albert Hufstadter, and James Burnham, who were young, energetic philosophers who would become leading scholars of their generation. In addition to philosophy, Seldin dabbled in subjects as diverse as literature, art history, economics, and political science. Enrolling in these courses did not necessarily imply that he attended them, however. A gifted test-taker, Seldin found that he could study for the exams and maintain an almost perfect grade point average while avoiding the burden of spending his precious time in classrooms. He befriended other students who shared his passions for the arts and humanities. Initially, Seldin fancied himself becoming a poet or a philosopher, but the harsh realities of the Depression squelched those ambitions. Jobs were difficult to obtain, and no employer was going to hire either a poet or a philosopher.[19]

Seldin decided that he needed to change direction and prepare himself for a career in which he could earn a decent living. His father, still reeling from his own financial reversal, thought that the road to success in America was through business rather than the professions. The younger Seldin, continuing to demonstrate his independent streak, ignored his father's advice and decided to pursue medicine instead. Unfortunately, Seldin was poorly prepared to apply to medical school, as he had not bothered to take any of the required science prerequisites in his first three years of college. During his senior year of college, he finally enrolled in biology and chemistry, satisfying the minimal requirements for medical school candidacy.[20]

Seldin applied to twenty or thirty medical schools and was admitted to NYU. While he was awaiting responses, he could not afford to pass up his assured seat in the class at NYU. Seldin paid the nonrefundable $50 fee—which was very difficult to spare—only to learn a month later that he was accepted at Yale. For a Jewish student at a time when religious quotas on admission were still in force at many Ivy League medical schools, acceptance at Yale was quite unexpected. Seldin also was placed on the waiting list at Harvard.[21]

Unlike most of his Jewish classmates, including many who would go on to distinguished careers in medicine, Seldin now had options. Should he stick with NYU, where he had already paid a hard-earned deposit, or lose his NYU deposit and accept the scholarship offer from Yale? Having little solid information on the relative merits of the two schools, Seldin made some inquiries and concluded that Yale was the superior choice. So, he parted with his deposit at NYU and headed for Connecticut.[22]

In many ways, arriving at Yale was like being born again for Seldin. He left behind the family tensions that marked life in Brooklyn and immersed himself in the rich intellectual environment that surrounded him in New Haven. He made connections and pursued scholarly and cultural interests across campus.

The academic environment of the medical school was totally different from what he had experienced at Washington Square College. As an undergraduate, the emphasis was placed on repeated examinations—test after test after test. At Yale, however, the focus was on the development of critical thinking skills rather than on rote memorization. A young faculty scientist, Ralph Meader, greeted the thirty-nine new Yale medical students at their orientation. Meader, a neuro-anato-mist, informed Seldin and his classmates that Yale operated on a tuto-rial system. Atypical of medical schools during that era, there were many more faculty members than students, so there was an oppor-tunity to develop close mentoring relationships with the professors.[23]

The disbelieving students were told by Meader that attendance at lectures was optional. Courses did not have required textbooks, although students were expected to read on their own. Even more remarkable, there were no tests during the first two years. Instead, a single, weeklong comprehensive examination was administered at the midpoint of medical school.[24]

For Seldin, the lack of a structured educational program was lib-erating but simultaneously unnerving. As someone who navigated through college by minimizing his class attendance, he felt at home with the laissez-faire attitude toward lectures at Yale. However, Seldin's mastery of the art of regular examinations would not be the ticket to easy success in medical school that it had been in college.

Adapting to the Yale system, Seldin took full advantage of the opportunity to explore topics outside the standard curriculum. He camped out in Sterling Library—built in the style of a European Gothic cathedral—where he could worship the written word. Although Sel-din continued to read widely, he discovered a new fascination with the latest advances in science. For instance, he was captivated by the work of Fritz Lipmann, a biochemist who had escaped from the Nazis just a few years earlier. Lipmann studied how certain chemical bonds served as a vehicle for storing and transferring energy within cells. A dozen years later, Lipmann would share the Nobel Prize in Physiology or Medicine for his subsequent discovery of coenzyme A, which con-tains these high energy bonds. This molecule is one of the key elements involved in the chemical digestion of sugars, proteins, and fatty acids. For Seldin, who had artfully avoided taking even basic biology and chemistry courses until his senior year of college, it was a huge leap to be reading about Lipmann's latest findings just a year or two later. He was awakening to the concept that science could be just as beautiful and captivating as poetry and art.

When not absorbed by the latest biochemical studies, Seldin was intrigued by the work of the Institute of Human Relations on campus.

Founded in 1931, the institute served as an interdisciplinary convening center for scholars from fields as diverse as medicine, psychology,
economics, and law. The brainchild of medical school dean Milton
Winternitz and the university president James Angell, the institute was
designed to tackle cross-cutting issues that could not be addressed adequately within traditional disciplinary boundaries. As a case in point,
Angell said at the institute's dedication: "In a given instance poverty
may be quite as much a medical problem as an economic one, and even
as an enduring social issue it inevitably involves many different factors."[25] Such a perspective was far ahead of its time, but more recently it
has been embraced widely under the rubric of "social determinants of
health." For Seldin, who only a few years earlier had considered philosophy as a possible career, the moral implications of these relationships
were compelling.

At the earliest stage of his Yale education, Donald Seldin was
exposed to the full spectrum of medical thought, from fundamental research on biological processes to societal influences on health.
He also was able to delve more deeply into a specific topic through a
federal government–funded program that allowed him to work for a
faculty member. Even with a scholarship, Seldin needed to earn extra
money to pay living expenses. He was assigned to work with a physiological chemist named Cyril Norman Hugh Long. Long, who would
later serve as dean of the medical school, was known for his work on
the pituitary and adrenal glands. He was preparing a review article on
hormones, and Seldin was assigned to collect and summarize references. The experience was positive because Long was a dedicated and
good-natured supervisor, but he was not a source of great personal
influence for Seldin.[26]

Inspiration would come only after Seldin completed his first
two years, excelled on the comprehensive examination, and began
his clinical rotations. On the medicine service, he encountered the
quintessential physician-scientist: John Punnett Peters. In Peters, Seldin found what he would later describe as "the epitome of a clinical
scholar."[27] By that, Seldin meant that Peters "on the one hand, had
a deep appreciation of medical science; on the other hand, this was
rooted to a meticulous care of patients. The two together turned out to
be a very exciting thing."[28]

For the first time in his life, Seldin encountered a teacher with an intellect, sense of purpose, and drive that could match his own. Until meeting Peters, Seldin had traveled a road of educational discovery that was largely self-directed. Now, he could be guided by someone who was further along on the path to pursuing a virtuous and transcendent life.

CHAPTER 3

PERFECT CHEMISTRY

For a man with so much wisdom to share, John "Jack" Punnett Peters spoke in a voice that was barely audible to the person standing next to him. Nowhere was this phenomenon more evident than during the "Metabolic Rounds" he conducted for more than three decades at New Haven Hospital, the teaching hospital of Yale University. Peters, affectionately known as "Whispering Jack," was surrounded by a gaggle of his trainees and colleagues, all of them leaning in as close as possible to catch his every word. Three times each week and every other Sunday, this tightly knit group weaved its way through the hospital visiting patient after patient. Following each encounter, the team gathered outside the patient's room, where Peters reviewed the clinical information and the pertinent medical literature, then seamlessly shifted into a discussion of the underlying biological abnormalities.[1] His ability to blend compassionate bedside care with the rapidly evolving science of medicine would shape future generations of academic physicians, including Donald Seldin.

When Seldin first encountered Peters in 1942, the professor was fifty-four years old and approaching the zenith of his storied career. He preferred to be addressed as "Jack" because his given name "John" had an unfortunate association with a certain piece of plumbing equipment. Every medical student and resident physician, however,

addressed him with reverence as "Dr. Peters." His red hair had begun
to thin decades earlier, leaving behind a prominent brow that was
marked with deep furrows, most evident in times of either deep concentration or stress. Peters had penetrating eyes and a warm, if tight-
lipped, smile. He was a driven man, and the strain of his rigorous life
was etched on his countenance and thin frame. Peters maintained high
standards, expecting the best efforts from his students and colleagues,
yet always demanding even more of himself.[2] This devotion to work
ethic was a lesson that Donald Seldin took to heart, and it served him
well throughout his own career.

Very much a product of his lineage and upbringing, Peters was born
in Philadelphia on December 4, 1887. The eldest son of the Reverend
John Punnett Peters and his wife, Gabriella Brooke Peters, young Jack
was introduced to international travel and to scholarly pursuits as an
infant. Reverend Peters was a professor of Hebrew at the University
of Pennsylvania when he proposed an archeological expedition to
Nippur, an ancient Mesopotamian city located about a hundred miles
southeast of Baghdad. Nippur was a religious and cultural center with
origins that could be traced back more than six millennia. Beginning
in January 1889, with his family in tow, Reverend Peters led the first
of two expeditions to Nippur sponsored by the university's archeological museum. After a second expedition the following year, Peters left
the university and any further explorations of Nippur, where an array
of cuneiform tablets were unearthed. Subsequent expedition leaders
claimed full credit for these discoveries, leaving Peters with a sense of
betrayal by his former colleagues. Jack was thus exposed at an early age
to the fiercely competitive and occasionally devious nature of scholarly pursuits. The elder Peters's departure from the University of Pennsylvania faculty was precipitated by the death of his own father, who
had been the rector of St. Michael's Protestant Episcopal Church in
Upper Manhattan. Reverend Peters returned to New York to succeed
his father in the pulpit at St. Michael's.

Formal education for young Jack began in 1896 at the nearby
Trinity School. He attended high school at St. John's Military Acad-
emy ten miles east of Syracuse in the little town of Manlius, New
York. Jack graduated at sixteen, winning honors as the "top boy," with

distinction in English and the classics. Following the family tradition, Jack enrolled at Yale University, where he was a gymnast as well as a diver on the swim team. He completed his four years at Yale in 1908, earning a BA degree. He then returned to St. John's, where he taught Latin and English for a year in order to earn enough money to attend medical school.[3]

In 1909, Peters matriculated at the College of Physicians and Surgeons of Columbia University. After graduating in 1913, he undertook two years of training at Presbyterian Hospital. Having distinguished himself there, Peters was selected as a Coolidge Fellow in Clinical Medicine for an additional two years.[4]

In May 1917, with the United States engaged in World War I, Peters was commissioned as a captain in the Army Medical Corps. Shortly after arriving in Europe and not yet thirty years old, he was assigned as chief of medical service for Base Hospital Number 2 in Etrétat, a summer resort town on the northern coast of France. During his year and a half of military service, Peters observed the horrific physical and emotional toll of war—lessons he would remember for the rest of his life. After his discharge as a major in early 1919, Peters returned to New York, where he held several appointments including, most importantly, a year at the Hospital of the Rockefeller Institute.[5]

During his brief tenure at the Rockefeller Institute, Peters met Donald Dexter Van Slyke, the founding chief chemist of this relatively new facility. Known to his friends by his nickname "Van," he was one of the first chemists to apply his knowledge and training to the analysis of patients' blood specimens. He devised an accurate method for measuring carbon dioxide in plasma, as well as oxygen saturation of blood hemoglobin. These tools quickly proved valuable in the diagnosis and management of patients with conditions as diverse as diabetes, kidney diseases, and respiratory illnesses. Partnering with his clinical colleagues, Van Slyke devised procedures for measuring an array of blood constituents, thereby helping to illuminate the underlying biological processes and facilitating improved patient care.[6]

A second relationship at the Rockefeller Institute also proved to be decisive in Peters's career. There, he befriended Francis Gilman Blake, a Harvard-educated physician who was a rising star in the field of infectious diseases. At only thirty-four years old, Blake was recruited away from the Rockefeller Institute to become professor and chairman of medicine at Yale University. Blake, in turn, recruited several of his former colleagues from the Rockefeller Institute, including Jack Peters.[7]

When Peters returned to New Haven in 1921, he found a medical school that was in the early stages of transformation. About a decade earlier, Abraham Flexner had reviewed the school as part of his national survey of medical education sponsored by the Carnegie Foundation. Flexner noted the strengths of the century-old Yale school, but his report also documented deficiencies, particularly Yale's inadequate investments in laboratories, professors, and support staff. Shortly before Peters arrived, the school had lost all but seven of its full-time faculty members and was at risk of losing more. Those who remained were housed in undesirable space that included a barracks constructed by the War Department during World War I for a laboratory school.[8]

With Flexner serving as an adviser to Yale medical dean Milton Winternitz, plans were developed to invigorate the medical school to rival its more prestigious competitors in Baltimore, New York, and Boston. The modernization initiative required a complete revision of the school's physical plant. First out of the ground was a privately endowed laboratory building for the basic sciences, accompanied by a medical library. Shortly thereafter, donors funded a new administration building, and a private patient pavilion was added to the hospital. Flexner was essential in securing foundation support for four additional buildings.[9]

As the gleaming new campus was rising in New Haven, Dean Winternitz also began to build a full-time faculty, shifting away from a· historical reliance on community practitioners who taught medical students in their spare time. With a dedicated faculty recruited, Winternitz undertook a visionary curricular revision decades ahead of its time. In the new Yale model, students were given greater personal responsibility for their own educations. Lectures were available, but not required, under the premise that students could learn the material in whatever manner best suited individual needs. Emphasis was placed on the acquisition of critical thinking skills rather than on rote memorization. Moreover, examinations were reduced to an absolute minimum in the hopes of instilling a more cooperative and less competitive culture. Finally, each student was required to complete a dissertation, allowing deep immersion in a single topic of interest. In this academic setting Peters became a master teacher and passed along his passion for the pursuit of knowledge to his students at Yale, including the young Donald Seldin.

The model of medical education that evolved at Yale was suited ideally to its young, progressive faculty—including Peters. Applying the knowledge he had acquired working with Van Slyke at the Rockefeller Institute, Peters developed a clinical chemistry laboratory at Yale that stood at the vanguard of the field. It is no exaggeration to say that Peters, along with other leading physicians who were grounded in laboratory-enhanced care, introduced science into the practice of medicine. For the first time in history, diagnoses could be driven by objective biological measurements. Serial determinations over time could be deployed to follow, and even to predict, patient outcomes. Equally important, illnesses could be understood on a biological level as normal physiological responses to conditions that were disordered by an underlying disease.

Peters's[10] academic unit at Yale—which he called the "Chemical Division" of the Department of Internal Medicine—was responsible for operating the clinical chemistry laboratory at New Haven Hospital. His unit came to be known by various names such as the Division of Clinical Chemistry, the Metabolism Section, and the Metabolic Service or Division; interns and residents simply referred to it as "metabolism." The lab served dual purposes: It provided routine chemical analyses for patients being treated in the hospital; and simultaneously it was used for research studies undertaken by members of the division. Whether analyses were undertaken for patient care or for scientific investigation, Peters insisted on the same high standards of measurement.[11]

In 1940, Peters appointed Miss Pauline Hald to be director of the laboratory. A chemistry graduate with a baccalaureate degree from Wellesley College, Hald had worked and published with Peters for nearly fifteen years. At a time when few women were encouraged to pursue scientific careers, Peters promoted Hald even though she did not have a graduate degree. One of the most impactful contributions of the lab was demonstrating the speed and accuracy of a new approach to measuring sodium and potassium in body fluids. The traditional methods were so slow and tedious that they were not useful in monitoring patients. The new instrument—the flame photometer—allowed rapid and precise measurements on minute samples and thus revolutionized the field. When the findings were written up, Peters left his own name off the paper so that Hald would get the full credit.[12] Years later, Donald Seldin would show the same interest in advancing the careers of his own students and colleagues.

Peters was not active in the lab himself, but his research fellows were expected to conduct their own analyses for investigations rather than rely on assistance from technicians.[13] The research questions Peters pursued came directly from the bedsides of his patients. Many of the protocols involved so-called balance studies, in which the intake of various compounds was measured and compared against the output. Even when conducted on healthy subjects, this type of investigation can be tedious, involving meticulous control of the diet and collection and measurement of all urine and stool output. In the context of patients that Peters studied, including those with serious physical and cognitive disorders, balance studies were almost a heroic exercise.[14]

Peters's stature as a leader in this field was established by the prodigious output from his research laboratory. However, it was the 1931 text by Peters and Van Slyke titled *Quantitative Clinical Chemistry, Volume I: Interpretations*,[15] followed a year later by *Volume II: Methods*,[16] that heralded his broad mastery of the field. This pair of books was conceived initially when Peters was approached by the publisher about writing a text on the subject. Peters sought Van Slyke's input as a reviewer, but during the course of their subsequent exchanges Peters concluded: "We have to do this together; it takes a chemist as well as an internist."[17] The author of another widely acclaimed textbook in the field described the tomes by Peters and Van Slyke as a "monumental work," adding that it "will doubtless last for many years as the best example of such writing."[18] These words proved prophetic, as *Quantitative Clinical Chemistry* quickly sold out three printings and became one of the most influential references of its day.

Beyond his acknowledged expertise in the methods and interpretation of clinical laboratory tests, Peters had strong beliefs about the appropriate use of these tests. He viewed his own laboratory as an exemplar for others. Peters believed that chemical analyses helped to illuminate, but did not replace, astute clinical observation and judgment. So, he was equally exacting when it came to bedside care. His expertise was sought for any patient with derangements of bodily fluids or their chemical components. With such an expansive scope of interest, Peters's patient population included a diversity of conditions, from kidney disease, to diabetes and other hormonal disorders, to cirrhosis of the liver and various gastrointestinal afflictions, to rheumatoid arthritis, to urinary tract infections, to high blood pressure, to heart failure.

As a practitioner, Peters was known for his obsessive attention to detail. He monitored the progress of each patient with round-the-clock visits to the hospital, returning, if necessary, well into the early morning hours. During an era before intensive-care units, he obtained blood samples at regular intervals to assess changes in oxygen saturation, carbon dioxide, or hydration. For Peters, every patient deserved the best care possible regardless of his or her financial means or social status. This exceptional devotion to patients in the clinical setting was yet another trait that separated Peters from many others, and he passed along that same passion to students like Donald Seldin. Peters followed patients meticulously during and after hospitalizations. Although he could be stern and demanding with colleagues and students, Peters was solicitous and compassionate with patients.

As a teacher, Peters preferred small group settings where he could interact individually with students. In these intimate settings, his broad command of the medical literature was both awe-inspiring and intimidating. Students quickly learned that Peters had little patience for anything less than their best effort. The same would be said of Donald Seldin during his career.

At the prime of his career, Peters was invited by First Lady Eleanor Roosevelt to join a small group of physicians and health care experts for a luncheon with the president at the White House. Peters likely had been selected for this April 1937 presidential briefing because he had served on an advisory committee for a recent independent review of health care. That report concluded that the cost of medical care was prohibitive for most Americans. It recommended the creation of a system for universal health insurance,[19] which even today some might consider to be controversial. At the time, a quarter-century before Medicare and Medicaid were launched, many in the medical world saw the proposed role of the federal government in health care financing as downright radical.

Within a year of the White House event, Peters organized the Committee of Physicians for the Improvement of Medical Care. This eighteen-member who's who of leading doctors issued a set of "Principles and Proposals" authored by Peters. Among the policies advocated were ensuring health care for the indigent population, providing public funding for medical education and research, and creating a federal agency to oversee these activities.[20]

Organized medicine, led by the powerful American Medical Association, did not simply disagree with the "Principles and Proposals"; it derided them as a form of socialism and belittled the proponents as "unthinking physicians."[21] Peters anticipated the criticism: "My social philosophy, I presume, would be termed radical, though I prefer to believe myself merely curious and intelligently open-minded."[22] Never demurring from a fight, Peters addressed the American College of Physicians a year after the White House event, stating: "The social responsibility of medicine, as I see it, is to provide to all classes of the population medical care of the highest quality."[23] His words echoed those of his father, Rector John Peters, who was known for challenging both his fellow clergy and the members of his prosperous congregation to meet their civic and social obligations.[24]

Jack Peters anticipated that his ideas would draw fire, but it is unlikely he could have foreseen the personal assault they provoked. In 1947—the same year he was elected to the National Academy of Sciences—Peters appeared before the United States Senate to testify against a bill supported by the American Medical Association. Peters opposed the legislation on the grounds that it did not ensure universal access to health care—a principal that by then he had advocated for a decade. With typical candor, he reminded the senators: "Medical care is meant for patients, not for doctors,"[25] a clear attack on the powerful influence of organized medicine.

Less than two years later, Peters received a letter from the Loyalty Review Board, which was responsible for screening employees for the Public Health Service. This review board, and similar organizations in other federal agencies, was established in 1947 by President Harry Truman's Executive Order No. 9835 at the height of the so-called Red Scare. The goal of the loyalty screening program was to prevent the appointment of Communists to positions within the federal government. In the letter to Peters, he was relieved of his position as a voluntary grant peer-reviewer for the National Institutes of Health (NIH), a position that was considered part-time federal employment. Eleven charges were leveled against Peters by anonymous sources claiming that he was associated with organizations deemed subversive. This flimsy evidence was used to disparage the national loyalty of a man who had served his country admirably during World War I and as a lecturer and adviser for the Army Medical School during World War II. Peters denied that he was a Communist; the loyalty board accepted his rebuttal of the charges and reinstated his NIH appointment.

This close call with smears alleged in anonymous allegations did not dissuade Peters from further activism for liberal causes. Almost three years later, he was charged again with being disloyal to the United States government. This time, sixteen charges were leveled against him without attribution, many being repeated from the earlier dismissed allegations. Again the board exonerated Peters, but a year later (and just a few weeks before President Dwight Eisenhower ended the Loyalty Review Board process) Peters was charged an unprecedented third time. In contrast to the two previous reviews, this third hearing found reasonable doubt as to Peters's loyalty to the federal government, and he lost his NIH position and grant support. Peters felt he had been denied the right to face his accusers or even to know their identity and the evidence they provided. He brought a legal action to challenge the absence of due process in the Loyalty Review Board proceedings. His argument was rejected by a federal district court, but after appellate review the United States Supreme Court ruled in his favor. It was not the victory that Peters sought, however, because the Court did not adjudicate on the issue of his right to due process. Instead, the justices ruled on a narrower procedural issue, stating that the executive authorities granted to the Loyalty Review Board did not include any provision to reverse earlier absolution by the board.[26]

The six-year hardship of unfounded disloyalty allegations took its toll on both the physical and emotional well-being of Peters. He bore these burdens with characteristic stoic courage and perseverance.

Sixteen months after the Supreme Court ruling, however, he suffered a heart attack while on teaching rounds at the hospital. It was perhaps fitting that the place where he spent so much of his life and gave so much to his patients and trainees would be where his own mortality came calling. He died two months later, at the age of sixty-seven, while still looking forward to professional goals that he had not yet realized.

Arguably, Peters's greatest legacy was not found in his own prodigious work but rather in the molding of future leaders of American medicine. Many who trained under him went on to distinguished careers themselves, extending Peters's influence nationwide. Of Peters, Seldin said: "I was impressed by his learning, scholarship, and dedication to medicine, all integrated together. On the one hand, he was a meticulous physician. On the other hand, he was a man of enormous learning. He applied himself with rigor." Seldin added: "I found Dr. Peters a very inspiring figure. He anchored me in the direction of medicine."[27] Elsewhere, Seldin expressed his admiration for "the sonorous tone, the Victorian richness that John Peters could infuse into his best writing."[28]

It is not surprising, therefore, that when the time came in his own education Seldin had chosen to pursue his required thesis under Peters's direction. As Seldin recalled: "The thesis had to be based on experimental work. Everybody in the Department of Medicine was attuned to research as a component of education, not merely as a search for new knowledge, and the atmosphere was exciting and electric." In the course of this experience, Seldin fell in love with academic medicine. "It was in the third year in medical school when I took medicine and worked with Dr. Peters, and I found academic medicine a very inspiring domain. And it was at that point that I thought I would try to enter academic medicine on graduation."[29]

After completing medical school in December 1943, Seldin, who was already in the United States Army, was permitted to remain at Yale for an additional two years of residency training. During this time, he continued under the tutelage of Peters in patient care and research. He conducted studies of rheumatic heart disease as well as diabetes. "We started out by calibrating pipettes and burettes, going through all the methods of the laboratory, and then ultimately embarking on a project where things like blood sugars and the like were done by each individual without any technical help whatsoever." Seldin pointed out that the research was layered on top of an already busy clinical schedule: "So you'd work through the night . . . but it was exciting, nevertheless. Exciting and thrilling. There was a sense of animation that went through the house staff."[30]

The first ten scientific papers that Seldin published all came from his work in the Division of Clinical Chemistry at Yale. Although Peters likely contributed to much of this work, only one of these papers listed him as a coauthor.[31] By the time this article appeared in print, three of the five authors, including Seldin, had departed Yale—part of a diaspora spreading Peters's influence across the country. The topic of this article was the influence that the central nervous system exerted on metabolic processes involving fluids and dissolved constituents, commonly known as electrolytes. In it, the authors presented a broad overview of the current state of knowledge, interspersed with illustrative patient vignettes drawn from the clinical service at Yale. This paper showcased two of the distinctive features of Peters's work. First, he possessed an exhaustive command of the relevant scientific literature. Second, he maintained detailed personal records on his patients and drew upon them for scholarly purposes.[32]

As much as Seldin was influenced by Peters's work ethic, devotion to his patients, pursuit of knowledge, and mastery of teaching, in the final analysis it was Peters's character that separated him from all other professors. At a symposium held at Yale to honor John Peters more than four decades after his death, Seldin elected to speak about the man's moral grandeur. In his tribute, Seldin praised his mentor's "unimpeachable integrity," declaring: "The plain fact of the matter is that he was a courageous and morally dignified man," adding "he dedicated himself selflessly to causes of social justice and equity." While acknowledging that his mentor was human—and therefore imperfect—Seldin concluded: "What transcends his flaws and idiosyncrasies is his dedication to academic medicine, his sense of social justice, and his capacity to live his moral principles. These define the man."[33]

These lessons learned from "Whispering Jack" would stay with Seldin throughout his career and played an essential role in shaping both his personal and professional life.

CHAPTER 4

WAR AND PEACE

In 1940, when Donald Seldin entered the Yale School of Medicine, World War II was well under way in both Europe and Asia. Germany had invaded Poland, followed by Denmark, Norway, the Netherlands, Belgium, and France. Great Britain was under an unrelenting German aerial bombardment. Japan had attacked China and soon would broker an alliance with Germany and Italy. As the fighting intensified, the United States remained officially on the sidelines, isolated from the European and Asian conflicts by wide ocean expanses. That all changed when the Imperial Japanese Navy Air Service launched a surprise attack on the United States naval base at Pearl Harbor on December 7, 1941. America declared war first on Japan and, shortly thereafter, on Germany and Italy as well.

As the United States mobilized for hostilities, many of its colleges and universities, including Yale, helped the war effort by educating officers and conducting military research. An Air Force Training Center was established at Yale in 1943, followed by specialized educational programs for the Army and Navy. More than eight thousand military personnel were housed on the New Haven campus. In addition, the federal Office of Scientific Research and Development (OSRD) sponsored research at Yale and other universities. The OSRD was created by executive order of President Franklin Roosevelt in 1941 to advance and coordinate military research. Led by an engineer, Vannevar Bush, head of the Carnegie Institution in Washington, the OSRD was charged with giving the United States the technological superiority needed to secure a military victory. The OSRD was civilian-controlled and sponsored research at private companies in addition to universities. Topics of interest to the OSRD ranged from the development of new weapons, to radar, to transportation, to medicine.

One of the OSRD's projects at Yale involved the dreaded poison gases that were introduced during World War I, resulting in nearly 100,000 deaths and more than a million casualties. Two Yale pharmacologists, Louis Goodman and Alfred Gilman, were engaged to study the effects of nitrogen mustards. These agents are derived from sulfur mustard, commonly known as mustard gas, which was introduced to battlefields by the Imperial German Army in 1916. This aerosolized yellow compound caused agonizing burns of the skin, eyes, and lungs. Despite the Geneva Protocol that banned the use of chemical weapons in 1925, there was understandable fear that they might be deployed again. Efforts were made to find antidotes for these agents and to study their underlying biological effects.

There was evidence, for example, that exposure to mustard gas reduced the number of lymphocytes, a type of circulating white blood cell. At Yale, Goodman and Gilman demonstrated that this property of nitrogen mustards could be exploited for beneficial effect in the treatment of certain cancers. In 1942, while Seldin was still in medical school, a forty-seven-year-old patient with a lymphosarcoma that had relapsed after treatment with surgery and radiation therapy became the test case. The tumors regressed but recurred subsequently; the patient died about three months later. Although this first test of nitrogen mustards revealed limited survival benefit, Goodman and Gilman had opened the door to a new way of treating cancer by introducing the concept of chemotherapy.[1]

Another medical advance at Yale derived by World War II research was a new piece of medical technology: the flame photometer. The American Cyanamid Company produced this machine and touted its value to the military. The OSRD was interested in whether the equipment could speed up the clinical assessment of downed pilots and other wounded warriors. The flame photometer measured the amount of positively charged compounds, such as sodium and potassium, by the wavelength of light emitted when the specimen of blood or urine was heated. Given his national reputation in the study of clinical chemistry, Jack Peters was selected to evaluate this new equipment. What took a day or two for a single measurement with traditional techniques could be performed in an hour for a dozen samples by using the flame photometer. Although the early machines were finicky and easily contaminated, with refinement the flame photometer became an essential tool for monitoring patients with kidney and other diseases.[2]

Beyond their engagement in military research, the faculty at Yale were involved in delivering medical care to service members as well. Yale physicians were responsible for staffing the 39th General Hospital in Auckland, New Zealand. Also known as the Yale University School of Medicine Unit, the 39th was mobilized in July 1942 and after a six-month training period embarked for New Zealand. Ever the academics, the Yale team conducted research on jungle rot, discovering that it was caused by a diphtheria bacterium. They also studied the natural history of hookworm infection. Following the atomic bombings at Hiroshima and Nagasaki, a medical commission was organized to study the health effects. Four of the seven physician members of this original commission were Yale faculty members from the 39th General Hospital.[3]

Even with many of the faculty called into military service, Yale's medical school educational programs continued to operate. Beyond research and patient care, the Army needed to secure its future medical workforce. Accordingly, Donald Seldin, like most of his classmates, was recruited into the Army. He received a modest stipend, wore a uniform, and was taught basic military practices. His medical school coursework was accelerated so that he completed his studies in three years, graduating in December 1943. Seldin finished first in his class and was selected to receive the Campbell Gold Medal, the highest academic award. By tradition, the president of Yale, at the time Charles Seymour, delivered the graduation address and bestowed the Campbell Medal on the top graduate. In order to prepare his remarks, Seymour called Peters to learn more about the top honors graduate.

Seymour began: "Doctor, I understand one of your students is getting the Campbell Gold Medal." When Peters confirmed the selection, the president replied: "I assume the recipient, Mr. Seldin, comes from a family that has attended Yale for many years." Peters, whose own family had a long line of Yale alumni, indicated that Seldin was the first person in his family to attend Yale. With obvious chagrin, Seymour ventured: "Then I assume that they went to other schools like Harvard or Dartmouth." Peters responded that the Seldins had no Ivy League tradition.[4]

Growing somewhat flustered, Seymour interjected: "Well, probably the family has been in this country for many years, many generations." It became clear to Peters that the university president was not getting the message. So, in language that could not be misunderstood, he replied: "Look, I should tell you that his [Seldin's] parents are immigrants. They never went to college here. He is the first member of his family to be in an American university."[5] Even if he was a surprising choice to Seymour, Seldin received the Campbell Gold Medal. In a class with only one or two other Jewish students because religious quotas were still in place, Donald Seldin managed to overcome the religious, economic, and cultural biases at Yale. His intellect and drive had earned the respect of the faculty and his fellow students.

The admiration of Seldin's Yale classmates was still evident at reunions six decades later. According to Robert Alpern, a former colleague of Seldin's at UT Southwestern who became dean of the Yale School of Medicine in 2004, the memories of Seldin's genius continued to burn bright among his fellow students six decades later. "At different reunions, I got to meet members of the class that he [Seldin] graduated with," Alpern recalled. "These are all brilliant people who got into Yale School of Medicine, but every one of them described Seldin as this unique intellect that stood out above the rest of the class."[6]

As might be expected of the top graduate, Seldin was rewarded with a position as a medical intern and resident physician at Yale. With the Army's need for doctors, Seldin's residency was compressed from three full years down to twenty-seven months. As he approached the end of training, Seldin was activated by the military in late 1945. Although the fighting had ended by that time, the Army still had large numbers of troops stationed abroad who required medical care. Initially, Seldin was sent to San Antonio, Texas, for a month of basic training. Then, he was assigned by the 7th Medical Command to join the staff of the 98th General Hospital in Munich, Germany.[7]

Officially opened in July 1945, the 98th General Hospital occupied the repaired and renovated former Krankenhaus Schwabing (a hospital in Schwabing, a northern borough of Munich). This medical complex was located on forty-five acres and consisted of seven hospital buildings, each of which was three stories tall. The grounds also included outpatient clinics with fifteen additional buildings to house personnel and support services. During its first year of military operation, the hospital admitted nearly 14,000 patients, maintaining an average daily census of between seven hundred and 850 patients. The 98th was one of two general hospitals operated by the US Army in Germany, with a sister facility located in Frankfurt.[8]

Initially, Seldin was appointed as an attending physician on the medical service. As many of the more senior medical officers were completing their tours of duty, the twenty-six-year-old Seldin quickly became head of the medical service. In this capacity, he led a team of about ten internists who were responsible for the roughly two hundred patients on the medical service. In addition, nearly two thousand outpatients were treated each month.[9]

Beyond his patient care responsibilities, Seldin was charged with expanding the capabilities of the clinical laboratory. Drawing on his experience under Jack Peters at Yale, Seldin wanted to use the most accurate methods available. The Army was more focused on standardization of procedures across facilities. The conflict between Seldin's scientific rigor and the Army's protocol standardization came to a head when Seldin abandoned the military's old, inaccurate method of measuring serum proteins for a more valid and reproducible approach. He even used his own money to buy the necessary equipment. When the laboratory was inspected by the Army, the new technology was called into question, but it was approved eventually.[10]

Seldin's time in the armed services was not entirely spent on the wards or arguing with military bureaucrats. In 1947 he was called as an expert witness in the ongoing trial of a Nazi physician accused of involuntary experimentation on prisoners of war. Seldin later wrote about and discussed this trial in several contexts, always relying on one of his greatest assets: his prodigious memory. Late in Seldin's life and with his encouragement, a friend and nephrology colleague named Michael Emmett wanted to learn more about the trial. Through the National Archives and Records Administration, Emmett was able to locate Seldin's original testimony. The following account of events is based largely on the records that Emmett uncovered and generously provided. To the extent that important details differ from Seldin's repeated earlier descriptions of the outcome, the official transcript is assumed to be more accurate (although it was imperfect, as Seldin's name was recorded erroneously as "Silden").

The war-crimes trial related to medical experimentation conducted on prisoners of war held at the Dachau concentration camp. Opened in 1933, Dachau was located about ten miles northwest of Munich and was the Nazis' first concentration camp. The forced labor prison occupied about five acres and was surrounded by a twenty-acre training center for the Schutzstaffel (SS). Led by Heinrich Himmler, the SS, among its other assignments, was responsible for operating the concentration camp system and executing the "Final Solution" plans for exterminating the Jewish population. In the dozen years that it functioned, Dachau housed nearly 200,000 prisoners, among whom at least one in five perished before the camp was liberated by American troops on April 29, 1945.

On November 2, 1945, about six months following liberation, a US General Military Government Court was appointed to prosecute forty defendants, including Claus Karl Schilling. A physician who was seventy-four years old at the time of his trial, Schilling had retired after three decades as head of tropical medicine at the prestigious Robert Koch Institute in Berlin. In 1942, Schilling sought and was granted permission to establish a special malaria research station at Dachau. Himmler personally authorized the research because of the high rate of malarial infections among Nazi soldiers deployed in North Africa. The research involved the involuntary exposure of more than a thousand prisoners, including many Polish priests, to mosquitoes carrying the malarial parasite. At least six different antimalarial agents, including an experimental drug identified only by a numerical code, were tested on the exposed internees. More than four hundred of the subjects died, and many of the survivors suffered permanent injury. The studies continued for three full years until April 1945, only one month before the Germans surrendered to the Allies.[11]

The defendants were tried for war crimes. The erudite and bespectacled Schilling had a graying shock of hair and a matching goatee that made him appear to be more of a scholar than a torturer. Nonetheless, he demonstrated no remorse for his actions or the many deaths that occurred, claiming that the knowledge gained would benefit mankind. Schilling was convicted on December 13, 1945, and was executed by hanging at the Landsberg prison on May 28, 1946.

Eighteen months later, a US General Military Government Court undertook a separate trial of another physician at Dachau, Rudolf Adalbert Brachtel. It was the prosecution of Brachtel for which Donald Seldin was called to testify as an expert witness. A native of Czechoslovakia, Brachtel studied medicine in Vienna and Prague. In 1938, he joined the SS and two years later became chief physician of a tuberculosis sanitarium. On April 17, 1941, the thirty-two-year-old Brachtel was transferred to Dachau, where he conducted tuberculosis research before being assigned to work as Schilling's assistant on malaria research. An outbreak of epidemic hepatitis at Dachau in 1942 led to a separate investigation. The research on hepatitis included at least eighty liver biopsies in which a needle was inserted into the liver and a plug of tissue was removed for examination under a microscope. Some of the patients who underwent these biopsies subsequently died, either from hepatitis and its complications or from the procedures themselves. In addition, it was alleged that liver biopsies were performed on other prisoners at Dachau who did not have hepatitis.[12]

The central question at the time of Seldin's testimony was whether the liver biopsies had any therapeutic benefit or, alternatively, were administered solely for experimental purposes without informed consent—or, even worse, as a form of torture. If the biopsies had value in guiding therapy, the deaths, though unfortunate, would not be considered murder by the court. However, if the biopsies had no value to the subjects who received them involuntarily, then the deaths would be construed as murder. Seldin was no authority on liver biopsies, but he was one of the few American medical officers available in Europe at the time and thus was asked to render an opinion on the status of liver biopsies.

Brachtel, thirty-eight years old at the time of his trial, spoke English and participated actively in his own defense, asking questions in both German and English. Seldin was called to testify on December 9, 1947, toward the end of the proceedings. He answered questions posed by both the prosecution and the defense counsel. In addition, the defendant was permitted to direct his own questions to Seldin. Much of the interrogation related to standards of medical practice concerning the use of liver biopsies for the diagnosis and management of epidemic hepatitis. Seldin testified that, in the United States, liver biopsies were neither needed nor used routinely for managing hepatitis. Except in unusual cases, Seldin asserted, the risk of the procedure, including bleeding, was not justified by the benefit of any diagnostic information to be gained.[13]

The defense's cross-examination then attempted to establish the experience that the twenty-seven-year-old Seldin had in treating epidemic hepatitis. Seldin testified that he had managed a recent outbreak involving about twenty officers and civilians who were treated at the 98th General Hospital. The defense counsel then probed Seldin's knowledge of other tests for liver impairment. Having studied under Peters, Seldin was well prepared to rattle off the various chemical tests then available. Seldin also was questioned about his knowledge regarding the practice patterns concerning liver biopsies in Europe. Seldin testified that he was not familiar with the standards of care in Europe and that there might be some variation from country to country.[14]

Two days after Seldin's testimony, a surprise verdict was rendered: Brachtel was acquitted of the charges. The court concluded that "liver punctures are accepted as a means of diagnosing liver disorders as well as getting a picture of the prognosis of a disease involving a disorder of the liver." The trial judges concluded that the biopsies were "beneficial for a decisive cure," and they likewise dismissed Brachtel's participation in the separate malaria studies, as he acted under the direction of Schilling.[15]

The malaria work may have been set aside for an entirely different reason. During the eighteen months between Schilling's conviction and Brachtel's trial, twenty-three Nazi physicians charged with war crimes were tried in Nuremberg. The nine months of court proceedings ended with verdicts delivered on August 19, 1947. Seven death sentences were handed down, nine defendants received prison sentences, and the remaining seven were acquitted. Some of the defendants argued that experimentation on prisoners in Nazi concentration camps was morally equivalent to medical experiments conducted on prisoners in other countries. For example, between 1944 and 1946 the United States Army had sponsored a study of malaria conducted by physicians from the University of Chicago at the nearby Stateville Penitentiary. Prisoners serving terms for criminal offenses were offered incentives to participate, and about five hundred volunteered. The selected subjects were infected with the malarial parasite to test whether existing or new experimental drugs could prevent the development of disease or its relapse.[16]

In the absence of generally accepted standards for the ethical conduct of experimentation on human subjects, the court included in its verdict a section titled "Permissible Medical Experimentation." Ten principles for the ethical conduct of human research were identified; later these became known as the Nuremberg Code. Among the criteria identified were voluntary consent to participate and withdraw, societal benefit, and minimization of harm. The Nuremberg Code was never formally adopted as law by any nation, but it served as a foundation for subsequent ethical guidelines.[17]

When Brachtel came to trial four months after the Nuremberg doctors' trial concluded, it was unclear how to apply the newly established Nuremberg Code to historical research practices. Not wanting to call into question the malarial research on prisoners in the States, several American medical organizations and consultants argued successfully against convicting Brachtel.[18] This surprising outcome was never cited by Seldin, so it is unlikely that he even knew about it. Brachtel subsequently entered private medical practice in the town of Giessen in central Germany and lived there until his death four decades later.[19]

The experience of confronting the brutal and inhumane actions of Nazi physicians would haunt Seldin for the remainder of his life. Three decades after the trial, he was selected to serve on a national commission that built upon the Nuremberg Code by defining core principles for protecting human research subjects in the United States. Without question, his experience with the horrors of Dachau helped to motivate and inform Seldin's contributions to this landmark effort.

For Captain Seldin at the 98th General Hospital, he and his colleagues were responsible for caring for patients, many of whom had recovered from their illnesses but were awaiting transport back to the United States. With the volume of military personnel heading home postwar, it was not unusual to experience a three-month delay to secure a spot on a troop transport ship. Army regulations dictated that the medical staff must enter a daily progress note on every patient, even when the patient had recovered already. Medical records would be filled with page after page of notes indicating "condition unchanged." Such military rules had to be followed, regardless of whether they made any sense. For Seldin, the Army provided a sharp contrast to the scholarly and stimulating environment he had enjoyed at Yale.

While off-duty, Seldin used his free time to travel around Europe, planning each trip carefully with a focus on fine arts, history, and culture. With the US military controlling the available supply of gasoline, Seldin could fuel up for Jeep excursions around the continent. Midway through his deployment, when Muriel was able to join him in Munich, the couple continued these educational jaunts around Europe. High on Seldin's priority list was to travel the historic pilgrimage routes he read about as a teenager in the New York Public Library. Retracing the steps that the faithful had traveled for more than a millennium, Donald and Muriel drove the roughly five hundred miles of the Camino de Santiago, from the south of France to Santiago de Compostela in northwestern Spain.

Having quenched his thirst for cultural immersion in Europe and after more than two years of military service, Seldin finally received his discharge orders. Now headed home, he had no idea what he would do upon his return. One option was to enter private practice. Another was to undertake further training. The third choice was to remain in the military, where he had been offered a substantial promotion. Having endured the frustrations of Army protocol for the previous two years, however, Seldin quickly ruled out a military career. On his very last day in Munich, awaiting assignment to a ship headed home, Seldin decided to stop by the hospital to check his mail. To his great surprise, there was a letter from Yale. This was the one and only piece of correspondence he had received from Yale during his time in the Army. Seldin opened it hurriedly and read the following brief message: "Dear

Don: I would like to offer you a position as instructor of medicine at a salary to begin at $2,500 a year. Why haven't you written? Sincerely yours, Jack."[20]

Seldin was stunned. "Jack" was, of course, Jack Peters. Seldin had placed his former mentor on such a high pedestal that he never imagined Peters would communicate with him on such an informal, first-name basis. Even more remarkable, this letter literally came out of nowhere. There had been no discussion about a return to Yale when Seldin departed after his foreshortened training. He presumed that any openings likely would be filled by returning faculty after they had completed their military obligations. The timing of Peters's letter could not have been more propitious. Had the offer arrived even a day later, Seldin may have been forced to make other arrangements. Looking back years later, he would refer to the letter as a "defining moment" in his life.[21]

In 1948, Yale's Division of Clinical Chemistry was stocked with current and future leaders in the field. In addition to Peters, there were about ten full-time faculty members. Four would go on to chair departments of medicine: Louis Welt at the University of North Carolina and Yale, Arnold Relman at the University of Pennsylvania, Frank Epstein at the Harvard-affiliated Beth Israel Hospital, and Seldin at UT Southwestern. In addition, two faculty members eventually became editors at leading medical journals: Arnold Relman at the *New England Journal of Medicine* and J. Russell Elkinton at the *Annals of Internal Medicine*. Seldin described the Yale environment as "stimulating," surrounded as he was by so many established and rising stars. It was an ideal setting to launch his own academic career. Nevertheless, as in the military, Seldin was required to play by the rules of the house.

The Division of Clinical Chemistry was built from the ground up by Peters, who carried strong opinions about how research should be conducted there. Rule No. 1 was to study the patients admitted to the hospital. Peters believed that his faculty had an obligation to focus their research on the patients on their clinical service. For Peters, the greatest insights into disease processes came from careful observation of human patients. Rule No. 2 was that all chemical measurements must be performed personally by the investigator rather than relying on a technician. In conducting the analysis with one's own hands, Peters believed, the investigator could have greater confidence that the protocol was followed correctly. Moreover, the best way to fully appreciate the limitations of any assay was to have direct experience in performing it.

Peters was a perfectionist who also demanded the same high standards from his faculty members. The expectation was that they would take care of their patients, teach their students and fellows, and do their own laboratory work. It was exhausting, but everyone played by Peters's rules. The division flourished under his steady, if demanding, guidance.

Seldin immersed himself in the work. Years later, he characterized his research interests from the earliest days: "My particular area of interest is the physiology of kidney function. In other words, when a person takes [in] a lot of water or salt, how do his kidneys become aware of this fact so as to excrete the excess?" Seldin continued: "On the other hand, when a person doesn't take in enough, how do his kidneys recognize the need to consume body stores? In short, what signals does the kidney receive that induce it to readjust automatically? What occurs in disease to disrupt this sensitive regulatory organ?"[22]

Over a period of three years, working primarily with fellow Robert Tarail, Seldin conducted a variety of studies. All but one of these research projects involved human subjects who were either normal or had a metabolic disorder such as diabetes. A particular emphasis was placed on measuring so-called electrolytes—chemical substances dissolved in the blood or urine that bear an electrical charge. Seldin assessed changes in positively charged electrolytes, such as sodium and potassium, as well as negatively charged electrolytes, such as chloride, under various conditions. He observed, for example, what happens when healthy subjects, including Seldin and his coauthor, were injected with highly concentrated sugar water. When injected rapidly, the sweet concoction sucked water out of the body's cells, thereby diluting the concentration of sodium in the serum. There was an associated increase in urine flow and loss of sodium from the body.[23] Separate studies in diabetic patients revealed that high amounts of sugar in their urine pulled sodium and chloride along with water out of cells, resulting in dehydration and salt depletion.[24]

Through these and other studies published in premier scientific journals, Seldin was beginning to attract notice as a promising investigator. In 1949, one of his papers was presented in preliminary form at the highly prestigious American Society for Clinical Investigation's annual meeting in Atlantic City, New Jersey. Even as his reputation was growing around the country, Seldin was uncertain about the opportunity for advancement at Yale. Although he was very happy in New Haven with the work and the social and cultural environment, Seldin became increasingly concerned about whether he could move up the academic ladder. As he would later recall: "The Department of Medicine at Yale was a very crowded department in the area I was working in. . . . What future was there for me at Yale in the long run?"[25] His former colleague, Arnold "Bud" Relman, had moved on to Boston University for a less crowded playing field. Relman had mentioned Seldin's name to Charles Burnett, a senior faculty member in the Department of Medicine at Boston University. In 1949, Burnett had gained notoriety for his published description of a complication of the treatment of peptic ulcer disease. Burnett reported that patients who consumed large amounts of milk and antacids were at risk for developing high levels of calcium in their blood, but not in their urine, leading to calcium deposits in tissues and kidney insufficiency.[26] Initially termed the "milk-alkali" syndrome, it later became known as Burnett's syndrome.

When Burnett was offered the position as chair of the Department of Medicine at a relatively new medical school in Dallas, Texas, he invited Seldin to join him on the faculty. Unlike the situation at Yale, where Seldin felt there was minimal opportunity to advance, at a new school he would not have to leapfrog over other faculty members. Burnett wanted Seldin to establish a metabolic lab and then direct it. Seldin could also develop a clinical ward devoted to patients with metabolic disorders.

Without question, the idea of developing his own program was appealing to the ambitious Seldin. In contrast, his mentor Jack Peters was not impressed with the offer in Dallas. Peters's reservations were not based entirely on an Ivy League prejudice, although he did question whether Seldin would encounter any truly bright students in Texas. Rather, Peters was concerned that Seldin's promising research career would be stymied by the heavy clinical and teaching demands of a new medical school with few full-time faculty members. Peters expressed his concerns, but when Seldin announced his intent to depart, Peters accepted the decision graciously and even hosted a farewell party to honor his junior colleague.

Without so much as an exploratory visit to Dallas, Donald Seldin, his wife, Muriel, and their young daughter, Leslie, headed south to the nation's capital—and then west to a new life in Texas.

CHAPTER 5

A NEW SHERIFF IN TOWN

Donald Seldin was appointed chairman of medicine at UT Southwestern at the close of 1951. He was only thirty-one years old and had been on the faculty for less than a year as an associate professor. Seldin's apparent meteoric rise to a position of authority was completely circumstantial. As he later characterized the situation: "This wasn't a sumptuous crowning of any sort. There was nobody else around."[1]

The previous chairman of medicine, Charles Burnett, lasted in the job only eight months. Burnett, the person who had recruited Seldin to Dallas, was himself recruited away to the University of North Carolina to chair the Department of Medicine there. He invited the two other full-time faculty members in the Department of Medicine at Southwestern Medical School to join him in Chapel Hill. Neurologist Tom Farmer accepted Burnett's officer, but Seldin remained in Dallas, leery of making another quick jump to a newly minted school.

As the sole remaining full-time faculty member in the Department of Medicine, Seldin was the obvious heir apparent to Burnett. Even so, things looked so grim in Dallas that Seldin turned down the offer initially. His former colleagues at Yale sought his return to New Haven, and Harvard, not to be outdone, was trying to convince him to come to Boston. Because Seldin's academic roots and his mentor Jack Peters were at Yale, he decided to head back there.

Much to Seldin's surprise, the situation in Dallas became remarkably more promising within a few months. First, a new dean, George Aagaard, was appointed. Only thirty-nine years old at the time, Aagaard was admired for his calm demeanor, wise counsel, and fairness. Equally important, the state of Texas, which had dithered about investing in the Southwestern Medical School, finally committed to constructing a permanent home for the second public medical school in the state. Lastly, Dallas County issued bonds to commence the long-awaited replacement of Parkland, the city's crowded and outdated public hospital.

When Aagaard approached Seldin about the medicine chairmanship a second time, the reluctant prospect had a change of heart. He could see some potential in Dallas. Three decades later, Seldin's decision to remain there was described by a journalist: he "stayed on at Southwestern during the bleak days of the early fifties, not because he was blind to the ruin around him, but because in that great emptiness he saw possibilities."[2] Not lacking in self-confidence, Seldin believed he was the right person to realize that potential. The lack of other full-time faculty members, rather than being a hindrance, provided Seldin with a clean slate from which he could build a premier academic enterprise. As Seldin later advised one of his prized recruits, Robert Alpern: "If you know what type of department you want and you know the type of faculty that you want in your department, it is best to move to an empty department."[3] Alpern, who came to UT Southwestern as chief of nephrology, later served as the school's dean before assuming the same position at Yale's medical school. As a dean at medical schools with established cultures and longtime traditions, Alpern could appreciate the free hand that Seldin wielded in the early days at the Southwestern Medical School.

At the time, others were less convinced that the young and inexperienced chair of medicine was prepared to run the department. The medical school was heavily dependent on private practice physicians in the community to perform most of the teaching. As Seldin recalled: "The ward services were conducted by practitioners who gave their time, free of charge, to the medical school. They were very competent and very loyal. . . . They received no remuneration either directly or indirectly by virtue of being clinical teachers at Parkland, but there was a very good spirit and a very warm dedication to the medical school."[4]

This goodwill was threatened when Seldin began imposing a new model of education. As was the case in most other schools, the roughly one hundred students per class completed two years of basic science instruction before starting clinical work during their third year. The foundation of the third year in Dallas was a seven-month block of time spent on the Department of Medicine rotation. The problem, at least from Seldin's perspective, was that the approach and content of the teaching was not under the direction of the department. The students were swamped with lectures, and in many cases the subject matter had little to do with internal medicine. Topics as diverse as orthopedics, urology, and surgery were taught during the internal medicine rotation. There was no overarching design to the range of topics covered. Even lectures that clearly focused on internal medicine were more a reflection of the interests of the speakers than of the knowledge base required for students.

Seldin concluded that the only way to deliver a coherent and logical educational program was for the department to take control of the internal medicine rotation. Drawing from the Yale tutorial model, where formal lectures were minimized and small-group learning was emphasized, Seldin slashed the number of lectures. Only Wednesday afternoons each week would be reserved for lectures; the rest of the week would be allocated to hands-on learning at patients' bedsides. Seldin started by eliminating the surgically oriented talks. Particularly deep cuts were made in the amount of lecture time devoted to dermatology. Dallas had a very prominent and influential dermatology community that controlled a major portion of the medical curriculum. The supposed justification for this concentration on skin diseases was that many of these conditions are very common in medical practice. Seldin argued that teaching time should not be apportioned based on the prevalence of various conditions but rather on the extent to which it helped to reveal general principles about disease causation and treatment.[5]

Seldin also subscribed to the view—again based on his experience at Yale—that the lectures should be delivered principally by the full-time academic faculty. As he was the only full-time faculty member in the Department of Medicine at the time, he delivered most of the lectures. With very limited financial resources, Seldin also was forced to stop providing the $100 honorarium that by tradition was paid to volunteer faculty to present a lecture. For some private practitioners, the discontinuation of the honoraria added insult to the injury of reduced lecture time. Seldin was walking a tightrope—he felt it essential to take tighter control of the educational program. At the same time, he needed to maintain the backing of the private practitioners who helped to teach students on the clinical wards.

To some extent, the friction with the local medical community probably also reflected cultural and personality clashes. Seldin was young and very new to the local scene. His irrepressible New York accent and brash attitude likely grated on the nerves of native Texans. As the locals might have phrased it: "He can strut sittin' down." Seldin's Ivy League pedigree did not endear him to his colleagues, either. Although he did not experience overt anti-Semitism, the fact that he was Jewish contributed to the overall perception that he was a stranger in a strange land. With the rapid turnover of his predecessor and the chairs of other clinical departments, it was reasonable for private practitioners to assume Seldin would be a short-timer himself. Unlike employed faculty who came and went, volunteer faculty were rooted deeply in the community and were there to stay.

Seldin freely admitted that his own personality did not help matters: "I'm no rose. I would hardly describe myself as an easy person."[6] A man of strong convictions, Seldin had no reservations about expressing them or challenging others who did not share his beliefs. For Seldin, it was never about winning a popularity contest—his priority in redesigning the medicine rotation was to ensure that the students got the best possible education. All other considerations were secondary, including the egos of colleagues whose volunteered services still were needed.

Seldin was fortunate to have some powerful allies within the private practice community. One such advocate was Alfred W. "Al" Harris. From the earliest days of the medical school, Harris was a leading supporter. He devoted considerable time to the school, despite the demands of a busy private practice. A large and gregarious man who was almost a decade older than Seldin, Harris ran his office practice with very unconventional hours, beginning to see patients at around ten o'clock at night and continuing into the wee hours of the morning.

He would call Seldin in the middle of the night with a cheery greeting: "Hello, Don, can we talk?" Then, Harris would launch into a conversation about the Department of Medicine and how he could assist in various ways, such as recruiting.[7]

Along with Al Harris, other private practitioners came to the aid of the revitalized medical school.[8] The volunteers included Paul "Brownie" Thomas, a graduate of the Baylor University College of Medicine; he typically had patients hospitalized all over the city but traveled to Parkland to teach students and resident physicians.[9] Elmer Russell "E. R." Hayes had also graduated from the Baylor University College of Medicine and spent several years conducting research at the University of Minnesota before returning to Dallas in 1950. Hayes worked fourteen-hour days so that he could both teach at the medical school and also take care of his private patients.[10] Others who helped to carry the teaching load included Seldin's close friend and former roommate Sam Shelburne, as well as a senior statesmen of the local medical community named Walter Grady Reddick. Without the generous contributions of these colleagues Seldin could not have survived the early years of his chairmanship.

As the sole full-time faculty member, Seldin was on the move constantly. Typically, his day started at 6 A.M., with a session known affectionately as "Sunshine Rounds." These were targeted primarily toward resident physicians at Parkland Hospital, and Seldin would often deliver a lecture or a clinical discussion. Afterward at the "Morning Report," the resident physicians would present patients admitted the previous day. Seldin would then ensure that appropriate care plans were implemented. With four or so students and resident physicians on a service at one time, Seldin would get to know each of the trainees in a very personal way.

John Fordtran, an early resident physician and later head of the Gastroenterology Division, recalled an encounter with Seldin on the wards at Parkland Hospital on the second day of his internship: "When diabetic ketoacidosis patients came in you were supposed to fill out this chart that documented everything you did, minute by minute." Diabetic ketoacidosis (DKA) is a life-threatening complication of diabetes mellitus characterized by high levels of both blood sugar and

ketones—the acidic breakdown by-products of fats. Fordtran continued: "The next morning, I hadn't done that. I had written it all in
the progress notes [in the medical record]."[11] Fordtran added: "I was
really proud that I'd taken care of this diabetic ketoacidosis patient and
I thought I'd done really good. He [Seldin] was furious that the document hadn't been filled out. I'd never been told about the document. . . .
He wasn't exactly mad, he just let me know I had room to improve."[12]

One former resident physician and later faculty colleague and
friend, Robert Haley, recalled how important it was to learn how to
manage patients with DKA. "That was the number one challenge on
the wards. . . . Back in that era . . . we didn't have all the [insulin] pumps
and all the stuff we have now." DKA often was a recurrent issue among
teenage patients who would rebel by not taking their insulin injections.
"In my era, there was this kid. . . . He trained a whole generation of
our house staff on how to take care of DKA." Haley described the
approach to lowering blood sugar: "You could do it gently. The key
was not to overshoot with either hypokalemia [low serum potassium]
or with low blood sugar. . . . If you gave insulin too long, you would
get hypoglycemia [low blood sugar]. Boy, if you had to record that on
the sheet, it was a disgrace." The trick, according to Haley, was to taper
the insulin before the blood sugar returned to normal. "If you wait
until the blood sugar normalizes, that's too late and they're going to get
hypoglycemic."[13]

Another aspect of the educational process that Seldin imported
from Yale was a student laboratory on the internal medicine ward of
the hospital. Haley described it: "One of the former patient rooms he
converted into a small lab. There was a big lab bench in this small room
and there were reagents up on the shelf. There was a microscope, a
centrifuge, a candle jar, an incubator, and glass slides and cover slips
and capillary tubes." Each junior student rotating through internal
medicine was required to personally perform certain laboratory tests.
Haley recalled: "You had to do the urinalysis and you would have to
put a drop of urine on a slide, put a cover slip on it and examine it. You
count the number of white cells per high power field and that's how
you diagnose a UTI [urinary tract infection]."[14]

After the urine was examined, it was spun on a centrifuge to examine it for casts (various microscopic structures indicative of kidney

disease). Haley continued: "Then, for anybody who was coughing up sputum, you did a Gram stain [a microscopic test used to visualize bacteria] and an AFB stain [a microscopic test used to detect tuberculosis organisms]. If you didn't do it and have it on the chart, you would hear about it." Haley added: "If the patient was bleeding, you would do a finger stick, get some blood in a capillary tube and spin it down. You would measure the hematocrit [the proportion of blood volume occupied by red blood cells]."[15]

This laboratory served generations of medical students and resident physicians at UT Southwestern before it came to an untimely and abrupt demise. John Warner, the current executive vice president for Health System Affairs, recalled the events. In 1996, when he was co-chief resident, Warner received an urgent telephone message from Seldin along these lines: "I observed something happening in the hospital today that if allowed to continue would threaten the very existence of American medicine." With some trepidation, Warner headed directly to Seldin's office. Amid the floor-to-ceiling stacks of papers that constituted Seldin's filing system sat the great man. Warner asked: "Dr. Seldin, I got your message. What on earth are we doing wrong?" Seldin replied: "The residents are no longer spinning their own urine specimens." The federal Occupational Safety and Health Administration had just released new guidelines on handling laboratory specimens. As Warner described: "We literally had to disassemble the lab where the residents could spin their own urine because it had to be in some sort of regulated environment. Well, that did not travel well with Dr. Seldin." Warner continued: "He was upset about it and wanted to know exactly why we'd done it—wanted to see the regulations and make sure that we weren't overreacting. He wanted us to push back on them [the federal regulators] so that we could continue."[16]

Back in the early days, in addition to supervising the busy wards at Parkland Hospital, Seldin had arrangements to oversee the care of patients at two Veterans Administration (VA) hospitals. One was located in Lisbon, a suburb about six miles south of downtown Dallas. The second was a former United States Army hospital in McKinney about thirty miles north of Dallas. After World War II, the McKinney facility was converted to the care of veterans. For their clinical rotations, medical students were distributed between the principal teaching service at Parkland and the ancillary sites at the VA hospitals. Seldin traveled to the VA facilities two to three times each week to make rounds on the patients and to teach the students.

Beyond his responsibilities caring for patients at the three teaching hospitals, Seldin also served as a consultant for physicians in private practice. If a local doctor wanted advice and guidance on the management of a patient with a metabolic disorder, a referral would be made to Seldin. As Neil Kurtzman, an early fellow who later became chairman of medicine at Texas Tech University, described it, Seldin "wasn't a hands-on clinician. You wouldn't want him to be your primary care doctor. But if you had a problem that you wanted analyzed, he could analyze it better than anybody."[17]

The whole subject of referrals was highly sensitive at the time. Many community physicians were concerned that, once an academic physician became involved with the care of their patients, subsequent management would be diverted from the original practice. With such a small number of full-time faculty members at the Southwestern Medical School at the time, concern about retention of patients by the consultants was more theoretical than real. Nevertheless, the fear persisted. To address these apprehensions, early negotiations were conducted between a delegation from the Dallas County Medical Society and representatives from the medical school.

The parties reached an agreement whereby the primary activities of the faculty members would be teaching and research; in addition, they would accept private patients only upon referral from private practitioners. A referred patient could be seen one or more times by the consultant but not on a long-term basis. The agreement further stipulated that the faculty members would admit patients only to the teaching hospital (Parkland). Limits also were placed on the amount of income that faculty members could derive from the care of private patients.[18]

In all instances, a referred patient was to be returned to the original private practice. Sometimes a consultation occurred on an outpatient basis. On other occasions, Seldin and his fellow consultants traveled to a private hospital, such as Baylor University Hospital, to evaluate the patient. Seldin later enjoyed consulting arrangements at both Presbyterian Hospital and Saint Paul's Hospital when they opened. In addition, he served as a consultant at more distant facilities, including William Beaumont General Hospital in El Paso and Wilford Hall Hospital at Lackland Air Force Base in San Antonio.

When Seldin was not running back and forth between hospitals, his time was devoted to writing, supervising students conducting research, and meeting with various constituents. His workday ended back at Parkland Hospital, where he conducted evening rounds with the resident physicians and students. Although the schedule varied somewhat day to day, typically he would not get home until eight or nine o'clock at night.

As if his hours during the week were not long enough, Seldin also came in on Saturday mornings to round on patients. Afterward, there was a teaching conference during which a resident physician would present a patient currently on the medical service. There was a general discussion of the clinical issues involved, as well as the underlying disease processes. Then, for good measure, a second patient was presented and discussed. For the resident physicians, these teaching conferences could be intimidating.

John Warner described these sessions: "Second- and third-year residents would give these conferences and he [Seldin] would come, which was completely terrifying." After each thirty-minute presentation, Seldin would ask the first question. According to Warner, "If you managed to answer the question, you were everybody's hero. If you missed the answer, you were pretty much like everybody else." Warner added: "If someone gave a terrible lecture, he would not critique that person in front of everyone, but he would let the chief residents know that the person needed some remediation."[19]

From the earliest days of Seldin's tenure as chairman, key aspects of his leadership style were apparent. Despite his youth and lack of prior administrative experience, Seldin was supremely firm in his convictions about how the educational program of the department should be organized. Although his autocratic—some might even say dictatorial—style may have ruffled some feathers, Seldin's charm, intellect, and wit won over key members of the private practice community. There was no denying his commitment to students and their educational experience. Nor was there any perception that he was motivated by personal gain. When Seldin accepted the chairmanship, he threw himself into it with abandon. Some observers described him as a whirlwind. He worked virtually around the clock, shouldering most of the responsibility for lectures, rounding with students and resident physicians, and caring for patients in multiple hospitals. One of his first star students, Floyd Rector, had vivid memories of Seldin literally running between his many obligations.[20]

Seldin made himself available to the resident physicians at all hours, day or night. An early former student, resident physician, and later Seldin's successor as chairman of medicine, Daniel Foster, recalled: "He was tough, but we all sort of adored him. He would come out in the middle of the night—we would call him and he would come over and see a patient at three o'clock in the morning and start giving a lecture."[21] With such personal sacrifice and dedication, Seldin won the respect and admiration of the trainees—even those who occasionally were the target of a caustic remark from him. The trainees sensed that Seldin had their best interests at heart, and they appreciated his commitment to their mastery of the knowledge and skills required for medical practice.

CHAPTER 6

TALENT SCOUT

One of the top priorities for Donald Seldin, as the sole full-time faculty member in the Department of Medicine, was to recruit promising candidates to join the faculty. He scraped together spare nickels to create some seed funds, but the departmental budget was so tight that he had little to offer potential recruits. Moreover, the teaching, research, and clinical facilities were embarrassingly primitive at that time. The school remained for another four years in the same deteriorating temporary shacks that Seldin discovered on his initial visit to campus in 1951. It was hardly a setting in which he could successfully compete for the best talent in the country.

Even if Seldin had both high-quality space and ample funding to offer, the market for medical school faculty was particularly tight at the time. In the decade following the end of World War II, seven new medical schools were established in the United States. Publicly supported schools were launched in the states of Washington, California, Florida, and New Jersey and in the commonwealth of Puerto Rico. In addition, private schools were created in New York (Albert Einstein) and Florida (Miami). The established schools also were in a growth mode, with average class sizes swelling from seventy-five to ninety-five students.[1] Even with this expansion, medical schools were struggling to keep up with demand. At the onset of World War II, there were fewer than 12,000 applicants each year to medical school. Fueled by a wave of veterans who attended college on the GI Bill, medical student applications more than doubled by 1948. In contrast, admissions increased by only about 10 percent during that same period. During the following decade, with surging class sizes, the annual number of medical school graduates increased by more than a third.[2]

As medical schools responded to the overflowing pool of applicants, they greatly expanded the ranks of full-time clinical faculty members. In 1951, there were 2,277 full-time clinical faculty members in the United States, accounting for slightly more than half of all full-time faculty members. Within a decade, the number of full-time clinical faculty members had more than tripled to 6,948, and by then this represented almost two-thirds of full-time medical school faculty members.[3] A major driver for the skewed increase in clinical faculty members was a loosening of prior constraints on their ability to care for private patients, thereby allowing them to earn an income more competitive with private practice.

The expansion of medical school faculties after World War II also was propelled by another driver. Prior to the war, the major funding for research in the United States came from the private sector, including companies and philanthropic foundations. The war effort led to the creation of the Office of Scientific Research and Development, which initiated and supported scientific research deemed essential to winning a military victory.

Before World War II ended, President Roosevelt turned to OSRD director Vannevar Bush to map out a national plan for the United States to retain scientific preeminence. Bush answered this lofty challenge with a report titled *Science: The Endless Frontier*, in which, among other recommendations, he wrote: "If we are to maintain the progress in medicine which has marked the last 25 years, the Government should extend financial support to basic medical research in the medical schools and in universities."[4]

Bush's counsel led directly to the creation of a mechanism by which the National Institutes of Health could make competitive grants to researchers outside the federal government. Once this door was opened, money flowed freely through it. In 1946, eighty projects were funded by the NIH with a total of less than $800,000. Just seven years later, the NIH's Division of Research Grants made two thousand grants totaling more than $20 million.[5] This more than twenty-fold increase in both the number and financial magnitude of federal grants in biomedical research spurred universities to recruit faculty who could compete successfully for these awards.

In the race to attract the best faculty, Donald Seldin was operating at a decided handicap. As he sat in his drafty office in the dilapidated shacks, Seldin contemplated how he could grow his faculty. As he later recalled: "The major resource we had was students. So, it seemed to me that if we were ever going to do anything at that time, we should take advantage of the students."[6] One of those students, Daniel Foster, who many years later would succeed Seldin as department chair, remembers Seldin telling the students: "One thing I know is: brains are not geographically distributed."[7]

Kern Wildenthal was another early student singled out by Seldin. Decades later, Wildenthal would be appointed president of UT Southwestern. He described the typical student in the following manner: "Those of us who were coming to Southwestern in those days usually had been trained in what were decent but not academically high-powered institutions. We were almost all Texans who had gone to Texas universities and gotten a good solid grounding, but had a lot to learn."[8] Seldin liked to refer to his earnest young charges from the Lone Star State as "milk-drinking Texans."

As the sole full-time faculty member in the Department of Medicine, Seldin had a front-row seat from which he could judge students and their abilities. In his words: "I knew them well. I was making rounds all the time. I knew the students on a personal basis."[9] The students, in turn, were drawn to Seldin. A lucky few were invited to join his research laboratory for the summer months following their third year. In the laboratory setting, Seldin could further judge the most promising candidates for scientific careers.

In a class of a hundred medical students, he might find at most four or five who had the talent and drive to become academicians. He would then suggest a plan for their career development, typically involving research training at a premier laboratory somewhere else. The Seldin plan would come full circle when the former students were recruited back to Dallas as faculty members.

The very first class of students that Seldin encountered at UT

Southwestern included several in whom he recognized raw potential. One was Norman Kaplan. The son of immigrants from Eastern Europe and the youngest of four children, Kaplan was born in 1931 and raised in an Orthodox Jewish household. The family ran a small grocery store in a poor neighborhood in Dallas, living next to the store. Kaplan was a good student, and at the age of sixteen he graduated as the salutatorian of his high-school class. He attended the University of Texas at Austin, where, like his older brothers before him, he studied pharmacy. Kaplan took extra credits each semester, as well as classes during the summer, which allowed him to graduate in three years at the age of nineteen.

Kaplan was accepted at the Southwestern Medical School in 1950. As he later reminisced: "As a junior medical student, I thought I wanted to become either a pediatrician or a psychiatrist, but then Dr. Seldin grabbed me one day and said: 'I'd like for you to go into internal medicine.' His presence and what was happening in the Department of Medicine influenced me."[10] Seldin encouraged Kaplan to remain in Dallas for his internship and residency at Parkland Hospital. During his third year of residency, Kaplan undertook several research studies on diabetes. Following his residency, he fulfilled a two-year military obligation. Given his work on diabetes, Kaplan was appointed chief of the endocrinology service at Wilford Hall Hospital at Lackland Air Force Base in San Antonio.

Seldin intervened again on Kaplan's behalf, arranging a fellowship at the National Heart Institute (part of the NIH) in Bethesda, Maryland. Kaplan worked for one year in the Clinical Endocrinology Branch under the supervision of its famed director Fred Bartter. Although Kaplan did not particularly enjoy the laboratory investigation, he benefited from the exposure to a wide range of endocrine disorders among the patients treated at the NIH's Clinical Center. Kaplan possessed a clear preference for patient-oriented studies, and when Seldin recruited him back to UT Southwestern in 1961 he focused on clinical research. His particular area of expertise was high blood pressure; in addition to more than five hundred research papers, he wrote a popular textbook on this subject and served on many national advisory committees.[11]

Another student in Seldin's inaugural class was Jere Mitchell. A native of Longview, Texas, Mitchell was raised in this small rural town about 120 miles east of Dallas. His parents were involved in the oil and cotton business, and Jere Mitchell was the first person in his immediate family to attend college. He enrolled at the Virginia Military Institute, jokingly noting that his mother liked uniforms and thought her son would look good in one. Mitchell chose a premedical curriculum, in part influenced by the two general practitioners in his hometown who had cared for him and his family.

Upon graduation in 1950, Mitchell enrolled at the Southwestern Medical School, selecting its shacks over the big, beautiful buildings of the Baylor University College of Medicine in Houston. In Dallas, Mitchell became interested in physiology, and Donald Seldin arrived just as Jere was transitioning into clinical studies. Mitchell, like most of his classmates, was in awe of Seldin, spellbound by the chairman's lectures. Nevertheless, when Seldin invited Mitchell to conduct laboratory research after his junior year, the East Texan chose instead to work as a student teacher. Upon Mitchell's graduation in 1954, Seldin convinced him to pursue a medical internship and residency at Parkland Hospital, followed by a two-year cardiology fellowship in Dallas. When his clinical training came to an end, Mitchell began research in Dallas on exercise physiology. Subsequently, he was invited to work in the Cardiovascular Physiology Laboratory run by Stanley Sarnoff at the NIH. After four years of basic research with Sarnoff and more than twenty scientific publications, Mitchell returned to UT Southwestern in 1962 as a faculty member. Four years later, he was appointed chief of cardiology.

Mitchell made many important contributions to both basic and applied cardiology research. Perhaps his most cited work examined the effect of bed rest on cardiac function. At the time, standard management for patients who suffered a heart attack (and many other conditions) was bed rest for weeks on end. Mitchell and his colleagues demonstrated that cardiac performance deteriorated when patients were subjected to prolonged bed rest. The team demonstrated that an exercise program dramatically improved cardiac performance and clinical recovery. These findings changed protocols for managing patients after heart attacks, as well as those undergoing surgery or other procedures where bed rest was the prior standard of care.[12]

A third standout among Seldin's inaugural group of medical students was Floyd Rector. He was a native of Slaton, Texas, about fifteen miles southeast of Lubbock in the Texas Panhandle. When Rector was born there in 1928, the population was less than four thousand. The local economy was built around the Santa Fe Railroad, which ran through the town. Rector left Slaton for nearby Lubbock to attend Texas Technological University, from which he graduated in 1950. He then enrolled at Southwestern, where the unexpected exodus of faculty left him discouraged; he considered dropping out to enroll in graduate school. During his sophomore year, a chance encounter with Donald Seldin changed his life forever. Rector was studying in the medical library and noticed that Seldin was searching unsuccessfully for a book. Rector went over to the professor and asked what he was trying to find. Seldin replied that he was searching for a physiology formula. Rector indicated that he didn't know where the reference book was, but he thought that they should be able to derive the equation on their own. He asked Seldin to describe the parameters of interest, and much to Seldin's amazement Rector was able to determine the formula.

That evening, Seldin told his wife, Muriel, about this talented medical student that he had met, and the following morning he called Rector into his office to get to know him better. A few months later, when Rector encountered Seldin again on the wards during his junior year, the admiration became mutual. Seldin's brilliance as a presenter at weekly "Grand Rounds" and student lectures was spellbinding. Rector decided that he should spend the summer of 1953 working in Seldin's laboratory.

The research experience in the sweltering heat of "the shacks" was quite literally a test by fire for Rector. He was assigned to set up the flame photometer that Seldin had brought with him from Yale. An instrument used for measuring charged particles, the aging flame photometer was, in Rector's words, "a horrible piece of equipment. It was run by propane and there would be occasional explosions."[13]

Rector did not sustain any permanent injuries; equally important, he produced two scientific papers that were published in leading journals, and his work was presented at a prominent national meeting in Atlantic City. His research focused on how a specific enzyme in the kidney responded to changes in blood levels of ammonia. Rector was able to demonstrate that the enzyme's activity increased as the circulating ammonia level increased. He would later characterize this finding as "one of the first demonstrations of an adaptive increase of an enzyme in the kidney to produce an effect."[14] At summer's end, Seldin invited Rector to his office again to discuss the young man's career path. In what was becoming a familiar pattern, Seldin had it all planned out for Rector. Six decades later, Rector remembered with precision how Seldin "sat down and told me what I was going to do with my life."[15]

Rector graduated from medical school in 1954 and, like his classmates Norman Kaplan and Jere Mitchell, remained in Dallas for his internship and residency at Parkland Hospital. Rector traveled to Bethesda to interview for a two-year research fellowship in the Laboratory of Kidney and Electrolyte Metabolism at the NIH, one of the leading centers for studying kidney function. Seldin accompanied Rector on the interview and spent an hour talking privately to the laboratory director, Robert Berliner.[16] Then, Rector had a five-minute interview with Berliner and was offered the fellowship. Working with a staff scientist named Jack Orloff, Rector extended his prior rat studies to dogs. Upon completion of his training in 1958, Rector accepted Seldin's invitation to return as a faculty member. He moved rapidly up the academic ladder, conducted kidney research with Seldin and others, and became director of the Division of Nephrology in 1966.

As described in more detail in chapter 9, Seldin and Rector published about ninety papers together, many of which included their colleague Norman Carter. As with Rector, Carter was a former student who also trained at Parkland Hospital. Rather than going to the NIH for a research fellowship, however, Carter remained in Dallas to work with Seldin. The threesome of Seldin, Rector, and Carter became the nidus for a growing kidney research program at UT Southwestern. Before long, it was considered one of the premier renal physiology programs in the country.

The collaboration was sustained for fifteen years until Rector departed to become the head of nephrology at the University of California, San Francisco (UCSF). He remained in that position for sixteen years before being appointed chairman of medicine there. Rector remained a highly productive investigator, contributing important insights into the mechanisms by which the kidney reabsorbs sodium and bicarbonate. One of his most accomplished trainees was Robert Alpern, who later reconnected the circle with UT Southwestern, where he was appointed to head the Division of Nephrology and then later served as the school's dean. The multigenerational inheritance of national recognition in nephrology, passing from Seldin to Rector to Alpern, was manifest in their sequential stewardship of the largest professional organization dedicated to the study of kidney disease—the American Society of Nephrology. Seldin was the society's second president in 1967–1968. Almost a decade later, Rector was elected president, and Robert Alpern followed in his footsteps a quarter-century later.

Seldin's trifecta in his first class of medical students was hardly a fluke. In his next class, he found equally promising candidates. One was a soft-spoken and bookish young man whose parents were public school teachers. Born in 1932 in a small town in West Texas (placing him in the middle of both the Great Depression and the Dust Bowl), Jean Wilson learned from his parents that education was a path to greater opportunity. He graduated from high school at fifteen and found his way to the University of Texas at Austin, where he majored in chemistry and minored in zoology. Graduating from college in 1951 at nineteen, Wilson's choices for medical school were constrained by his family's tight finances. His father encouraged Wilson to enroll at the Southwestern Medical School, largely on the basis of the reputation of its chairman of medicine at the time, the brilliant Tinsley Harrison.[17]

Between Wilson's acceptance and his enrollment seven months later, however, Harrison decided to return to his home state of Alabama to lead its new medical school. So, Wilson arrived in Dallas to find only the shacks that Harrison had forsaken. The first two years of medical school did not capture Wilson's fancy, and he, like Rector, even considered leaving to pursue a graduate degree. Again, mirroring Rector's experience, Wilson found a much-needed role model during his junior year of medical school when he encountered Donald Seldin. Seldin's intellect, knowledge of medicine, and commitment to excellence immediately convinced Wilson that academic medicine was the place for him to be.

The summer of 1954 provided an early test of this chosen career path. Again, following Rector's example from the prior year, Wilson was selected to conduct research in Seldin's laboratory. Wilson was assigned a project based on the prior work of Robert Pitts, a pioneer in the field of kidney research. At the time, Pitts was chairman of physiology at Cornell University School of Medicine. Seldin wrote of Pitts that he had "an incisive capacity to focus and identify critical issues, to design meticulous studies of great experimental ingenuity, and to integrate the results thus obtained into an overall theoretical framework of formidable explanatory power."[18] Pitts had published two studies indicating that the removal of the adrenal glands, and thus the hormones they produce, impaired the ability of experimental animals to handle acids. Seldin designed an experiment for Wilson to elucidate the possible mechanism by which adrenal hormones could affect the kidney's processing of acids. Learning how to remove the tiny adrenal glands from rats without causing mortal injury occupied much of Wilson's summer. When he finally mastered the surgical technique, his findings were surprising.

Rather than displaying the anticipated reduction in ability to handle acids, Wilson's adrenal-free rats responded normally. He gathered his data together and made an appointment to discuss the results with Seldin. Unable to contain his excitement, Wilson exclaimed: "Dr. Seldin, Pitts is wrong!" Astonished by the outburst, and even more alarmed that a junior medical student would contest the work of a renowned scientist, Seldin asked Wilson to explain. After reviewing the data, Seldin concluded: "Pitts is right! Wilson is wrong! Repeat the entire summer's work."[19] It took two more years for Wilson to fully convince Seldin that his results were correct. The following year, their findings were published in the esteemed *Journal of Physiology*,[20] but the novice investigator never had the satisfaction of hearing his professor concede to him "Wilson is right! Pitts is wrong!"

During his senior year, Wilson had an epiphany while listening to a seminar at which Seldin discussed a patient who produced a hormone normally but whose body was unable to respond to the signals appropriately. Wilson wanted to understand how hormones worked, and at the time little was known about their modes to action. By studying conditions such as the one in the patient presentation, where a person was resistant to hormone action, Wilson thought that he might be able to gain insight into normal hormonal processes. This would become a major focus of his subsequent research career.[21]

In the familiar Seldin grooming strategy, Wilson remained at Parkland Hospital for his internship and residency. During his training, he spent a six-month elective doing research with one of Seldin's first faculty recruits from outside of Texas. With a wry smile, Wilson recalled how Seldin passed the baton of supervision to the newcomer, Marvin Siperstein: "When I finished my scientific problem with him [Seldin], he fired me. He informed me one day that he decided to move my appointment from his lab to the laboratory of a new faculty member whom he recruited, Marvin Siperstein." Wilson added that Seldin "explained that the reason for it was that Marvin had fewer things to break."[22]

Siperstein was an expert on metabolism who had come to Dallas from the NIH. Siperstein assigned Wilson a project examining whether the consumption of saturated and unsaturated fats affected the way rats processed cholesterol. Wilson was able to publish several papers from this work. Equally important, Siperstein, who maintained strong contacts with his former colleagues at the NIH, could advocate for Wilson to be accepted there for further training.

Wilson was selected to work with Sidney Udenfriend at the Laboratory of Clinical Biochemistry of the National Heart Institute in 1960. He spent two years in Bethesda learning how to perform biochemical studies, especially the importance of doing control experiments. After completing his fellowship, Wilson returned as planned to UT Southwestern; among other topics, he began to pursue his interest in the action of hormones. Of particular fascination to him was how testosterone impacted the organs of the male urinary and genital tracts. Along with his postdoctoral fellow, Nicholas Bruchovsky, Wilson discovered that the hormone that most stimulated activity in the prostate was not, as had been expected, testosterone per se but rather a closely related breakdown product, dihydrotestosterone (DHT). Wilson then demonstrated that a genetic deficiency of the enzyme that converts testosterone to DHT impedes the embryonic development of male genitalia.[23]

Wilson and his colleagues also demonstrated that DHT caused benign enlargement of the prostate in two species—man and man's best friend, the dog. The pharmaceutical company Merck then discovered that a drug, finasteride, could block the formation of DHT and thereby shrink an enlarged prostate. Finasteride was approved in 1992 as the first medication for treating an enlarged prostate.

In addition to numerous awards and honors, Wilson served

as the editor-in-chief of the prestigious *Journal of Clinical Investigation* from 1972 to 1977. Against Seldin's advice, Wilson also served as an editor for five editions, and editor-in-chief for one edition, of *Harrison's Principles of Internal Medicine*. Named in honor of its founding editor-in-chief, Tinsley Harrison, this textbook has been venerated as a bible of medicine since it first appeared in 1950 when Harrison was still the chairman of medicine in Dallas. Seldin was not a fan of textbooks in general, preferring to read and teach from the original scientific literature. Wilson, however, had missed the chance to study under Harrison, and he more than made up for it decades later when he carried the mantle forward for Harrison's textbook.

One of Wilson's classmates in Dallas was Daniel Foster, a native of the small town of Marling, Texas, about a hundred miles south of Dallas. Raised in El Paso, Foster graduated from Texas Western (later renamed the University of Texas at El Paso) in 1951. He matriculated at the Southwestern Medical School and, like Wilson, came under the influence of both Donald Seldin and Marvin Siperstein. Foster went on to graduate first in his class in 1955, and like his fellow superstar classmates he remained at Parkland Hospital for his internship and residency, serving as the chief resident in 1958–1959.

Upon the recommendation of Seldin and Siperstein, Foster was accepted as a research fellow at the NIH. Once he was exposed to the bright lights of a major research institution, Foster's only view of Dallas was in his rearview mirror: "I really wasn't planning on coming back," he later recalled. He noted, however, that "Seldin's very persuasive."[24] When he arrived back at his alma mater in 1962, Foster was mentored by Marvin Siperstein. In fact, many of the young faculty recruits were drawn to Siperstein. Foster credited Siperstein with implementing Seldin's vision for a scientifically based practice of medicine.

Foster's own research career was just beginning to bloom when a young British biochemist named J. Denis McGarry arrived in his laboratory in 1968 for a postdoctoral fellowship. Within a year, McGarry was appointed to the faculty and invited by Foster to codirect the laboratory. This partnership was sustained for thirty-three years until McGarry's untimely death. The pair seamlessly blended Foster's expertise in the clinical manifestations of diabetes with McGarry's background in the biochemistry of metabolic processes. They chose to focus on how two hormones—glucagon and insulin—impact the body's consumption of fats as a fuel source. A series of elegant experiments led to the discovery in 1977 of a specific molecule (malonyl Co-A) that inhibits the consumption of long-chain fatty acids. This pathway is particularly important in patients with insulin-dependent diabetes mellitus, where defective utilization of sugars as a source of energy leads to burning fats for fuel and the accumulation of acidic by-products. This work also proved to be fundamental to understanding many bodily processes, including the regulation of food intake, weight loss, and the development and progression of liver disease and heart attacks.

As with Wilson, Foster's scientific discoveries were recognized by his election to the Institute of Medicine (later renamed the National Academy of Medicine). He also won the Banting Medal—the highest scientific recognition of the American Diabetes Association. Perhaps the greatest honor of his career, however, was to be asked in 1987 to succeed Donald Seldin as chairman of medicine. He followed in the footsteps of his mentor, continuing to build the national stature of the department. He also received the Robert H. Williams Distinguished Chair of Medicine Award from the Association of Professors of Medicine, twenty-four years after his mentor won the same award.

These five early students, and many others that Seldin later identified and nurtured, helped him to realize his dream of building a premier medical school in Dallas. Even competitors at venerable medical schools began to pay attention. One early admirer was the famed cardiologist Eugene Braunwald, who spent twenty-four years as chairman of the Department of Medicine at the Harvard-affiliated Brigham and Women's Hospital. Of Seldin, Braunwald smiled and said: "It was easy for me to see that he was really a pied piper and would attract . . . the best people. . . . I have said that one of Don Seldin's wonderful qualities is that he has the best taste in academic horseflesh of anyone who's been around in the last half century."[25]

Seldin was not unique in his ability to identify talented students. Braunwald and other leaders of academic medicine had their own strong track records in selecting future luminaries. In Braunwald's words, Seldin "did what we all do, only he did it much faster and much better. I don't think there was anything mystical about it. It's just that he was able to analyze people as he was able to analyze experiments, without the struggle that the rest of us have."[26]

One former fellow, Neil Kurtzman, was trained by Seldin for a career in academic nephrology. Kurtzman noted that Seldin "picked out a lot of talented people, identified them, and sent them away to get trained. That was a wonderful trait, but a lot of people could do that. What he did that nobody else that I know of could do is he got them to come back. And he got them to come back when the school wasn't that great a place."[27]

This raises the obvious question of why Seldin was so successful in drawing his protégés back to UT Southwestern after they were polished at the best institutions in the country and had many competing job options. Kurtzman believes the answer is clear: "It was his personality; his intellect." Even if Seldin could be demanding and difficult to work for, his former students admired his work ethic, his honesty, and his loyalty. Kurtzman added: "He attracted people who were tough. You had to be able to withstand a lot. There were some people who were not attracted. . . . They didn't live up to his standards, which were really high. So, he attracted a certain type of person. He attracted the super alpha male . . . in spades."[28]

Yet another returnee was David Hillis, who served as chief resident at UT Southwestern before Seldin recommended him to Braunwald for a cardiology fellowship. The only admission requirement was a ten-minute interview during which Braunwald told Hillis: "Don [Seldin] says you're a good guy. How would you like to come to the Brigham?"[29] Braunwald confirmed that if Seldin "recommended somebody, there would be no question" about acceptance into his fellowship program.[30] When the training came to an end, Hillis recalled Braunwald telling him with a chuckle: "I would love for you to stay here, but if you're not back in Dallas by July 1, Don will kill me."[31] Hillis attributed his decision to return to Seldin's charisma: "It was the magnetism surrounding him personally." Moreover, Seldin created an "atmosphere in the department . . . that was just magical. Every day was just incredibly exciting and interesting."[32]

Mike Brown, one of Seldin's faculty recruits who trained previously at the University of Pennsylvania, Massachusetts General Hospital (MGH), and the NIH, agreed that Seldin had nurtured an environment that did not exist at other institutions: "There was incredible camaraderie. Maybe it's because it was Dallas—there isn't much else to do in Dallas. Maybe that's why the department was so cohesive . . . everybody was young; this place hadn't been around long enough for anybody to be old."[33]

Through a mix of his towering intellect, high standards, personal magnetism, and superior knack for spotting rising stars, Donald Seldin attracted and developed homegrown talent. Together, he and his acolytes from the Lone Star State and beyond built a premier department of medicine from the flat prairie, ground-up. Across the country, even in venerable Boston, others took notice.

CHAPTER 7

HERE'S A DIME

For a half-century or more, one of the rites of passage for medical students and internal medicine resident physicians at UT Southwestern was to be taught by Donald Seldin. Even when the department grew and there were many other faculty members to share the teaching load, Seldin devoted a substantial portion of his schedule to educational activities. Each week he would deliver at least one student lecture and hold a separate conference with interns and chief residents. In addition, every weekday he would discuss with the six ward resident physicians and the chief residents the care of the patients admitted to Parkland Hospital the preceding day.

A former chief resident and later eminent faculty scientist, Helen Hobbs, recalled Seldin's approach to these morning reports: "He was brilliant. . . . Sometimes people would present cases that were very obtuse to me. He would ask three questions and then it would be apparent. He'd get right to the diagnosis."[1] David Johnson, the current chair of the Department of Medicine, described Seldin's clinical acumen: "He was always remarkably adept at making diagnoses. It wasn't by magic. He systematically worked through every case and it was an incredible display of how implicitly his brain worked." Johnson continued: "Anyone paying attention would do their best to try to mimic his approach because it was so sophisticated, but so logical."[2] Hobbs noted that Seldin had subtle mannerisms that added to the trepidation, whether by intention or otherwise: "He had this watch that had a thick gold band. He used to take it on and off and play with the change in his pockets. Everything [else] would be quiet and he'd be grilling somebody about some aspect of the presentation. I found it very intimidating, but also very compelling and I learned a lot."[3]

On Wednesdays, Seldin conducted a chart conference in which the medical records of patients discharged from Parkland Hospital over the prior several months were reviewed with the first-year resident physicians—the interns. The former student, resident physician, and faculty colleague Robert Haley described the scene before the conference: "Going into that, all my fellow interns would gather in the hall. I played high school football here in Dallas. It was just like before a game. You're with your buddies and you look out there and you see the opposing team. The battle is about to begin and you anticipate it with great excitement." Haley added: "You were just buzzing with excitement and people were saying: 'He's going to get one of my patients. Who's he going to get today?' It was excitement. It wasn't fear. . . . You went in there keyed up for the competition and the challenge."[4]

In the chart conference, Seldin would open a thick paper file and say: "This is the chart of so-and-so." Then the intern who cared for that patient would give a short synopsis of that patient from memory, often supplemented by notes scribbled on pocket-sized index cards. The discussion that ensued would focus on the care that was delivered during the hospitalization. Haley elaborated: "Oh, my gosh, he had a laser eye. He would find that abnormal lab test that you didn't explain. He would say: 'Dr. Haley, this is a lady with low potassium. When she was discharged, the potassium was still low. Did you think that was nothing to worry about?'" Each intern was caring for so many desperately ill patients at Parkland Hospital that it was almost impossible to recall specific laboratory results for each one. Haley continued: "He would just mercilessly drill you on why that [abnormal test result] was important and what you should have done about it. Then he would slam the chart as if he was disgusted and go on to the next chart. You'd go: 'I survived that one.'"[5]

Although the chart conference was a stress test for the interns, the master class taught by Donald Seldin was his virtuoso performance at Metabolic Rounds on Friday afternoons. These sessions were held in a classroom on the sixth floor of Parkland Hospital adjoining the internal medicine ward. The patient to be presented would be selected by the chief residents but not discussed in advance with Seldin. Typically, it involved a patient who was in the hospital or who had been discharged recently. Not knowing anything about the patient in question, Seldin would have to fit together the information presented to him like pieces of a jigsaw puzzle. The resident physicians would begin by describing the patient's chief complaint, then proceed to the past medical history, then physical examination, and finally laboratory studies. As David Hillis, a former chief resident and later a faculty colleague, described: "When the presentation was completed, and he [Seldin] had taken a few notes at the board, he would then proceed. Now, he might proceed by asking the presenter additional questions. He might proceed by asking pointed questions at members of the audience sitting there. He would simply call on somebody or point at somebody and ask them what they thought."[6]

If the patient was still in the hospital, Seldin might lead the entourage out of the classroom and down the hall to the patient's room. It could be an intimidating experience for a patient lying in bed to be surrounded suddenly by a professor and as many as two dozen protégés. Hillis recalled that the chairman, like Seldin's own mentor, John Peters, "was very precise and careful in his questions; very kind and considerate and very warm in his interactions with patients."[7]

Another former chief resident who later joined the faculty, John Warner, painted a similar portrait of Seldin's bedside manner: "He was very interested in patients' opinions and their symptoms and describing their illness, but he always treated patients with utmost respect. He was very formal with them in many ways. He would come in and explain who he is, who all the people in the room are . . . then, he would ask them questions. . . . He wanted to hear it in their words."[8] Juha Kokko, a former head of nephrology and later chairman of medicine at Emory University, recalled one of the ways that Seldin put his patients at ease: "He made rounds with the patients and always held the patients' hands when he talked to them. The patients loved him."[9]

While Seldin was engaged with a patient, the medical students and resident physicians were observing, but their minds were racing ahead to the questions that might ensue. According to Warner: "We were sitting there thinking 'What's he going to ask as soon as we leave the room?' We were all listening to the patient, [and] we were listening to Dr. Seldin thinking: 'Oh, no, here we go. What is he going to get us on next?'"[10] The team would return to the classroom and Seldin would take center stage. Fredric Coe, a former fellow who went on to head nephrology at the University of Chicago, recalled that Seldin "would stand up while everyone else was sitting down. He was kind of tall and he would have a blackboard. He'd march around pointing to people or sometimes tap someone on the top of the head and say: 'You, say something.'"[11]

David Hillis described Seldin's teaching style as "very interactive. . . . You couldn't hide from him. . . . If you hoped to come to the conference and enjoy the show and learn something without participating, the chances are pretty good that you would not succeed in avoiding participation."[12] Coe recalled that medical students and resident physicians "were fair game, but they weren't the fairest game. The fairest game were the [nephrology] fellows. They were expected to be able to do this."[13] Coe described a typical interaction: Seldin would "stop with the serum sodium and he would turn to one of the fellows and he would say: 'You.' That's how he referred to us. He'd say, 'You say something about that.' Whatever you said, it would be hopeless, utterly hopeless, and then there'd be a second number. He'd say: 'Somebody else say something about that.' You'd say something and then that would be hopeless."[14]

Helen Hobbs had vivid memories of Seldin's approach: "He would ask a million questions and really put you on the spot, but everybody got used to it. . . . I actually think it was a really good thing. He really made you think about things in a very deep way and held you highly accountable. So that when you didn't know, you felt badly about it."[15] Hobbs thought that these sessions provided great personal insight: "Yes, you were embarrassed, but it was a process that had nothing to do with him trying to embarrass you, but with him letting you put the mirror up to your face to realize: this is what I know; this is what I don't know; this is what I should know."[16]

Hobbs described her mentor Seldin as "a very direct person. He would ask you very pointed questions and you either knew the answer or you didn't. If you didn't know the answer, you had to get comfortable saying, 'I don't know.' If he caught you trying to figure out a way not to answer the question, but talk a lot, he just would not put up with it." Hobbs added: "I really liked his ability to ask tough questions and not make it personal. It wasn't about you as a person. It was about the patient."[17]

Sometimes, the street-smart kid from Brooklyn in Seldin would emerge from somewhere deep inside the erudite professor. He had a few trademark lines that he would deliver when he thought a trainee was being evasive or not giving his or her best effort. Perhaps the most familiar refrain, while he towered over a student and again jangled his pocket change, was: "Here's a dime. Go call your mother. She will know the answer to my question. Tell her that you are coming home." Another favorite line was: "Your patient could have received better care at J.C. Penney." A classic Seldin assessment was: "This is a beautiful example of therapeutic frenzy combined with abysmal ignorance."[18]

Often, the repartee was accompanied by a physical gesture that could be equally unsettling. William Henrich, who served on the faculty before leaving for a series of academic appointments culminating in the presidency of the University of Texas Health Science Center at San Antonio, recalled such encounters. Seldin would grab a person by the scruff of the neck "and squeeze it while he was talking to you, which gave you a sense of [physical] discomfort at the same time that you're mentally uncomfortable. So, it was a very carefully orchestrated one-two punch to the recipient."[19] Robert Haley had similar recollections: "You were sitting there chilled over—were you going to feel the cold hand squeezing your shoulder as he walked among us? You would suddenly feel the grip on your shoulder and he would say: 'Bob, what do you say about this? What's the answer to this?'"[20]

At only 155 pounds, Seldin would have been listed as a lightweight if he were a boxer. In the world of academic medicine, however, he was a heavyweight who packed a powerful punch—both literally and figuratively. Henrich remembered being poked in the chest by Seldin: "He would hit you more than just touching you. He would actually make the point so that I've seen people actually take a step backwards because they thought they were going to lose some of their balance from it." Henrich continued: "Now, he did this to everybody, so it wasn't personal, and it was very effective. It made people pay close attention. All of my friends who knew him and respected him, and in some ways loved him, were recipients of that treatment."[21]

John Warner noted: "When you were scolded, either you didn't understand something, or you had done it wrong. If you were incomplete in your diagnosis or treatment, he would certainly point it out in the most granular of ways." Warner added: "Coming from many people, that would make you feel despondent or disappointed. . . . but you never felt that way with him. . . . You didn't leave feeling defeated. You left feeling inspired."[22] Henrich agreed: "There was an uplift at the end where you could see a path forward. . . . There was, underneath it all, without any question, his desire to make you better. He wasn't going to sugarcoat the elements that he thought you were lacking in to make you better."[23]

Still, the way that the message was delivered often was hard to swallow. On occasion, his theatrics reportedly included opening a window and yelling out of it: "Police! Police! Help! Someone is trying to kill my patient!" When his temper flared on rounds, Seldin was not averse to tossing an aluminum-clad medical record down a hospital corridor, clattering noisily until, mercifully, it came to a rest.

Warner cited one conference in which Seldin paused and declared: "We've quickly got to stop the conference and go straight to the patient's bedside because your care was so bad that this patient could be in dire circumstances." Warner recalled that, as the team headed to the ward, the natural response was to think: "This is the worst day of my life. . . . Not only have I made a mistake, but now we're going to amplify it by trying to get him to talk about it in front of the patient." In the end, Warner still felt that Seldin had a way of ending the encounter on a positive note.[24]

Warner offered an analogy to playing a video game: "At the end of it, you get destroyed—you die or something bad happens to you, so you don't get to the next level." With Dr. Seldin, Warner indicated that "a lot of your inspiration was to see how far you could go before he got you. . . . So, every time you saw him, the next time you're thinking, 'I could go one level higher.' . . . So you could get further down playing the Seldin video game." Rather than feeling defeated, "you went back wanting to get better. . . . I've seen very few people get upset even though they might have been heavily criticized. . . . You didn't leave feeling like you were a bad doctor. You just felt like you could have done better and here's how."[25] Juha Kokko recalled that the trainees "responded to it and sometimes I was surprised that they really didn't take issue with him [Seldin], but they never did." Kokko thought that Seldin came across to the resident physicians as a demanding parent: "They always felt like it's the father telling the son, 'Dammit, you've got to do a better job.'"[26]

There was even good-natured joking between the resident physicians and Seldin about his style of teaching. One group of trainees presented Seldin with a cartoon caricature of a vulture, with an inscription under it reading: "To the Chief from the Boys." The framed drawing occupied a position of honor on the wall of Seldin's cluttered office, surrounded by his numerous prestigious awards and certificates.

The medical students also enjoyed the opportunity to poke fun at Seldin. The senior students began a tradition of making a graduation video that was a parody of a famous movie or television program. The students often chose Seldin as the main character, and Seldin enjoyed hamming it up in the various featured roles. One take-off on the *Seinfeld* television series was titled *Seldinfeld*. In a spoof of *The Godfather*, the chairman of medicine played the lead role, Don Seldini. In a film fashioned after *Star Trek II: The Wrath of Khan*, the students produced *The Wrath of Don*. This good-natured ribbing from the students reflected how much they appreciated Seldin's commitment to their education, even if his instructional style left a few bruised egos and dented medical charts. To some extent, Seldin's willingness to join in the fun was an indication of the fact that he did not want to be perceived as remote or unapproachable to the students.

His former student and long-time faculty colleague Jean Wilson observed that Seldin "told me in later years that he never really criticized people that he thought couldn't stand it. He only criticized people who he thought were tough enough to stand it. But, I don't think that's true. I think he found out who was tough enough to stand it ex post facto."[27]

Seldin was aware that some trainees found his teaching style to be unpleasant and even distasteful. Looking back over the years, he confided to Bill Henrich: "Sometimes people have taken this the wrong way." Seldin then followed up with a rhetorical question: "What am I going to do? I have to tell people what I'm thinking, and I have to be honest with them because I wouldn't be honest with myself if I didn't do that."[28]

Robert Alpern, the former head of nephrology before becoming dean at UT Southwestern and later Yale, underscored Seldin's absolute commitment to the values that he learned at Yale from John Peters. "He stood for truth and hard work and commitment to knowledge, and people wanted to be around him because of that. . . . He could never tell a lie. . . . If he thought something wasn't perfect, he could keep quiet, but he could never lie. . . . If you asked, you got the truth."[29]

Thomas DuBose, a former trainee and later faculty member who became chairman of medicine at Kansas and then Wake Forest, remembered one occasion when he thought Seldin had been too aggressive in his interrogation of a trainee. DuBose was a junior faculty member at the time, and after the conference ended he walked with Seldin back to his office. "I told him what I thought, and he received that very well. I asked him if he would apologize to this young lady." DuBose reported that Seldin paused, apparently surprised, and asked, "Do you really think I need to?" DuBose replied: "Yes, sir, I do." To his credit, Seldin followed this advice and apologized to the trainee.[30]

When viewed from current norms of how faculty members may engage with trainees, the Seldin style seems painfully anachronistic. In Seldin's day, the professor was king (there were strikingly few queens) who ruled with absolute authority. Some monarchs were more benevolent than others, but nobody questioned the royal authority. Today, a faculty member who touches a student in an unwanted manner, or even addresses a student in a challenging way, could be brought up on charges of harassment. Much has been gained in the evolution of classroom codes of conduct, but perhaps something has been lost as well. Seldin's students may have been motivated, in part, by fear of being called out, but they were motivated nevertheless.

The current chief of nephrology at UT Southwestern, Orson Moe, will never forget his first introduction to Seldin as a fellow. "He [Seldin] was talking about steroid metabolism. He had chalk [and] he said: 'Draw cortisone.'" Moe was paralyzed by fear and Seldin continued

"C-O-R-T . . . are you deaf? Draw the structure." Moe replied, "I can't. I can't draw them." Seldin looked at the nervous trainee square in the eye and told him that if he couldn't draw the chemical structure of this steroid molecule, then he could not possibly understand anything about it and had no business prescribing steroids to patients or ordering hormone levels. Seldin concluded: "You either know this or you don't." Moe confesses that he was "reduced after this." He continued: "That evening, I remember that I studied that pathway all night. I said, 'If this S.O.B. asks me this again, I'm going to blow him up.' He didn't ask me again, but I know the structure."[31]

Moe saw the method in the madness: "I personally found that these torture sessions were extremely helpful because I'd always leave the room feeling that: 'OK, there's something that needs to be done.' I will do it and feel pretty good about it." In Moe's mind, the message from Seldin was: "You cannot say, 'I've learned enough.' No, there is no limit. . . . Bruises were accompanied by something very, very inspirational."[32]

While the interactive parts of these teaching sessions were seared into the memories of trainees, the most spellbinding part of the lecture was Seldin's command of medical information. At the Metabolism Conference, he would not know anything in advance about the patient, so he had no notes or preparation to guide him. He would download information from his seemingly infinite memory banks, writing it all on the blackboard as he spoke. One former trainee who later became an academic leader at multiple institutions, Jay Stein, referred to Seldin as a "chalkboard clinician." As he talked, Seldin would illustrate his points with elaborate drawings and diagrams on the blackboard.

Robert Alpern described one such lecture: "I saw him give a talk to the residents on the porphyrias . . . just off the top of his head." Porphyrias are rare, usually inherited disorders in which the oxygen-carrying protein of hemoglobin is not manufactured appropriately. There are eight separate steps, each controlled by a different enzyme, and a defect in any one of these chemical catalysts can lead to a porphyria. Seldin identified "the entire pathway from bilirubin to metabolism with every intermediate, every enzyme. [He] showed where each of the blockages were in each of the porphyrias." The most amazing part was "this was an unknown case in which he got it wrong, so he wasn't in any way prepared to talk about porphyrias. . . . He just sat there for an hour at the blackboard and did this. . . . I've never seen anything like it and he did this repeatedly."[33]

The former fellow Fredric Coe described a similar scene when he invited Seldin to come to the University of Chicago as a visiting professor. At the morning report, a resident physician presented a patient who had just been admitted to the hospital. As was the custom, the patient and his or her diagnosis were unknown to the discussant. In this particular presentation, virtually all that Seldin was told was that the patient was found lying on the street while intoxicated, with both low body temperature and low blood sugar. Seldin rose to begin his analysis and said to the assembled group of resident physicians: "Would one of you young men [and they were all men] kindly draw on the blackboard the main pathways for glucose [blood sugar] metabolism? Which ones are temperature sensitive and how might hypothermia [low body temperature] have contributed to the hypoglycemia [low blood sugar] in terms of temperature sensitive reactions?" The silence in the room was deafening, so Seldin began "tapping people on the shoulder and top of the head, saying, 'You, you're young and smart and very attractive looking. You get up. Take my piece of chalk. I'm an old, tired man. Write something on the board."[34]

When nobody in the room could muster the courage to stand up, Seldin continued: "Alright, anybody in the room, write anything on the board about glucose. Anything at all—just anything." Still, the crowd remained motionless. Then, in Coe's words, Seldin "turned his back on the group and started writing on the board—sketched out the entire glycolytic [sugar breakdown] pathway and glucose production pathway. . . . All these enzymes were included [and he] pointed out which ones were notoriously temperature sensitive and where the hypoglycemia might have come from." Coe continued: "Now, it took him about eight to ten minutes to draw it all with a running commentary about every step. He dusted his hands off, turned to the group, and said: 'You picked the case. You were here all night. You have books. . . . You could have read a book. . . . None of you did it. What good are doctors who won't get a book and read?' With that, he said, 'I'm done' and walked out of the room."[35]

In Coe's opinion, Seldin could pull off this performance without seeming haughty because "he was truly erudite. He really had the stuff, so you would forgive him. More than that, you admired him for his knowledge."[36] Coe introduced a Fluid and Electrolyte Conference at the University of Chicago modeled after Seldin's Metabolism Conference. Having run these conferences for many years, Coe understood how challenging it was to deliver a cogent presentation without any advance knowledge of the case. "It was a high-wire act in which he put himself out there completely doing an unknown in a public space. He was completely confident. He had such knowledge. It was just beyond anything."[37]

Coe pointed out that although Seldin's powers usually appeared to be superhuman, he was not infallible. One such event occurred when Seldin was at the blackboard writing a set of equations and there was an error in one. "I knew that," Coe admitted, "because he had done something I had done, so I said it was wrong." Complete silence. Seldin responded: "Well, Hans Krebs [Nobel laureate in Physiology or Medicine] wrote it this way. I wrote it this way and Dr. Coe says I am wrong." Coe persisted: "It's just wrong. The math is wrong." Coe got up, took the chalk from Seldin, and wrote the correct equation.[38]

As Coe recalled: "Seldin walked out of the room. He didn't say anything. He just walked out. And everybody was angry with me. . . . Floyd [Rector] looked at me like: Did you have to do that, Fred?" Coe continued: "The next morning, I was sitting in the conference room and Seldin came up to me and ran his fingers through my hair and he called everybody back into the conference room—all the fellows, all the faculty, everybody." Then, Seldin went to the chalkboard and rewrote all the equations from the preceding evening. He said: "This is what Dr. Coe said and he was right, and I was wrong." Coe continued: "Then he went into an elegant discourse into exactly where he was wrong and exactly where I was right. . . . He spent in the evening some time really looking at the math. He was perfectly willing in a public space to say he was wrong." Coe concluded: "I gave him a lot of credit for that. If you gave him something, he would give you a lot back."[39]

One of Seldin's greatest gifts was his ability to integrate biomedical science into his discussion of a clinical presentation. This was a direct inheritance from his Yale mentor, John Peters. As Seldin wrote about clinical investigation at Yale: "Its presence in non-investigative clinical settings [would] inculcate into students and house staff the habits of critical inquiry so necessary to medicine. The ultimate expression of this model was the concept that each patient on a university service should be approached with an investigative attitude."[40]

This integration of science and patient care permeated Seldin's lectures. Juha Kokko gave an illustrative example. If the patient under discussion was someone with heart failure, "Don would start his discussion about calcium transport and isolated myocytes [heart muscle cells] and how that would affect the contractility of the myocardium [heart muscle]. Then he would go into the studies from the cell to the heart—what's been done in isolated [cell] preparations. Then, he would go to the humans, and then he'd go to the population types of studies."[41]

A naturally gifted teacher, Seldin had little tolerance for a poorly constructed or delivered lecture. Faculty colleagues, particularly those at junior ranks, learned from him how to deliver an effective lecture. These lessons could be humbling, even when the recipients knew they were motivated by the best of intentions. One of the first faculty members to experience a Seldin teaching tutorial was Jean Wilson. A member of Seldin's second class of medical students, Wilson was hand-picked by Seldin for further development.

Wilson described his first teaching assignment as a newly minted faculty member: Seldin "wanted me to introduce genetics lectures into the curriculum for the junior and senior students. I was thrilled to have this opportunity. . . . July and August and part of September I spent working on two lectures." Wilson's extensive preparations began to unravel when Seldin arrived unexpectedly at the first lecture and sat down immediately in front of Wilson. "If you knew Seldin, he has a very peculiar tic. When he really doesn't like something, he says it by taking off his glasses and pinching his nose."[42]

The lecture had barely started when Seldin removed his glasses, clasped his nose, and "simply put his head and arms down on the desk and spent the rest of the hour shaking his head." Wilson, who would go on to a distinguished career, including election to the National Academy of Sciences, recalled six decades later exactly how Seldin's reaction affected him: "I've always been proud of myself that I didn't wet my pants," he quipped.[43]

After the talk ended, Seldin came up to Wilson, and "he put his left arm around my right arm, pulled me to the blackboard. He picked up a piece of chalk and he restated that lecture as he would have given it. It was a painful experience, but I appreciated the fact that he wanted me to be a good teacher."[44] Wilson pointed out that medical education typically does not focus on how to nurture pedagogic skills: "As an MD, you're expected to be able to teach, yet we're not taught how to teach. He [Seldin] did that. He went to a lot of trouble to do that."[45]

Wilson was not the only future superstar professor to have a lesson in teaching from Seldin. Michael Brown, who along with Joseph Goldstein would share the first Nobel Prize awarded to UT Southwestern faculty members, reminisced about a research presentation that he gave early on. "So, I gave a talk on this great breakthrough, which I thought was fantastic. Dr. Seldin just sort of sat there." Brown continued: "When it was over, it was probably about seven o'clock in the evening. He immediately ushered me into his office and said: 'Now listen, that was a terrible talk. Let me show you.' He took all my slides that I had used and rearranged them in a much more logical order and threw out things that were irrelevant."[46] The impromptu lesson continued for a full two hours. "We were there until about nine o'clock. In fact, his wife, Muriel, called up. . . . He had missed his supper, but that was the kind of person he was and here I was—just a young fellow, really."[47]

Robert Alpern recalled one Grand Rounds lecture that he had delivered in Dallas. "I got a standing ovation . . . I felt really good. . . . Don Seldin was walking out with me and I said to him: 'So, what did you think of that?' Then he proceeded to explain to me why he thought it was awful." Alpern could not hide the fact that he was crushed by Seldin's comments. "After about four minutes of explaining to me why it was awful, he turned to me and said: 'You asked.' He told the truth . . . and sometimes it hurt, but he never wanted to be mean."[48]

Whether he was teaching trainees or teaching other faculty members how to lecture, Seldin was totally committed to the educational process. If his style sometimes appeared more drill sergeant than professor, his motivation was to make the learners better physicians. He believed in hard work and was unforgiving if he felt a trainee was not delivering his or her best effort. His former student and then faculty colleague Floyd Rector stated aptly of Seldin that "there was no place to hide from the power of his probing intellect. The standards he set seemed at times to be outrageous and unattainable. He was intolerant of the illogical and poorly informed argument, the disorganized lecture, pedestrian research, indifferent patient care." Rector added: "Seldin does not suffer in silence, his rage is never inarticulate."[49]

For generations of UT Southwestern medical students, resident physicians, and fellows, the chalkboard lectures delivered by Donald Seldin are the most enduring memories of their medical education. To be taught by a true master, even when the lessons were painful, was the experience of a lifetime.

CHAPTER 8

THE TRIPLE THREAT

When Donald Seldin assumed the mantle of chairman of medicine at UT Southwestern in 1952, he brought an unfamiliar philosophy and expectations to the Dallas campus. Seldin's approach can be traced in large measure to that of his mentor at Yale, John Peters. A less direct connection, but still a powerful influence, went back a generation earlier. The template for the modern American medical school was forged in Baltimore at the close of the nineteenth century. At that time, medical education in the United States typically was delivered in proprietary schools that, by and large, were little more than diploma mills (for-profit outfits that were a poor substitute for university-affiliated institutions). In establishing its own medical school, Johns Hopkins University sought to create a more academic model. Among the innovations introduced at Johns Hopkins were stringent admissions requirements and a four-year curriculum with an emphasis on the growing scientific foundations of medicine, including laboratory instruction and bedside teaching of clinical medicine in a university-owned hospital. Johns Hopkins also created a model for an apprenticeship after graduation, in which selected candidates lived and worked at the teaching hospital and therefore were called either "resident physicians" or "house staff." Over time, the once avant-garde educational prototype at Johns Hopkins became the standard for medical schools in the United States.

Johns Hopkins was fortunate to recruit four of the leading physicians of the day to become the founding fathers of the medical school: William Welch (pathology), William Halstead (surgery), Howard Kelley (gynecology), and William Osler (medicine). They were attracted, in part, by the offer of a full-time salary, allowing them to focus their energies on research and teaching in addition to patient care. Among this Mount Rushmore of medicine at Johns Hopkins, Osler arguably was the most celebrated for his contributions to the profession, so much so that frequently he is characterized as the "father of modern medicine."

A native of what is now Ontario, Canada, Osler received his medical degree from McGill University in Montreal. He extended his studies in the major European medical centers of London, Vienna, and Berlin. Osler returned to North America and pursued a series of academic chairs, first at McGill University, then at the University of Pennsylvania, and finally, in 1888, at Johns Hopkins.

With a clean slate at a brand-new medical school, Osler established three mutually reinforcing priorities: to offer the best medical care to patients at the newly opened Johns Hopkins Hospital, to provide scientifically grounded education to the medical students, and to contribute to the knowledge base relating to disease development and treatment.[1] Osler was accomplished in each of these three domains. He was widely recognized as an astute diagnostician, and his services as a consultant were in high demand. As a scholar with diverse clinical interests and a background in pathology, Osler published papers on topics ranging from blood disorders, to infectious diseases, to cancer, to heart and vascular conditions. He wrote the preeminent medical textbook of the day, *The Principles and Practice of Medicine*,[2] which remained a best-seller for four decades.

As prodigious as his talents were as a clinician and scholar, it was as an educator that Osler left his most enduring mark. He believed that the passive lecture format employed at most other schools was less effective than hands-on learning. So, at Johns Hopkins, Osler brought the students into the dispensary (outpatient clinic) and onto the hospital wards for clinical instruction. Students were teamed with and supervised by the more experienced resident physicians. Three times a week, Osler conducted teaching rounds with the trainees. Osler quizzed the trainees, probing for gaps in their knowledge. He encouraged his charges to fill those voids by reading further, even allowing access to his extensive personal library. As he famously remarked: "To study the phenomena of disease without books is to sail an uncharted sea, while to study books without patients is not to go to sea at all."[3]

Although he could be demanding, Osler also saw education as a continuing process and thought of himself as a perpetual student. In his words: "When a simple, earnest spirit animates a college, there is no appreciable interval between the teacher and the taught—both are in the same class, the one a little more advanced than the other."[4] It is no surprise, therefore, that Osler found his greatest satisfaction in his role as a teacher. As he wrote: "I desire no other epitaph—no hurry about it, I may say—than the statement that I taught medical students in the wards, as I regard this as by far the most useful and important work I have been called upon to do."[5]

Six decades after Osler arrived at Johns Hopkins, Donald Seldin was appointed to the faculty of UT Southwestern. There were remarkable similarities between their situations. Both joined newly established medical schools and became chairmen of the departments of medicine. They assumed their responsibilities at young ages—Osler was forty, and Seldin, at only thirty-one, was even more of a tenderfoot. Both profited from prior faculty appointments at Ivy League medical schools—Osler at the University of Pennsylvania and Seldin at Yale. They shared reputations as superb clinicians and outstanding teachers. Both were committed to advancing the scientific knowledge base of medicine. They favored instruction in small group settings, with hospital wards serving as their classrooms. Their trainees went on to distinguished careers as leaders of academic medicine in the United States and beyond. Finally, Osler and Seldin read broadly, had diverse intellectual interests outside their chosen profession, and also possessed an encyclopedic command of medical information.

Yet there were striking differences between the circumstances that greeted Osler and Seldin. Osler was recruited to a private university with considerable resources, including state-of-the-art laboratories, library, and hospital facilities. Seldin, in contrast, was employed by a public university that was underfunded and housed in decrepit facilities. Osler was surrounded by colleagues who were distinguished in their respective areas of specialization, whereas Seldin encountered an exodus of other leaders from his institution and was literally the last man standing. It is no exaggeration, therefore, to contend that Osler began his tenure as chairman of medicine with major built-in advantages when compared with Seldin. As Eugene Braunwald, the distinguished and long-serving chairman of medicine at the Harvard-affiliated Brigham and Women's Hospital, surmised: "This was handed to Osler on a platter—a silver platter—and Seldin had to create the platter."[6]

Osler is such an iconic figure in American medicine that to mention any other mere mortal in the same breath might be considered a form of heresy. And even though Seldin most certainly was not the second coming of Osler, their shared values and priorities are undeniable. Osler died on December 29, 1919, almost exactly ten months before Seldin was born, yet there is a striking continuity of thought and values that stretches across the generations that separated them.

Donald Seldin admitted that he was guided by principles that he later characterized as "old-fashioned."[7] Even though he worked at a medical school that was not part of a comprehensive university, Seldin viewed the medical school as part and parcel of the larger academy. From that perspective, he believed that the common denominator between medical faculty and their colleagues in other scholarly disciplines was a shared commitment to scholarship.

In the medical school microenvironment, and particularly within its clinical ranks, Seldin stated that he "always thought that the model should be what I would call the clinical scholar; someone who is interested in medicine and competent in medicine but can illuminate it with first rate research and teaching."[8] An individual who fits this definition of "clinical scholar" glides between separate but interconnected roles as a scientist, a teacher, and a clinician. In medical school circles, such an individual often is described with envy as a "triple threat."

Seldin summarized his profile for the ideal faculty member: "We want someone who would be surpassingly brilliant as an investigator, a dazzling clinician and a marvelous teacher." He quickly added: "That doesn't happen usually. Occasionally it does, but usually not."[9] In more practical terms, Seldin described what he sought in a faculty member: "Someone who is interested in medicine, in clinical disease in patients, and at the same time wants to illuminate that experience by research as basic as he or she is capable of, and who finally enjoys contact with students."[10]

The type of scholarly activity that Seldin most valued was, in his view, knowledge of underlying fundamental sciences such as biochemistry and physiology. Today, such a view might be construed as overly narrow, excluding important areas of research such as clinical trials, informatics, behavioral sciences, health economics, medical ethics, and population health, among other examples. Seldin was quick to defend his priority, however. "Now, this is often misconstrued. I don't mean to sound heartless and I recognize that there are many other aspects of medicine, but the necessary condition for a physician is the mastery of biomedical science." Seldin noted: "That is not a sufficient condition. There are many other qualities we look for, but that would be critical."[11] Later in his life, he adopted a somewhat broader view, but he never abandoned his belief in the primacy of biomedical science.

As a physiologist, Seldin was partial to scholarship in that domain. As he wrote: "It is characteristic of the laws of medicine that they usually have this physiologic character. They organize vast amounts of data into broad generalizations that apply within an organ system or link together several organ systems."[12] Seldin continued: "It is by virtue of physiologic laws of this type that normal and deranged regulatory functions are formulated. . . . From the point of view of clinical medicine, therefore, such laws are 'basic,' and investigations designed to discover them are, properly speaking, basic research."[13]

From Seldin's vantage point, someone who was immersed in the study of basic research was uniquely able to translate these concepts into medical practice: "The only person who can meaningfully bring the developments of biochemistry, physiology, and other sciences into a clinical context, where they have relevance to the management and understanding of disease, is the clinical scholar who himself is concerned with these issues."[14] For this reason, Seldin believed that it was imperative that a clinical scholar be engaged both in research and the practice of medicine, and he saw each patient encounter as presenting a research question.

In addition to excellent patient care and basic research, the third, and in many ways the most important, leg of the tripartite stool for the clinical scholar was teaching. Seldin felt strongly that a medical school should be more than a trade school with a goal of churning out practitioners who simply apply the tools of the trade. This was, in fact, the nature of most American medical schools—including his own in Dallas before he brought a different vision to it. He would characterize the prior reliance on private practitioners who did much of the teaching as follows: "In clinical departments particularly, the educational program was developed by physicians who, however conscientious and competent, were occupied with the responsibilities of private medical practice, and who had neither the time nor the training to develop medical science or instill into students the habits of critical inquiry so necessary for scholarly growth."[15] Seldin added: "The practice of medicine, no matter how skillfully and responsibly conducted, becomes progressively removed from the science of medicine to the extent that the clinician is no longer simultaneously an investigator."[16]

Seldin favored an educational model where the instruction was performed by full-time faculty members who met his definition of clinical scholars. In his words: "Quality of mind and habit of thought distinguish the scholar and entitle him to mediate between student and patient."[17] His experience as a student, resident physician, and faculty member at Yale convinced him of the merits of the tutorial system. In that model, a small number of trainees care for patients under the direct supervision and guidance of a faculty member. As Seldin affirmed: "I think the tutorial model was a strong one. It's after all an old renaissance model. If you wanted to be a painter, you worked with Leonardo."[18] In the same vein, if you wanted to be a clinical scholar, you worked with Seldin.

In Seldin's Department of Medicine, the expectations of the faculty were clear. As the former student and long-time faculty colleague Jean Wilson described it: "You were assigned teaching and clinical duties and you had to figure out how to do research and the academic part on the side. So, you had to create longer days."[19] Wilson and many of his faculty colleagues could be found working in their laboratories into the dead of the night. Another of Seldin's former faculty members, William Henrich, who went on to become a chairman, dean, and university president, summarized Seldin's expectations: "You had to have a grant—a peer-reviewed grant, preferably two. You had to teach the students and be good at it, and you had to take superb care of people. You had to publish your findings. There were no excuses. There just were no easy exceptions."[20]

David Johnson, the current chairman of the Department of Medicine at UT Southwestern, captured Seldin's style with a colorful analogy: "Don Seldin was like the coxswain on a rowing team. He was the guy barking out the instructions and he was the guy always looking forward. The rest of us were looking backward, thinking about how to make what we had done better. He was always thinking about how we could do new things that would make us better." Channeling Seldin, Johnson bellowed the cadence: "'Work harder. Do your best. Give it your all.' [That's] what a coxswain does and that's what Don Seldin was to me." Johnson continued the analogy: "If you're worn out toward the end of the race and you feel like you just can't pull that oar one more time, the [coxswain] is yelling at you: 'Pull, pull!' You dig deeper down for yourself, for your teammates, and for your leader."[21]

Under Seldin, when it came to teaching, the faculty were expected to be authorities in their own subspecialty, but also to be knowledgeable about the full spectrum of medical conditions. The former resident physician, faculty colleague, and friend David Hillis paraphrased his former boss by pointing out "that everyone—junior faculty, senior faculty—ought to have this fundamental core of medical knowledge."[22]

A master educator himself, Seldin saw the professorial role as paramount: "It is the teacher who sets the climate for learning in a cordial spirit. It is he who directs the energies and enthusiasms and animates the good student and the mediocre student as well."[23] To Seldin's mind, the emphasis should not be placed on which specific topics were covered, but rather on how the students were taught to think about a clinical issue. As he wrote: "It seems to me far more critical that the methodology of modern science be placed at the disposal of the student in an exciting clinical circumstance."[24]

Seldin viewed education as the raison d'être of the medical school. As Robert Alpern, the former nephrology chief and later dean of both the UT Southwestern and Yale medical schools, recalled: Seldin "continuously talked about the fact that if you just want to do research,

you should go to a research institute—you shouldn't be at a medical
school. . . . He felt that was the essence—that students should learn
from people who do research and clinical medicine." Alpern added:
"They should learn the beauty of tying research and clinical medicine
together. . . . The only way that you could do that was to have people do
all three."[25] Not surprisingly, when it came to the selection of academic
lieutenants, Seldin was strongly biased toward those who were triple
threats. As Alpern observed: "If you look at who he would appoint as
division chiefs in his department, every one of them was a triple threat.
He never would appoint a researcher who wasn't a great teacher and a
great clinician."[26]

Seldin also believed that the volume of clinical work performed
at a medical school should be confined to that which was necessary
to fulfill its educational and scientific missions. In his words: "The
magnitude of patient care should be delimited by the requirements of
teaching and research."[27] He worried that social and political pressures
could distort a medical school's priorities. At the same time, Seldin was
deeply committed to Parkland, the public hospital where most of the
clinical education at UT Southwestern occurred. Many of the unin-
sured patients who sought care there had no other options, and Seldin
treated these patients with dignity and respect. At the same time, he
was concerned that if the medical school was expected to fill in all
the gaps in the delivery of health care, it could be overwhelmed with
patient demand. "Some people think a medical school is like a public
utility," Seldin noted, "where physicians are available to mitigate community and other problems."[28] Elsewhere, he wrote: "The price for the
solution of community service requirements may be the inexorable
erosion of academic activity."[29]

If such words seem austere or insensitive, it is useful to recall
that Seldin was molded by a liberal social activist: John Peters. In the
1940s, the Yale professor was one of the first physicians in the country
to advocate for universal access to medical care. Echoing his mentor,
Seldin wrote that medical service needs "are pressing, and no responsible citizen can question the social value of legislation designed to
bring the fruits of medical science to all people."[30] Parkland Hospital
was a great equalizer, where persons without financial means could
receive high-quality medical services. Robert Alpern noted that "with
Parkland, we were able to care for the indigent, which he [Seldin]

really cared about."[31] Seldin championed the mission of Parkland Hospital, but he also felt that unconstrained growth of the clinical enterprise could distract the faculty from the important educational and research missions of the school. As Alpern noted, Seldin "felt that once [UT] Southwestern built a private hospital . . . making that hospital financially successful would dominate and would distract us from the triple threat."[32]

In later years, while Seldin remained deeply committed to the role of the clinical scholar in education, research, and patient care, he acknowledged that "the model is in the midst of a crisis."[33] He pointed to the financial pressures that most medical schools face: "Now, almost everywhere there is a requirement to generate resources through largely clinical activities and this has imposed a tremendous burden on any clinical faculty member." Seldin further noted: "Previously, the reward system was focused largely on scholarship—not only scholarship, but scholarship principally. But now, issues that are seemingly remote from scholarly activity, like money generation, begin to assume a dominating feature on the scene." In essence, faculty members are being asked to "do teaching, but we won't reward you for teaching. Do research, but you better generate clinical income. And the net effect is a certain schizophrenia."[34]

As medical schools evolved from the earlier Osler era, to the Peters era, to the Seldin era and beyond, the one constant was the need for visionary leaders. Each in his own way adapted the best parts of the prior model to the prevailing circumstances of a new generation. As a result, there was both continuity and progression in American medical education.

To this day, prominent leaders of academic medicine find themselves placing Seldin in the Oslerian stratosphere. Barry Brenner, former head of the renal division of the Harvard-affiliated Brigham and Women's Hospital, asserted that Seldin's "undistracted long-range vision over the past seven decades led as much to the current excellence and stature of the University of Texas Southwestern Medical School and affiliated hospitals as did Osler a century before in establishing and ensuring the future greatness of Johns Hopkins Medical Hospital and Medical School."[35]

Brenner's boss at the Brigham and Women's Hospital, Eugene

Braunwald, concluded that there were two giants of modern medicine: "I think that the first was William Osler. He was a great physician. He was a keen observer. He was an extraordinary teacher. He created a medical school—Johns Hopkins. I think a person who is his equal in terms of impact would be Donald Seldin."[36]

John Dirks, former head of nephrology at Osler's original academic base, McGill University, and later dean of the medical school at the University of Toronto, endorsed this judgment. Speaking of Seldin, Dirks concluded: "I'd say he is the closest analogy in the world to Osler."[37] Dirks conceded that comparisons across generations are just as difficult in medicine as in other human endeavors. He suggested that the Osler-Seldin comparison was a bit like weighing the relative merits of home-run sluggers Babe Ruth versus Hank Aaron—a generation apart—each with his own strengths and neither diminished by the other. Braunwald, a lover of classical music, preferred an analogy to legendary composers: "It's like comparing Beethoven to Mozart."[38]

Certainly, there were other titans in academic medicine during the Seldin era. Braunwald himself, sometimes described as the "father of modern American cardiology," was born nine years after Seldin and became chairman of medicine first at the newly opened University of California, San Diego medical school (1968–1972), then four years later at Brigham and Women's Hospital (1972–1996). Lloyd Hollingsworth "Holly" Smith, an endocrinologist, was four years younger than Seldin and was appointed chair of medicine at the University of California, San Francisco (1964–1985). James Wyngaarden, a rheumatologist, was four years younger than Seldin and was appointed chair of medicine first at the University of Pennsylvania (1964–1967) and then at Duke University (1967–1982). Robert Petersdorf, an infectious disease expert, was five years younger than Seldin and was appointed chair of medicine at the University of Washington (1964–1979), later serving in senior positions at Harvard and the University of California, San Diego.

Any list of prominent chairs of medicine in the second half of the twentieth century might be drawn too narrowly. When Seldin was asked to name his own pantheon of great chairs, in addition to Braunwald and Smith, he suggested three others who were a decade older than him (Eugene Stead, Duke University, chair, 1947–1967;

Carl Moore, Washington University in St. Louis, chair, 1955–1972; and Robert Williams, University of Washington, chair, 1948–1963). Seldin also mentioned his fellow nephrologist Robert Schrier, who was sixteen years his junior and chair of medicine at the University of Colorado (1976–2002).[39]

For simplicity, the following comparisons are drawn among the quintet closest in age: Seldin, Braunwald, Smith, Wyngaarden, and Petersdorf had many parallels in their careers. Each began as a clinician scientist and was deeply committed to the model of the triple threat. Each became a chairman of medicine at a relatively early age. Seldin was by far the youngest at thirty-one, while the others (much like Osler) were all around forty. Each was trained at preeminent institutions, yet three (Seldin, Braunwald, and Smith) of the five joined either new or struggling schools. They were drawn by the opportunity to build excellence from the ground up. Especially when measured by today's norms, all remained in their principal chairmanships for extended tenures, ranging from fifteen years for Wyngaarden and Petersdorf to thirty-six years for Seldin. In building their respective departments, each had a critical eye for talent and the force of personality to attract it. Their trainees and junior colleagues went on to distinguished careers in academic medicine at institutions across the country.

These five leaders of academic medicine had another thing in common: all were recipients of the prestigious George M. Kober Medal from the Association of American Physicians (AAP). The AAP is a highly selective organization of distinguished physician-scientists. One of the seven founders of the AAP was William Osler. Established in 1925, the Kober Medal has been awarded annually to a member for lifetime contributions to internal medicine through their own research and the training of other leading physician-scientists. In 1985, Seldin was the first of the quintet to win the Kober Medal, followed in quick succession by Smith (1986), Wyngaarden (1991), Petersdorf (1996), and Braunwald (1998).

Joe Goldstein, who shared both a Kober Medal and a Nobel Prize with collaborator Michael Brown, noted of his mentor: "One thing about Dr. Seldin's erudition—he didn't always wear it lightly."[40] To underscore the point, Goldstein recalled the words of another Seldin acolyte, Floyd Rector, who made the Kober Award presentation to Seldin and remarked that his mentor "received the news that he would be the recipient of this year's award with mixed emotions. He was deeply moved at the prospect of joining the distinguished company of the Kober medalists, individuals whom he had admired and respected throughout his career, yet he was disappointed that he would not be able to make this presentation himself."[41] Goldstein smiled and then added a footnote: "He was particularly annoyed about the allocation of time given to the presenter—thirty minutes—and to him—three minutes."[42]

When it came his turn to accept a Kober Medal in 2002, Goldstein was quick to acknowledge his mentor: "I fell under the spell of Donald Seldin, a man of towering intellect, immense erudition, keen zest for life, irrepressible curiosity, and deep respect for clinical scholarship. As a teacher, Dr. Seldin was a true maestro in the way he taught clinical medicine to third-year medical students."[43] Goldstein's scientific partner, Michael Brown, in his own Kober Medal acceptance speech also acknowledged his debt to Seldin: "When I arrived in Dallas, I was thrilled by the departmental conferences that Seldin dominated like a great oracle. These conferences were peppered with fiery arguments and salted by Seldin's demand for evidence to support every assertion." Brown elaborated further on the environment that Seldin fostered: "The whole department focused on disease mechanisms. Everyone had a laboratory. You could have called it the Department of Applied Physiology except that they took very good care of the patients at Parkland Hospital."[44]

Among this quintet of great leaders of academic medicine, two were particularly close colleagues and friends: Seldin and Braunwald. They started life under similar circumstances. Both grew up in Jewish families in Brooklyn and were "subway students" living at home and commuting to the Washington Square campus of New York University as undergraduates. Braunwald remained at NYU for medical school, whereas Seldin headed off to New Haven. The two first met in the early 1960s when Braunwald, then a leading scientist at the NIH, came to UT Southwestern as a visiting professor in cardiology. Braunwald recalled: "I was sort of carried away by his [Seldin's] enthusiasm and his dedication to the academic process."[45] Elsewhere, Braunwald noted that his decision to leave the NIH and return to a university setting was heavily influenced by the examples set by others: "The people who were rising to the top were people like Donald Seldin and Holly Smith." Braunwald added: "They were a half-generation older than I was, and by the end of the 1960s these people had taken over and were changing the whole landscape of academic medicine. I admired so much what they were doing—a combination of teaching, research, and clinical medicine, all in synergy."[46]

The rise of UT Southwestern stood out in Braunwald's mind: "I was particularly wowed by Don Seldin and what he was developing in Dallas. I watched what he did, and thought, 'Now I know what I want to be.' Like him, I wanted to create an environment in which talented young physicians could become triple threats. I wanted to be one of them. I realized that I wanted to become a chairman of medicine."[47] That opportunity arose when the newly created medical school at the University of California, San Diego recruited Braunwald to serve as its first chairman of medicine. "I was influenced by the contacts I had with Seldin. . . . He made it seem that it would be thrilling, absolutely thrilling, to start a new department."[48]

Braunwald used the phrase "role model" when he talked about his friend in Dallas. Braunwald credited Seldin with "building what would become the strongest academic department of medicine in the nation and perhaps the world."[49] Following Seldin's example, during his tenure as chairman, Braunwald continued "to maintain my clinical skills—whatever I had—and maintain a research program."[50] One further recommendation from Seldin to Braunwald was to support the other departments, particularly the basic sciences.[51] Seldin also helped Braunwald think through tough departmental political and management decisions. According to Braunwald, Seldin "was a very good sounding board. . . . He gave me the courage to do unpopular things, and that really was enormously helpful."[52]

Seldin, Braunwald, and their contemporaries, including Smith, Wyngaarden, and Petersdorf, transformed American medicine after World War II. Even within this elite group, however, Seldin stood out. As his protégé Michael Brown declared: "Medicine has never seen and will never see his equal."[53] Seldin assumed a leadership role in an institution that had been an academic wilderness. He began at a younger age, with less prior preparation, and fewer resources than the others. He set an endurance record as a chairman of medicine that was half again longer than any of these peers and is unlikely to be equaled by any other chairman of a major department of medicine. It was a record that even William Osler would have admired.

CHAPTER 9

LAB PARTNERS

Donald Seldin began his research career under the tutelage of John Peters at Yale School of Medicine.[1] His early papers reflected the diverse clinical conditions under investigation within the Chemical Division of the Department of Internal Medicine, with two studies of diabetes, two on edema (fluid leakage from the bloodstream into tissues), and four about the kidney's control of the levels of various chemical compounds. Even at the very beginning of his science career, Seldin's work was attracting notice. A paper on the metabolism of sugar and electrolytes (dissolved charged particles) in the blood of patients in diabetic crisis was reported in preliminary form at the preeminent national clinical research meeting in Atlantic City, New Jersey, in May 1949.[2] Two years later, after Seldin moved to Dallas, one of his papers from his time at Yale was selected for presentation at a major session of the Atlantic City meeting, where it was introduced by none other than John Peters.[3]

After Seldin left Yale, he no longer had his mentor, or a state-of-the-art chemistry laboratory, or a crowd of dazzling young faculty colleagues. But one thing he did find at UT Southwestern was a bright former research fellow who transitioned onto the faculty. Mackenzie Walser, a graduate of the Columbia University College of Physicians and Surgeons, trained in internal medicine at Massachusetts General

Hospital before commencing his fellowship at UT Southwestern. Walser later joined the faculty of Johns Hopkins University, where he spent a distinguished career in nephrology. In the year that Walser overlapped with Donald Seldin in Dallas, they amassed data for five separate published papers.

After Walser departed, Seldin relied on the students at UT Southwestern as his summer workforce in the laboratory he had set up in the medical school's decaying shacks. One of the first students to join Seldin was Floyd Rector, a native of West Texas and graduate of Texas Tech University. In their very first encounter in 1952, while Rector was still a sophomore medical student, he astounded Seldin by his ability to derive a physiological equation from basic information that Seldin provided. Mathematics was one of the few subjects that did not come naturally to Seldin, and he immediately recognized that Rector brought a complementary skill set. In 1953, Seldin offered Rector a summer research experience after his junior year, and that study resulted in two presentations and two published papers.

Years later, Seldin had the opportunity to recall some of the lighter moments of Rector's introduction to research. One of the pieces of equipment that Rector was assigned to install and operate was a flame photometer, which was used to measure charged particles such as sodium and potassium. Seldin noted that "when activated, it had a tendency to explode," adding that Rector "succeeded in destroying the laboratory and flooding the place on numerous occasions. It was a terrifying experience when he ventured to the bench. Everyone within eyesight scattered."[4]

As with other promising medical students, Seldin mapped out a career development plan for Rector, beginning with an internship and residency at Parkland Hospital. From there, Rector completed a two-year research fellowship under Robert Berliner at the Laboratory of Kidney and Electrolyte Metabolism at NIH. Seldin's ultimate goal was for Rector to return to Dallas as a faculty member.

Berliner, only four years older than Seldin, already was established as one of the most prominent renal physiologists in the country. Born in New York, he was a mathematics major at Yale and graduated from the Columbia University College of Physicians and Surgeons. Berliner undertook his residency training at the affiliated Presbyterian

Hospital and during World War II worked under James Shannon on malaria research in New York. In 1950, Shannon, who by then had become associate director of science for the National Heart Institute at NIH, recruited Berliner to run the Laboratory of Kidney and Electrolyte Metabolism.

At NIH, Berliner assigned Rector to work with Jack Orloff, who had also trained with John Peters at Yale. Orloff was interested in Rector's student project on the kidney enzyme adaptation; they repeated the study, originally conducted in laboratory rats, in dogs. Those experiments resulted in a publication that confirmed the earlier work, and Rector headed back to Dallas in August 1958, first as an instructor and then as assistant professor of medicine. In Dallas, he rejoined Seldin and another former student, Norman Carter. A year ahead of Rector in medical school, Carter remained in Dallas for clinical and research training. For the first couple years, the trio continued to rely on clearance studies, where the chemical composition of blood was compared with that of urine, allowing them to make an educated guess about what happened in between in the kidney.

Clearance studies were analogous to counting vehicles entering at the start of a toll road and comparing that number to the number of vehicles exiting at the final toll booth, but without being able to view the traffic flow or the intervening entrances and exits. The papers published during this period were short on measurements and long on discussion. As Robert Alpern, later the head of nephrology and then dean at both UT Southwestern and Yale, described: "They would make three measurements and then you'd have a four-page discussion section explaining what it meant." Alpern added: "They would start talking about which segment of the kidney did what, but they actually had no technology to measure the individual segments. . . . Years later, when the technology evolved to measure the individual segments, most of what that generation of researchers concluded turned out to be true."[5] Orson Moe, who later became head of nephrology at UT Southwestern, agreed: "It was pioneering at the time because I think they pushed the technical limits. The interpretation of the data was brilliant. . . . He [Seldin] predicted the site of action of a lot of the diuretics before they [could] actually get down to [investigate] the tubule."[6]

Rector was not content with the limited view that could be

achieved with clearance studies—he wanted to penetrate the "black box" of the kidney by making direct measurements using a new technique. More precisely, he wanted to deploy an old methodology that was born again. The technique of micropuncture involved the use of a tiny glass pipette to sample fluid from within the microscopic functional unit of the kidney—the nephron. Along the course of the nephron, urine is formed by the sequential processes of blood filtration, then reabsorption of needed water and nutrients, followed by active elimination of waste products. There are about a million nephrons in a single human kidney, each of which contains a fine tube that is between one and two inches long, with a diameter as narrow as a human hair in places.

To penetrate this diminutive structure and then sample fluid from it required both skill and specialized equipment. The technique was pioneered in 1921 by A. Newton Richards at the University of Pennsylvania with a young colleague, Joseph Wearn. It was an amazing feat at the time, requiring the ability to construct and insert a minute sampling device under microscopic visualization and analyze the chemical composition of infinitesimally small amounts of extracted fluid. Using micropuncture, one could measure the chemical composition of samples at various sections within the nephron. The paper that Wearn and Richards produced in 1924 from their studies of frog nephrons remains a landmark in renal physiology.[7] Wearn and Richards chose to work initially with amphibian kidneys, as the functional units in frogs were more accessible than those in mammals.

Through World War II, Richards's laboratory was the only site performing micropuncture, which they extended for the first time into a mammalian species (rodents) in 1941. After the war, several other investigators adopted the technique, including Gerhard Giebisch, a native of Vienna who joined the faculty at Cornell University's Department of Physiology in 1957. Giebisch used micropuncture to study, among other things, how potassium is handled by the rat kidney. About two years after returning to Dallas, Rector became interested in setting up a micropuncture laboratory and visited Giebisch to learn more about the technique. The instrument shop at UT Southwestern proved invaluable in helping establish what was at the time only the second laboratory in the country performing micropuncture. Working with research fellow James Clapp, Rector published the first micro-puncture study at UT Southwestern on how chloride is handled by the rat kidney.[8] At risk of falling behind, Berliner recruited Clapp to help set up a micropuncture facility at the Laboratory of Kidney and Electrolyte Metabolism at NIH, where studies were extended to dogs.

Competition between the Seldin-Rector lab and the Berliner lab heated up during the 1960s. As Neil Kurtzman, a former UT Southwestern fellow who later became chairman of medicine at Texas Tech, described: "There's the Seldin School and the Berliner School. . . . Berliner was very physiologically oriented. Seldin's trainees all were taught, no matter how basic the physiology, you had to try to apply it to clinical medicine. Seldin was always trying to figure out how the physiology related to disease, even when they were doing very, very basic stuff."[9] A former fellow and later chief of nephrology at the University of Chicago, Fred Coe, highlighted a conceptual difference between the two labs: "One of the things about the Berliner lab is they worked segment by segment. Seldin's approach, which I think he got from John Peters, was to look at the nephron in terms of longitudinal integration. . . . Things that happened at one place along the nephron are passed down the nephron to other sites." Coe continued: "Seldin thought of the nephron as a continuous functioning element. . . . Seldin had this integrative approach which frankly still holds sway."[10]

John Dirks was a fellow in Berliner's lab who went on to become a chairman of medicine and a medical school dean. Dirks offered the following perspective on the NIH Laboratory of Kidney and Electrolyte Metabolism: "Berliner taught people to do very careful experiments, often chosen to disprove what others might have postulated and where there wasn't certainty about the validity of the data. So, he was kind of a last call. Once Berliner put his seal of approval on it, it usually held for the next number of decades." Dirks used the expression "unassailable experimentalist" to describe Berliner.[11]

Barry Brenner, who also trained with Berliner and later went on to lead the nephrology program at the Harvard-affiliated Brigham and Women's Hospital, described the somewhat frosty relationship between Berliner and Seldin: "There was an ongoing personal competition between Berliner and Seldin. They were both luminaries. They were both very smart and they had a running competition. . . . They were not pals. Berliner didn't have any pals. He was a very quiet, shy man."[12]

Brenner got an up-close-and-personal view of the lab competition during his fellowship. After he learned the technique of micropuncture in Berliner's lab, Brenner decided to test the so-called geometry hypothesis that had been put forward by a German investigator, Karl-Heinz Gertz, and then supported experimentally by Seldin and Rector.[13] The underlying question was: How does the kidney adjust its rate of handling salt and water absorption based upon changes in the amount of fluid filtered out of the bloodstream? Gertz had proposed that an increased flow of filtrate caused the tubule to swell and the change in geometry augmented the reabsorption of salt and water. Experimentally, the diameter of the tubule could be increased by placing an oil blockage distal to the site of measurement. The technical problem with this approach that Brenner discovered is that, if the oil blockage is not long enough, fluid can leak around it and contaminate the measurements. In his words: "I showed that it took a much, much longer column of oil placed into the tubule downstream to my sampling site to prevent fluid from coming back into my pipette."[14] In Dallas, where a shorter oil block was used, a leakage around the intended barrier distorted the findings.

When shown the results, Berliner wanted to go straight to publication. As Brenner later noted: "Nothing pleased Berliner more than for results of his lab to counter results from Dallas. As soon as he saw my results, he said, 'Write it up.' We went over the manuscript, he made a few changes and he said, 'Send it in.'"[15] Brenner indicated that he would do so, but first he wanted to extend the courtesy of sharing his findings with Seldin and Rector. Berliner did not see a reason to disclose the conflicting results, so Brenner bought his own airplane ticket and flew to Dallas in October 1967. As Brenner described: "I showed the data to Rector. It took him ten minutes to realize that they were wrong and I was right." Seldin graciously hosted Brenner and a group of faculty and fellows at a dinner that evening at one of the finer eating establishments in Dallas—The Old Warsaw restaurant. It was an elaborate meal that began with the waiter displaying an eel that was to be prepared as the appetizer. Once Brenner recovered from the idea that he would be consuming this slimy creature from the deep, he was

wined and dined by Seldin. The dessert was served, figuratively speaking, by Brenner himself when his paper was published.[16] According to
Brenner, Seldin and Rector "never said another word in any meeting or
in any publication about the geometry hypothesis."[17]

The inaugural meeting of the American Society of Nephrology took
place soon thereafter in Los Angeles on October 18 and 19, 1967. Berliner had been invited to deliver a forty-minute talk on renal physiology—one of the three main lectures at the meeting. As Brenner
described, Berliner "showed my data as the main thrust of his talk with
relish because he was disproving his competitor's theory."[18] As uncomfortable as it must have been to sit through this lecture, for Seldin and
Rector the following year must have felt like déjà vu all over again.

   This episode likewise began with a hypothesis developed elsewhere. In 1961, Hugh de Wardener, a preeminent British renal physiologist, had suggested that, beyond the two known determinants of
sodium excretion, there was what later came to be known as a "third
factor."[19] The two established determinants of sodium excretion were
the rate of filtration of the blood by the kidney and the steroid hormone aldosterone. Produced by the adrenal gland, aldosterone acts on
the kidney to conserve sodium. De Wardener's postulated additional
agent, also referred to as "natriuretic [sodium excretion] hormone,"
was suggested in studies by Rector and Seldin to be an inhibitor of
sodium reabsorption in the first part of the nephron.[20]

   It turned out that Brenner played the spoiler a second time when
he and colleague Fred Wright from NIH were unable to replicate the
findings from Dallas.[21] Brenner and Wright brought blinded plasma
samples of experimental and control dogs to Dallas, and the investigators there were unable to detect any differences in natriuresis. The
Dallas team also was unable to replicate their earlier findings when the
identities of their own samples were hidden. In retrospect, there were
several potential problems with their earlier experiments.

   First, the fellows in Dallas who were making the original measurements about natriuresis were not blinded to the experimental status of
their own canine subjects. Consciously or unconsciously, the team's
knowledge of the treatment status of the dogs may have impacted their
observations. As Fred Coe, a fellow who was present but not involved

in these experiments, noted: "It was clear; you know the answer, so you make the data fit the answer."[22] Moreover, the measurements themselves were subjective, involving visual inspection of the rate of disappearance of a small droplet of fluid that was placed between oil plugs within the renal tubule. From the speed of disappearance, the investigators inferred the rate at which the fluid was absorbed, hence the name "shrinking drop."

Seldin invited Brenner into his office. In Brenner's words: "The desk was covered with mountains of slides. I had never seen any place more disheveled in my life . . . papers on the floor, on shelves. It was a mess." Amid the chaos, Seldin "sits me down in a high-back chair . . . and he pulls another one up in front of me. Our knees are touching. He does what he has done to me repeatedly over the years. . . . He sticks his index finger into your chest and pokes at you as he's talking."[23] Brenner, alarmed by Seldin's confrontational style, braced himself for a personal attack. What Brenner did not see coming was a job offer (which he politely declined). Although Seldin could not persuade Brenner to join the Dallas team, the two nevertheless became close friends. A half-century later, at a small private dinner that Brenner hosted, Seldin confessed his regrets about the natriuretic hormone studies with some chagrin: "What Brenner did was he shrunk us. We used the shrinking drop and Brenner shrunk us."[24]

One of the great ironies of this "third factor story" is that in 1981—thirteen years after Brenner's second trip to Dallas—a research group from Toronto demonstrated that an extract from the atria of rat hearts was able to create a dramatic natriuresis.[25] This "atrial natriuretic factor," when released from the heart into the circulation, causes a wasting of salt, as well as the accompanying water, through urine output. This diuresis can have beneficial effects for a failing heart by lowering blood pressure, improving heart function, and reducing the abnormal accumulation of fluids within tissues. Later discoveries would reveal that there is a whole family of natriuretic factors.[26] So, ironically, Seldin turned out to be correct in predicting that natriuretic factors existed, even if the shrinking drop experiments were unable to demonstrate them.

In the late 1960s, despite an occasional setback, the Seldin-Rector lab was viewed as one of the most respected contributors to renal physiology. The team cemented its reputation through a series of important scientific contributions. Orson Moe reflected on the heyday of the Seldin-Rector lab: the team there "covered many areas of research, but in terms of making the most impact, I would think acid-base physiology is one and the second is extracellular fluid volume regulation and sodium balance. . . . A lot of what we know today can be traced back to [the lab's research]."[27]

Among the noteworthy studies was one conducted in 1963 whereby Seldin and Rector, with the assistance of fellow Allan Bloomer, demonstrated that potassium is reabsorbed by an active transport mechanism in the proximal part of the nephron.[28] In 1965, in conjunction with their faculty colleague Norman Carter, Seldin and Rector studied the reabsorption of the alkaline compound (bicarbonate) by the kidney.[29] By adjusting the amount of bicarbonate that is reabsorbed, the kidney can help to control the acid-base balance within the body. That same year, the Dallas team reported on the site of action within the nephron of a newly discovered, powerful, and fast-acting diuretic: furosemide. Seldin and Rector, working with the fellow Wadi Suki, demonstrated that the new agent—which would eventually become a widely utilized medication—operated differently within the kidney than the older, more established thiazide diuretics.[30]

The team, led by Norman Carter's technical skills, developed microscopic glass electrodes that could be used reliably to measure the pH within cells.[31] John Dirks (who had been a fellow in Berliner's lab) felt this work was truly innovative: "I remember enthusiastically when Rector and Carter measured the internal pH of a renal tubule cell. That was a technical feat of some measure and that work has stayed the test of time."[32] Rector himself described one of the studies that was made possible by this technical breakthrough: "Using those electrodes, I was able to show that the reabsorption of bicarbonate in the proximal [kidney] tubule" occurred by the secretion of hydrogen ions into the tubule, where they combined with bicarbonate, forming carbonic acid. In this instance, the presence of the enzyme carbonic anhydrase on the lining of the tubular cells served to break down the carbonic acid that was created.[33] In Rector's own assessment: "That probably was the most influential experiment that came out of the laboratory during my time there."[34]

The magic of the Seldin-Rector partnership resulted from the fact that they possessed complementary interests and skills. Of Seldin, Rector said this: "He always had sort of a big picture of what we were working on—heart failure, acid-base disturbances, potassium metabolism." In contrast, Rector saw his own contributions in ferreting out the details of the physiology: "I always tended to focus more on mechanisms. . . . So, we sort of reinforced each other's view."[35] In weighing their relative contributions to the research, Rector characterized Seldin and himself as "coequals." Rector noted that, even though he had started as Seldin's student, he never felt subordinate in their joint laboratory: "That didn't mean that I didn't still call him Dr. Seldin, which to this day, if I saw him, I would call him 'Dr. Seldin.' Jean Wilson and I were plagued with this problem. We never called him 'Donald,' but he treated me as an equal."[36]

Rector went on to describe how others might have viewed the partnership: "Some people thought I was more responsible for the content of the research we were doing than he was. Other people thought that he was a better spokesman for the research. . . . It was a path that we took together."[37] Brenner endorsed a more nuanced view: "I think most of the ideas, in fact, came from Rector. . . . Seldin was very good at promoting the ideas as a salesman. He was the better speaker. He had a larger audience to speak to because he was all over the place. . . . He was invited [to speak] much more I think than Rector was."[38]

For his part, Fredric Coe saw Seldin as the theoretician: "Seldin was freewheeling—highly intellectual—highly analytic. The interaction between them was that Floyd [Rector] would try very hard to keep Seldin anchored to the data at hand. Seldin was synthesizing all the time and he had a terrific flair for conceptualization and, therefore, for hypothesis generation—new hypotheses. He was very imaginative."[39] But Coe likewise saw Rector as the driver of pragmatism in the lab: "Floyd's idea was always to try to keep things on target so there could be some kind of experimental outcome. They were a good match and an excellent pairing. . . . Seldin's intellectuality and flair were transformed by Floyd's quantitative experimentalism into something really good."[40]

One venue where these two colleagues' perspectives would be witnessed was the weekly research conference attended by the nephrology faculty members along with the trainees. One former fellow (and later chairman of medicine at two institutions), Thomas DuBose, described these sessions: Seldin "always came in as the conference was to begin. He sat there and that was sort of command central."[41] For each of the fellows, the seating arrangement identified the pecking order. Another attendee at these presentations was Neil Kurtzman: "Seldin sat at the head of the table and Floyd sat to his left usually. It was a long table and all of the fellows were around it."[42] According to DuBose, Seldin "could look like he was asleep and wake up and just nail the most critical questions—something you needed to do and may have failed to do, or something that you'd thought about and dismissed, but he always made it extremely beneficial and helpful."[43] On occasion, there would be a noisy collision between Seldin's generation of big ideas and Rector's data-driven practicality. Rector himself described these weekly research conferences: "He [Seldin] and I would argue constantly about things. I never had any reservations about arguing with him. We tended to have slightly different points of view and he respected mine and I respected his."[44] Kurtzman affirmed that Rector was not bashful about challenging Seldin: "Floyd didn't hesitate to argue with him [Seldin] by telling him he was wrong when he thought he was wrong—sometimes in very colorful language."[45]

Professional to their cores, Seldin and Rector reserved private time to write together. "The last ten years that I was there," Rector recalled, "[Seldin] and I would meet every Sunday morning to work on writing papers on the basis of work done by the research fellows. That was, to me, just a very exciting thing to do."[46] The two also partnered on preparing Rector's research for presentation at important conferences. Rector described the process: "When I would give a talk at a national meeting, he and I would work on the talk four or five hours putting it together." When they arrived at the session, "The first thing he'd say: 'Let me see the talk. There's some changes I think we need to make,' and he would grab my copy of the talk and start scribbling. That created real confusion while trying to give a talk." Rector thought he had come up with the perfect solution, however: "After he had done that, oh, four or five times, I started memorizing my talks, so I didn't have anything on paper I could give him. The first time I did that, his wife Muriel was at the meeting sitting next to him. When I got up to talk, he had taken his handkerchief and rolled it up into a long roll and

put it in his mouth with the two ends hanging out, one on each side."
Rector laughed and continued: "As I looked over there and saw him,
his wife Muriel put her finger up and twirled it like he's a real nut."[47]

Even when he felt bound and gagged, Seldin could not repress his
admiration for Rector. In his later years, Seldin confided to David Hillis, a former trainee, faculty colleague, and later a department of medicine chair, that Rector was the brightest student or faculty member that
he had encountered.[48] This is high praise coming from someone who
had helped to nurture the careers of Nobel laureates. Seldin appointed
Rector associate director of the Division of Nephrology at UT Southwestern after only four years; three years later, Seldin promoted him
to division director. Even with a title suggesting that he was in charge,
Rector always knew that Seldin was in control. As Jay Stein, a former
fellow who went on to lead academic health centers, observed: "Seldin
was the boss, Floyd was the kid. That is just the way it was. Seldin had
an overwhelming personality."[49] Reflecting back on his days as division
director, Rector confessed that "I have trouble remembering specific
times where we had a meeting of the Division of Nephrology that he
was not there and running it. That was one of the factors that finally,
after many years, pushed me in the direction of leaving."[50] Rector continued: "When I decided that I might want to leave, I took a sabbatical
and spent six months in Germany, just to see what it was like to get
away. When I got back, within a month or two, I received an offer from
[the University of California, San Francisco]. It was an ideal position
for what I wanted to do."[51]

In 1973, after fifteen years of partnership with Donald Seldin, Floyd
Rector decided to head to the West Coast for new opportunities as
division director of nephrology at UCSF. In Rector's words: "I really
wanted to run a division and all aspects of it with the research conferences and the rounds, as well as conducting research."[52] Rector did not
discuss the offer with Seldin until after he had visited San Francisco
and accepted the position. Seldin did not see it coming and told Rector that, if he knew that Rector had been unhappy, Seldin would have
arranged an endowed research professorship so that Rector could be
freed up from his clinical and administrative duties. Although Rector appreciated this counteroffer, it did not really address what Rector

most wanted: to run all aspects of the Division of Nephrology. For
Seldin, Rector's departure was akin to having a son leave home, but
Rector reported that the separation "was very amicable. He [Seldin]
continued to keep in touch with me. He came out to San Francisco on
many occasions for a visit."[53]

For the decade and a half that the Seldin-Rector lab operated at UT
Southwestern, it proved to be a powerhouse in the field of renal physiology. Its leaders jointly published seventy-one scholarly works, which
represented almost four-fifths of Seldin's work during this period.
After Rector left for San Francisco, Seldin's rate of publication of scholarly articles dropped by more than half, and Rector's number of scientific papers fell by a third. They achieved a professional pinnacle while
working together, in part because they were young and hungry, and in
part because of the unique relationship they shared.

Robert Alpern had the privilege of working separately with Rector in San Francisco before coming to head nephrology at UT Southwestern and work directly with Seldin. In Alpern's assessment: "Seldin
was just the giant among giants, but everyone thought that Seldin's best
work was with Rector. . . . Both of them were intellectual giants."[54]

CHAPTER 10

THE ROAD TO STOCKHOLM

Among the many talented medical students that Donald Seldin nurtured, none was more remarkable than Joseph "Joe" Goldstein, a young man from rural Kingstree, South Carolina. Raised in a town of barely three thousand people, Joe was an only child. His father, Isadore, ran a dry-goods store and was a prominent citizen, serving on the city council and many other civic organizations. Joe was a standout student at Kingstree High School, where he served repeatedly as class president and as editor of the student newspaper.

For college, Goldstein attended Washington and Lee University in Lexington, Virginia, which was an all-male institution at the time. Goldstein was a gifted student, at one point earning a near-perfect grade in organic chemistry, with a thirty-point drop to the second-highest performer. Elected to the Phi Beta Kappa honor society as a junior, Goldstein also served as editor-in-chief of the yearbook and was the valedictorian of his graduating class in 1962.

When it came to choosing a medical school, Goldstein was admitted to Washington University in St. Louis, but when a college friend from Dallas encouraged Goldstein to apply to UT Southwestern, Goldstein visited the campus with his friend during spring break. Although it was late in the recruitment season, and few out-of-state students had ever been accepted at UT Southwestern, Goldstein was admitted.

Uncertain of which school to select, Goldstein conferred with a cousin who was an internal medicine physician. As chance would have it, this cousin had just returned from a national medical meeting where one of the most impressive speakers was Donald Seldin. The cousin was convinced that UT Southwestern would be an excellent place for Joe to attend medical school.

As soon as classes began, faculty members were awed by the new student from South Carolina. One such observer was Leonard Madison, who later stated: "We always thought that Joe was something super special. There's Joe Goldstein, and then there's nobody, and then there's nobody, and then there's nobody, and then there's the second one [in the class]. He was just head and shoulders above everybody else."[1] After his freshman year of medical school, Goldstein remained in Dallas for the summer to undertake a research project. His original plan was to pursue an investigation under the direction of the neurosurgeon William Kemp Clark. When Jean Wilson, the former star student who now ran the student research program, learned of Goldstein's plan, he quickly redirected the trainee to a more research-oriented supervisor, Burton Combes. An expert in liver disease, Combes was interested in studying a specific marker in the blood of patients whose hepatic function was compromised. Although a research novice, Goldstein was able to discover a new and more efficient approach to measuring this diagnostic marker. Goldstein later recalled: "This was my first scientific discovery, and I became hooked on the thrill of scientific research."[2] Goldstein was the lead author on three publications resulting from his three summers of research in medical school.

When Goldstein advanced to clinical rotations during his third year of medical school, his internal medicine faculty attending physician was Floyd Rector. Rector concluded that Goldstein was the best student he had ever seen. Wilson confirmed this assessment, and it was not long before Donald Seldin was working his career development magic again. Together, Seldin and Goldstein mapped out a four-step pathway. First, Goldstein would go to the Massachusetts General Hospital (MGH) for two years of clinical training. Next, he would head to the National Institutes of Health (NIH) to acquire research laboratory experience, followed by a fellowship in the emerging field of medical genetics. Finally, he would return to UT Southwestern to establish a medical genetics program.

The first step—gaining admission to MGH's internal medicine training program—was no mean feat even for Joe Goldstein, who graduated first in his medical school class. In 1966, the MGH medicine program took only a dozen internal medicine interns per year, and half of those slots were reserved for graduates of Harvard Medical School. The door was opened for Goldstein by Seldin when the head of gastroenterology at MGH, Kurt Isselbacher, came to UT Southwestern to give a lecture. Seldin introduced Isselbacher to Goldstein, which was enough to help his application stand out among the many hoping to train at the esteemed hospital. Similarly, UT Southwestern faculty member Marvin Siperstein, formerly on the staff of NIH, made contacts on Goldstein's behalf there.

When Joe Goldstein arrived at MGH in 1966, one of his fellow interns was a bright and high-spirited young man named Michael "Mike" Brown. A native of Brooklyn, Brown at the age of eleven moved with his family to Elkins Park, a suburb north of Philadelphia. Mike's father, Harvey, was a salesman for a textile company that served the clothing industry. Mike graduated from Cheltenham High School, where he excelled at scholastics and played third base on the baseball team. As for college, Brown dreamed of attending Princeton and had visions of himself as an alumnus wearing an ascot and smoking a pipe. Brown was admitted to Princeton but received only a partial scholarship. Family finances dictated that he attend the University of Pennsylvania instead, where he was supported on a full scholarship underwritten by Proctor & Gamble.

At Penn, Brown spent a substantial portion of his time writing for the student newspaper, the *Daily Pennsylvanian*. The paper was funded by the university, but the activist staff often took positions that were frowned upon by the conservative administration; some were unpopular even among large portions of the student body. When the paper was shut down because of a parody issue that not everyone found amusing, Brown led a resistance effort that ultimately prevailed, leading to his brief service as editor-in-chief. Despite his rabble-rousing days as an undergraduate, Brown was admitted to the university's medical school.

From the moment he matriculated, Brown contended for the top spot in his medical school class, winning the David Drabkin Prize in biochemistry during his freshman year. Brown's first research experience took place during the two summers before and after his first year of medical school. He worked at the pharmaceutical giant Smith, Kline & French, studying bowel motility in rats treated with an antacid medication. Although the work was not intellectually stimulating, on his own initiative Brown derived an equation to predict bowel motility. He wrote up his results, and they were accepted for presentation at the prestigious Federation of American Societies of Experimental Biology (FASEB) meeting in Atlantic City. Brown also conducted a mentored research project on diabetes under the guidance of the endocrinologist Albert Winegrad and was the recipient of the Frederick L. Packard Award for the best student in internal medicine. Upon Winegrad's recommendation, the newly appointed chairman of medicine, James Wyngaarden, who was well connected at MGH, recommended Brown for training there. It had been nearly a decade since another University of Pennsylvania graduate was chosen by MGH, so Brown was pleasantly surprised when he made the cut.

Upon receiving the list of his fellow interns, however, Brown could not help but notice that one of them had graduated from the Southwestern Medical School in Dallas: Joe Goldstein. With an impish smile, Brown recalled his initial impression of the school in the hinterlands: "I thought it was a Bible school. And, I figured, well, if they're accepting this guy, then maybe nobody applied this year." Shortly after meeting Goldstein, however, Brown came to a very different conclusion: "I remember admiring Joe's intellect and experience very early. Within the first two or three days of internship, it was clear that he knew more than anybody else, not only in the internship group, but more than most of the senior residents and half of the faculty. It was clear that this guy was going someplace and I just decided to ride along."[3]

For his part, Goldstein felt perfectly comfortable with the clinical and intellectual rigors of MGH. After all, he had been groomed by Donald Seldin. Equally important, he and his fellow UT Southwestern medical students at Parkland Hospital were active participants in the care of very sick patients. As Goldstein recalled later: "I didn't really feel intimidated by the other interns. About half of [them] were from Harvard Medical School and they had very little clinical experience."[4] What became apparent quickly, however, was that Goldstein and Brown were cut from the same inquisitive cloth. Brown remembered their regular interactions: "In those days, the interns would have a midnight meal— you'd be working all night, but you'd take a break and the cafeteria would open up for the interns. I remember many conversations that I had with Joe early on, talking about patients. 'Who did you just admit? What's wrong with them? What should be done?'" Brown continued: "Then we would get into the science. We would try to figure out . . . deeper than just simply what was wrong with the patients, but really, why did the patient have it [the disease]? What's the physiology going on? It struck a chord—we were both interested in getting deeper below the surface of the disease."[5]

During their residency, UT Southwestern's own Donald Seldin was invited to MGH as a visiting professor. Of course, Joe Goldstein knew what to expect from his old mentor, but for Mike Brown it was an eye-opening experience. Seldin made rounds with the resident physicians and gave conferences. Brown fondly recalls Seldin's aura: "He was so erudite. . . . That was my first impression: this man from Texas knew more about medicine than the folks at the Massachusetts General Hospital."[6]

While immersed in patient care, Brown and Goldstein had little time to contemplate their futures, but as luck would have it, their time together would be extended when both were accepted into the Clinical Associate training program at NIH. For Goldstein, NIH was step two in the Seldin-designed career development path. For Brown, admittance into the program was no sure bet, but it was one of the few alternatives for graduating physicians to being drafted into the military medical corps during the Vietnam War.

The Clinical Associate application form had spaces for each candidate to rank his (or, in rare instances at the time, her) top thirteen choices. For good measure, Brown wrote in a fourteenth and fifteenth choice. When the labs indicated their own separate rankings, Brown was matched to the NIH gastroenterologist Leonard Laster (Brown's fourteenth choice). Brown was not about to look a gift horse in the mouth, but he was curious about why Laster had picked him. Five decades later, Brown recalled: "After I was there for a little while I asked him [Laster]: 'You know, the other thirteen labs didn't choose me.

Why did you choose me?' He said: 'Well, I was in the audience when you gave that talk on the restrained rats [the bowel motility study]. I thought that was kind of cool what you did. The fact that you actually wrote a formula and you could explain things."'[7] Laster was referring to the talk that Brown had delivered as a senior medical student to a gastroenterology subsection of the FASEB meeting in Atlantic City. By pure coincidence, Laster happened to be one of the couple dozen attendees who wandered into his talk, and thus Brown was saved from a tour of duty in Vietnam.

Working for Laster proved to be a heavy dose of clinical obligations caring for patients referred to the NIH for study. But it was relatively light on the laboratory supervision side, especially when he compared notes with his buddy Joe Goldstein. Brown developed the distinct impression that more exciting science was happening elsewhere. Goldstein had matched into the National Heart Institute at NIH. When his intended supervisor accepted a job elsewhere, Goldstein was reassigned to the laboratory of Marshall Nirenberg. This was a fortuitous choice, as Nirenberg had played a lead role in the highly competitive race to crack the genetic code. In a brilliant series of experiments, Nirenberg and his colleagues solved how the four-letter language of the genetic material was used as instructions for assembling proteins from the twenty amino acid building blocks. Three months after Goldstein arrived in the lab, Nirenberg was announced as a corecipient of the Nobel Prize in Physiology or Medicine for this work. While the champagne corks were still flying, Goldstein and other fellows in the lab were mopping up the final stages of the decoding by studying the coding "stop signs" that appear when a protein is completely assembled.

Even the patients that Goldstein saw at the NIH Clinical Center were fascinating. One special patient was a young girl from Houston and her brother, both of whom had a genetic defect known as familial hypercholesterolemia (FH). This young patient had a cholesterol level that was eight times higher than normal, leading to fatty plaque buildup in her blood vessels, including the arteries of her heart. By age three, she experienced chest pain—a sign that the arteries of her heart already had blockages. Both this little girl and her brother had two copies of an abnormal gene, one inherited from each parent, giving them the severe form of the disease. This double whammy occurs rarely—about once in a million persons. Each parent, with only one copy of the defective gene and a prevalence of about one in five hundred, had a milder form of the disease in which cholesterol levels are twice the normal and heart disease first occurs in young adulthood. Although it was known that this condition had a genetic basis, the mechanism by which the cholesterol accumulated was unclear, and in the days before cholesterol-lowering drugs there was little one could do to treat it. Goldstein and Brown were intrigued by this patient and became determined to figure out what was causing her elevated cholesterol.

Meanwhile, Brown was inserting instruments in the top and bottom ends of patients with various gastrointestinal disorders and imagining glory in the laboratory. His big break came when Laster was called to serve as a health adviser in the President's Office of Science and Technology. With his supervisor gone, Brown was able to negotiate a position in the laboratory of Earl Stadtman, one of the premier biochemists at NIH. Stadtman was studying an enzyme that helped bacteria make the chemical substance glutamine, which in turn was used for energy, detoxification, and building proteins. Because he started a year late in Stadtman's lab, Brown extended his fellowship for an additional year. Toward the end of his commitment, he discovered that the process of enzyme deactivation involved the same agents that were needed for the activation process. The addition of one background chemical ingredient changed the activator to a deactivator.

As Brown was working with his enzyme systems, he was beginning to think about job opportunities beyond his appointment as a Clinical Associate. One possibility was to build on his experience in gastroenterology at NIH and pursue a fellowship in that area. Rudi Schmid, a native of Switzerland who trained in the United States, including at NIH, was a liver specialist at the University of California, San Francisco who was interested in recruiting Brown. Another possibility was to join Joe Goldstein in his trek back to Dallas.

Brown had continued to interact with Donald Seldin at dinners that Goldstein arranged for a group of former MGH resident physicians who were Clinical Associates at NIH. These small group sessions, held in conjunction with the annual meeting of the American Society for Clinical Investigation in Atlantic City, were the perfect venue for Seldin to demonstrate his command of the breadth and depth of biomedical research. "He was so magnificent at these dinners because he could discuss whatever research anybody in that group was doing," Brown recalled nostalgically. "The discussion just moved on to opera and art and football. I mean, it was just amazing to see this man."[8]

Brown took an interview trip out to San Francisco, accompanied by his wife, Alice. For the return, Brown encouraged Alice to fly back to Washington, DC, directly while he took a detour to visit Dallas, in his words "just to be kind to Joe."[9] Much to his surprise, however, when Brown met the other faculty at UT Southwestern, he found them to be equally impressive. Seldin put on the full-court press, encouraging Brown to come to Dallas sooner rather than later and not to get "overtrained" at NIH. Brown was convinced that he needed more time under Stadtman's tutelage, reaffirming that decision in retrospect: "If I had not had that year and a half with Stadtman, then I would have never been able to do anything."[10]

Alice Brown, who like her husband had grown up in the Northeast, was not enchanted with the idea of moving to Dallas. As Mike Brown recalled: "I always tell people that when we were living in Bethesda [when he worked at NIH], we thought that was the Deep South—literally."[11] Somehow, Brown convinced his wife to give Dallas a try, in part by suggesting that likely they would remain there only for a year or so. In the meantime, Joe Goldstein had already started on the third leg of his Seldin-designed professional development tour, having elected to pursue his medical genetics training with Arno Motulsky at the University of Washington in Seattle.

Still haunted by the young patient that he met at NIH with FH, Goldstein proposed to conduct a study of the occurrence of this genetic defect among persons in the Seattle area. With guidance from Motulsky and Edwin Bierman, a clinical researcher, Goldstein surveyed thirteen hospitals in Seattle that provided most of the region's cardiac care. He identified about 1,200 heart attack survivors. From this population, he was able to identify sixteen FH families and was able to estimate the prevalence of the underlying single copy of the genetic defect as between one in five hundred and one in a thousand.[12]

While fully engaged with his population genetics project,

Goldstein also learned what would prove to be an invaluable laboratory skill. By chance, the occupant of the office next door was Stanley
Gartler, who was one of the few people in the world at the time who
was growing human fibroblasts in tissue culture. The main cells of con-
nective tissue, fibroblasts are easily obtained from skin samples and
can be used to detect a variety of metabolic defects. The challenge was
getting them to grow in the artificial conditions of a laboratory, but this
is where Gartler's expertise was invaluable. As Goldstein described: "I
sort of nestled my way into his [Gartler's] lab and he let me work with
one of his technicians, so I learned how to do skin biopsies and how to
start cultures, and so forth."[13]

Back in Dallas, Michael Brown was beginning to set up his own
research program. As a newcomer, he felt that there was some advantage to arriving before Goldstein: "The fact that I came here and had
a year before Joe was extremely important. . . . Joe had already been
recognized as a genius here, as a medical student. So, if we had come
together, then everybody would have thought that I was just on his
coattails."[14] The project that Brown elected to pursue also related to the
patients with high cholesterol levels that he had seen at NIH. With the
expertise he had acquired in isolating and purifying enzymes under
Stadtman's guidance, Brown decided he would work on one of the critical enzymes used to construct the twenty-seven–carbon cholesterol
molecule in the body. That enzyme, HMG-CoA reductase, was notoriously difficult to purify. Even its discoverer, the German biochemist
Feodor Lynen, who shared the 1964 Nobel Prize in Physiology or Medicine for this work, was unable to purify it.

    With a wry smile, Brown recalled his NIH mentor's reaction to the
proposed project: "When I told Stadtman that was what I was going to
do, that's the only time I have ever heard him laugh. He just broke out
and said: 'Wait a second. You're going to do something that this other
guy—this great biochemist—says is impossible? You're going to do it?'
And I said: 'Yes, sir.' Well luckily, I stumbled onto a method and I was
able to at least remove the enzyme from the membrane and partially
purify it."[15] Brown's early success served to establish his bona fides with
Seldin and the other medicine faculty members: "The Department here
had such an interest in that enzyme and the whole cholesterol work,"

Brown observed, "so, I got an opportunity to demonstrate to them that I could do something on my own. They gave me my own laboratory, and when Joe came [back to Dallas], he had his own laboratory."[16]

Goldstein's homecoming to UT Southwestern occurred in 1972. "To begin with," he explained, "our labs were geographically separate."[17] Brown added: "This idea of uniting the two labs—that was never in the plan. We wanted to collaborate on one project dealing with children with high cholesterol, but other than that, the plan was to have separate laboratories."[18] Their collaborative project was on FH. Their initial working hypothesis was that affected persons had a defect in their HMG-CoA reductase enzyme. Normally, this enzyme would be turned off when there were high levels of circulating cholesterol so that the cholesterol manufacturing process would be halted. Brown and Goldstein thought that persons with FH must have an inability of the HMG-CoA enzyme to shut down, leading to excessive production of cholesterol.

To test their hypothesis, the team combined Goldstein's newly acquired expertise with fibroblast tissue culture with Brown's skill at working with enzymes. They successfully demonstrated that HMG-CoA reductase activity could be measured in normal human fibroblasts and that it was reduced in the presence of low-density lipoprotein (LDL) cholesterol. Lipoproteins are the water-loving packages that surround cholesterol molecules, allowing them to be transported around the body within the aqueous bloodstream. LDL often is referred to as "bad cholesterol" because it can be deposited into obstructive plaques within arterial walls, blocking the flow of oxygen-carrying blood to the tissues.

Having demonstrated how LDL levels suppressed HMG-CoA reductase activity in normal fibroblasts, Goldstein and Brown now needed to measure the enzyme activity in cells derived from patients affected with FH. There was only one problem: unlike at the NIH, where FH patients came for study and care, Brown and Goldstein had no ready supply of FH patients in Dallas. Almost as if there was some sort of divine intervention, the telephone rang. The call was placed by a pediatrician in Denver and was intended for the established cholesterol expert at UT Southwestern, Marvin Siperstein, who was out of the country at the time. Brown picked up the narrative: "The secretary answers the phone and this is the most amazing thing. If she hadn't done this, I don't know what would have happened. . . . She said: 'I'm sorry, Dr. Siperstein is away in Switzerland. He's on a sabbatical in Geneva, but he has a young associate, Dr. Brown. Would you like to speak to him?' 'Okay.' She didn't have to say that he had a young associate. Nine times out of ten, a secretary would say: 'I'm sorry, he's not here.'"[19]

Brown continued: "So, I get on the phone and this guy tells me about a twelve-year-old girl and she has this enormously high cholesterol. She's had multiple heart attacks and two days from now, Dr. Starzl is going to do an operation in her abdomen and he will have access to her liver and he will do a liver biopsy. He wanted Dr. Siperstein to come up there and take this liver biopsy and measure the rate at which it was producing cholesterol."[20] The caller was referring to Thomas Starzl, famed for performing the first successful liver transplant; he became chairman of surgery at the University of Colorado School of Medicine. Starzl's plan to measure cholesterol production by the FH patient's liver cells was a bit naive, as there were no comparison values for normal persons. Still, Brown immediately saw the opportunity that Goldstein and he had been praying for and replied: "'I know all of the methods of Dr. Siperstein. I can do that, but all I want is a piece of the skin from the incision,' because that is the way we had gotten the fibroblasts. He said: 'I am sure Dr. Starzl would have no objection to that.'"[21]

Starzl's patient, J. P., had a cholesterol level that was ten times higher than normal and had undergone nine years of dietary and medication interventions without success. She began experiencing chest pain, and studies revealed blockages in the arteries of her heart. After she experienced a heart attack, she underwent the liver shunting procedure on March 1, 1973, that Starzl hoped might lead to cholesterol reduction. Brown was present to receive the skin biopsies, which he transported back to Dallas, where Goldstein began the tissue culture process.

After several weeks, the cells had grown sufficiently for testing. Mike Brown was in Atlantic City to give a talk at the FASEB meeting, so Joe Goldstein ran the HMG-CoA reductase experiment. When the technician Suzy Dana shared the results with Goldstein, the normally sedate, soft-spoken Southerner could not contain himself. In Dana's words: "Dr. Goldstein came back and was looking at the results and was just bouncing off the walls and was saying: 'Do you know what this means? Do you know what this means?' And I kept saying: 'Well, yeah, it looks like it worked.'"[22]

Still basking in the glory of the moment years later, Goldstein noted: "The amazing finding was that when the cells were grown with lipoproteins in the serum, there was about a hundred or two-hundred-fold increase in the cholesterol synthesis enzyme (HMG-CoA reductase) from the girl (J. P.) who had the familial hypercholesterolemia compared with the normal individual. It's very rare that you see a difference like this."[23] Serum LDL had ratcheted down cholesterol production in normal fibroblasts, but in J. P.'s cells cholesterol manufacturing was operating at full throttle, oblivious to the LDL levels outside of the fibroblasts.

With Brown out of town, Goldstein turned to his next closest confidante, Donald Seldin, to convey the exciting news. For Seldin, the eureka moment of the fibroblast experiment was the payoff of the six-year investment that he had made in the professional development of his former student Joe Goldstein. Later that evening, Goldstein was able to connect with Brown by telephone. Brown described the brief conversation: "I get Joe on the phone and he says: 'You can't believe the experiment.' I said: 'What are you talking about?' He said: 'Suzy, the technician, came in and showed me the data. It's unbelievable—I mean, the patient's cells have an activity of the enzyme that's a hundredfold above normal. I really questioned her. There's no question that she did the experiment right, but maybe it's some fluke. Of course, we have to repeat it, but if it's real, we have an incredible discovery.'"[24]

Brown headed back to Dallas the next morning and, with Goldstein, began to plot out the next steps. After confirming their dramatic results on multiple different days, both were eager to rush their findings into print. But the observations, although highly reproducible, were based on a single FH patient, and they needed to replicate it in others before they could claim that it was generalizable. The referral from Starzl had been a chance phenomenon: they needed to find another source of FH patients. They hit pay dirt when they contacted Jean Davignon at the Institut de recherches cliniques de Montréal. The

Canadian province of Québec had an unusually high prevalence of FH, and Davignon was more than happy to collaborate with Goldstein and Brown. The team from Dallas flew up to Montreal and retrieved skin biopsies from two patients—a ten-year-old boy and a twenty-three-year-old woman.

When Brown and Goldstein tested the fibroblasts of the two additional FH patients, they found the same absence of LDL suppression of enzyme activity. They wrote up their results for publication[25] and then turned their attention to why HMG-CoA reductase was not responding normally in FH patients. A year of hard work led them to the conclusion that the genetic aberration was not in the enzyme itself but rather in the inability of LDL cholesterol to get inside the cell where the enzyme was located.[26] The task for Goldstein and Brown now was to study the process by which LDL normally crosses the cell's protective envelope—the cell membrane. They discovered that LDL bound tightly to the membranes of normal cells, but there was no binding of LDL on the surface of cells from FH patients with the double dose of abnormal genes. These observations led Brown and Goldstein to conclude that there was "an interaction of LDL with a physiological receptor."[27] Further studies reinforced their belief that "the primary genetic abnormality in familial hypercholesterolemia resides in a gene whose product is necessary for the production of a high affinity cell surface receptor for LDL."[28]

Cell surface receptors were relatively newly discovered entities in 1974, and not all reviewers were convinced that LDL entered cells through specific binding to a receptor. Undeterred, Goldstein and Brown went on to determine that LDL remained on the cell surface for only about ten minutes,[29] and once it was within the cell it was completely metabolized into cholesterol within an hour.[30] The intake of the bound LDL occurred after the lipoprotein bound to receptors that were localized in specialized regions of the surface membrane called "coated pits."[31] The pits pinched off from the surrounding membrane and carried the receptor-bound LDL into the cell's interior, where it entered lysosomes—cellular chop shops—which degraded the LDL, releasing its cholesterol for metabolic functions.

Brown and Goldstein were able to purify the cell surface receptor,[32] clone its DNA, and determine the amino acid sequence of the protein.[33] The clinical significance of the LDL receptor became apparent when a new class of drugs, the so-called statins, were shown to increase the number of cell surface receptors and thereby remove high levels of circulating LDL from the blood.[34] The contribution that Goldstein and Brown made to the understanding of cholesterol metabolism was recognized with multiple awards, including Canada's Gairdner Foundation International Award in 1981 and the Albert Lasker Award in Basic Medical Research in 1985. In the early morning hours of October 14, 1985, while in Boston with Joe Goldstein to give a talk at the Massachusetts Institute of Technology, Michael Brown received a telephone call. As he recalled: "I pick it up and it's a woman's voice and she says: 'Is this Dr. Brown?' And I said: 'Yes,' in a very groggy voice. 'Well, how do you feel?' And I said: 'What are you talking about?' She said: 'How do you feel? What's your reaction?' I said: 'I'm sorry, I don't know what you're talking about.' She said: 'I'm calling from the Reuters News Service in Washington and it's just come over the wire that you and your colleague, Dr. Goldstein, will share the Nobel Prize.'"[35]

Joe Goldstein picked up the story from there: "The New York Times, the Wall Street Journal, all had scientific correspondents in Boston. They all wanted interviews." Brown added: "One of the people said: 'When are you going to come out and make a statement?' And I said: 'Well, we don't want to do anything in Boston. We did all our work in Texas and we want to go home to Texas.'"[36] The pair got on the next flight to the Lone Star State, and although the skies over Dallas were filled with threatening clouds, the atmosphere at the packed press conference on campus was euphoric. Nobody in the audience could have been prouder than Donald Seldin, the foresighted genius who had nurtured the two superstar researchers from their earliest days. Since 1979, Seldin had orchestrated annual efforts to nominate Brown and Goldstein for the Nobel Prize. He had solicited support from, among others, Marshall Nirenberg, the Nobel laureate and former mentor to Goldstein at NIH.

Along with other dignitaries from UT Southwestern, Seldin was invited to attend the Nobel Prize ceremonies in Stockholm Concert Hall on December 10, 1985, followed by the banquet at the Stockholm

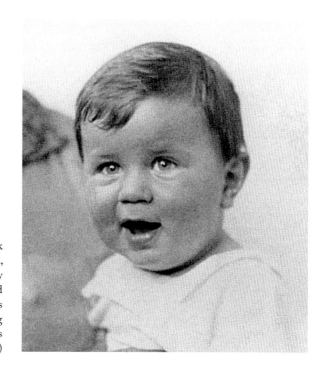

Donald Seldin, already a quick study as a toddler. Undated, likely 1921–1922. (Courtesy of Special Collections and Archives, Health Sciences Digital Library and Learning Center, University of Texas Southwestern Medical Center)

A young Donald Seldin displaying his lifelong affinity for fine clothing and automobiles. Undated, likely 1926–1928. (Courtesy of Dr. Ellen Seldin)

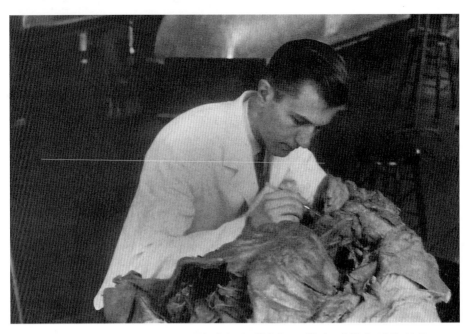

Donald Seldin studying gross anatomy at Yale School of Medicine. Undated, likely 1940–1941. (Courtesy of Dr. Ellen Seldin)

Dr. John Punnett Peters Jr., the John Slade Ely Professor of Medicine at Yale University and mentor to Donald Seldin. (Courtesy of Yale University, Harvey Cushing/John Hay Whitney Medical Library)

CLASS OF DECEMBER 1943 M

Class of 1943, Yale School of Medicine, mostly attired in their military uniforms, including Donald Seldin (*fourth row, fourth from right*). Undated, likely December 1943. (Courtesy of Yale University, Harvey Cushing/John Hay Whitney Medical Library)

Yale School of Medicine graduation ceremony at which Donald Seldin received the Campbell Prize as the top graduate. December 1943. (Courtesy of Yale University, Harvey Cushing/John Hay Whitney Medical Library)

Muriel and Donald Seldin on their wedding day, April 1, 1943. (Courtesy of Special Collections and Archives, Health Sciences Digital Library and Learning Center, University of Texas Southwestern Medical Center)

Captain Donald Seldin, US Army Medical Corps. Undated, likely 1946–1948. (Courtesy of Special Collections and Archives, Health Sciences Digital Library and Learning Center, University of Texas Southwestern Medical Center)

Captain Donald Seldin admiring the architecture of the Colosseum in Rome. Undated, likely 1946–1948. (Courtesy of Dr. Ellen Seldin)

Captain Donald Seldin testifying at the trial of the Nazi physician Rudolf Brachtel, who was accused of cruelties and mistreatment of prisoners of war at the Dachau concentration camp. Undated, likely December 1947. (Courtesy of Dr. Ellen Seldin)

The Department of Internal Medicine of the Yale School of Medicine, 1949–1950 (*first row, left to right beginning with fourth person*: Drs. John Punnett Peters, Francis G. Blake [chairman], and Donald Seldin). (Courtesy of Yale University, Harvey Cushing/John Hay Whitney Medical Library)

The shacks of the Southwestern Medical School of the University of Texas around the time Dr. Donald Seldin arrived in Dallas. Undated, likely circa 1950. (Courtesy of Special Collections and Archives, Health Sciences Digital Library and Learning Center, University of Texas Southwestern Medical Center)

Entrance to the Department of Internal Medicine at the Southwestern Medical School of the University of Texas around the time that Donald Seldin became chairman. Undated, likely circa 1950. (Courtesy of Special Collections and Archives, Health Sciences Digital Library and Learning Center, University of Texas Southwestern Medical Center)

Interns

Seated, left to right, Doctors: Jere Mitchell, Emmett Royer, Watt Salmon, Charles Baxter, Charles Fielder, Melvin Vaughn, Glenn Henderson. Standing, left to right, second row, Doctors: Marvin Gerard, Phillip Morrow, Robert Cohn, John Smale, Andrew Gwynne, George Pakis, Edgar Allen, Albert Roberts, Augustin Ruiz, Jack Cooper, Thomas Hair. Third row, left to right, Doctors: Richard Porterwood, John Rumsfeld, Berry Moore, Robert Bass, John Scogin. Not pictured, Doctors: Rector, Campbell, Ford, Fraser, Gunn, Kapland, Kuykendall, LaPrade, Leland, McAdams, Ross, Weiner, Somer, Cushing and McLeroy.

Dr. Donald Seldin's third group of interns in internal medicine at Parkland Memorial Hospital, including future faculty member Dr. Jere Mitchell (*front row, far left*). Drs. Floyd Rector and Norman Kaplan (*not pictured*) were also members of the group. Likely 1954–1955. (Courtesy of Special Collections and Archives, Health Sciences Digital Library and Learning Center, University of Texas Southwestern Medical Center)

Dr. Donald Seldin giving one of his celebrated chalkboard lectures. Undated. (Courtesy of Dr. Ellen Seldin)

A troika of nephrology leaders at the University of Texas Southwestern Medical School: Drs. Floyd Rector (*left*), Donald Seldin (*center*), and Juha Kokko (*right*). Undated. (Courtesy of Special Collections and Archives, Health Sciences Digital Library and Learning Center, University of Texas Southwestern Medical Center)

Donald Seldin (*center*) with faculty colleagues and 1985 Nobel laureates Joseph Goldstein (*left*) and Michael Brown (*right*), 1985. (Courtesy of Special Collections and Archives, Health Sciences Digital Library and Learning Center, University of Texas Southwestern Medical Center)

Dr. Donald Seldin with his family (*seated*: Seldin and wife Muriel; *standing, left to right*: children Leslie, Craig, and Donna). Undated. (Courtesy of Special Collections and Archives, Health Sciences Digital Library and Learning Center, University of Texas Southwestern Medical Center)

Poster for one of the annual senior medical student films starring Dr. Donald Seldin, in this case *Seldinfeld* (a parody of the television series *Seinfeld*), 1999. (Courtesy of Special Collections and Archives, Health Sciences Digital Library and Learning Center, University of Texas Southwestern Medical Center)

Dr. Donald Seldin at work amid his highly organized files masquerading as chaos. Undated. (Courtesy of Special Collections and Archives, Health Sciences Digital Library and Learning Center, University of Texas Southwestern Medical Center)

Drs. Donald and Ellen Seldin. Undated. (Courtesy of Special Collections and Archives, Health Sciences Digital Library and Learning Center, University of Texas Southwestern Medical Center)

Nephrology textbook coeditors and close friends Drs. Gerhard Giebisch (*left*) and Donald Seldin (*right*) on a trip retracing the Camino de Santiago pilgrimage route in the Pyrenees Mountains, May 2005. (Courtesy of Dr. David Hillis)

Donald Seldin (*right*) with former protégé and close friend David Hillis (*left*) at Hotel de La Fenice, Venice, Italy, December 2003. (Courtesy of Dr. David Hillis)

Dr. Donald Seldin accompanied by the larger-than-life bronze version of himself at the Seldin Plaza at the University of Texas Southwestern Medical Center. May 16, 2015. (Courtesy of Special Collections and Archives, Health Sciences Digital Library and Learning Center, University of Texas Southwestern Medical Center)

Drs. Ellen and Donald Seldin sharing a moment on the dance floor at the Ball for Eye Research, April 2017. Photograph by Kristina Bowman. (Courtesy of the Department of Ophthalmology, University of Texas Southwestern Medical Center)

Dr. Donald Seldin at home during his final illness, surrounded by former internal medicine chief residents and current faculty members (*seated, left to right*: Drs. Gail Peterson, Seldin, and Carol Croft; *second row, left to right*: Drs. James de Lemos and John Warner). April 2018. (Courtesy of Dr. John Warner)

Nine days before his death, Dr. Donald Seldin (reclining) met with his former student, faculty colleague, and Nobel laureate Dr. Joseph Goldstein (standing). The two devoted friends are shown on April 16, 2018, reviewing plans for a work by American sculptor Joel Shapiro to be commissioned by Goldstein and installed in honor of Dr. Seldin the following year on the Seldin Plaza. (Courtesy of Dr. Ellen Seldin)

City Hall. One can only imagine the thrill of observing two of his intellectual progeny decorated with the highest award for scientific achievement. In retrospect, the decision to recruit and develop Goldstein and Brown may have seemed obvious, but in 1966, when Seldin was mapping out a career pathway for Joe Goldstein, a senior medical student, success was hardly assured. Several years after reaching agreement with Goldstein, Seldin was confronted with a true dilemma: a former standout resident physician, William Kelley, whom Seldin had handpicked for training at NIH followed by a return to UT Southwestern, was ready to come back to Dallas. At NIH, Kelley worked in the Section on Human Biochemical Genetics under Jarvis Edwin "Jay" Seegmiller, an expert on the genetics of arthritis. There, Kelley discovered that a genetic deficiency in an enzyme known as "HGPRT" was responsible for a rare neurologic syndrome. Kelley went on to ascertain that a partial deficit of the same enzyme led to the more common problem of excessive accumulation of uric acid in the body, leading to gout. He published about ten scientific papers in his two years at NIH, then went to MGH for additional clinical training, and he was now ready to come back to Dallas.

The version of the story that Seldin later shared with a former trainee, colleague, and friend, David Hillis, went as follows: "Bill Kelley in the world of academic medicine is a rock star . . . and Joe Goldstein is a resident at the MGH that nobody's ever heard of."[37] Kelley reportedly told his mentor: "'Dr. Seldin, I know I told you that I wanted to come back and I do want to come back, but rather than being in the metabolism section, I want to start a new section in genetics.' Without a moment's hesitation, Seldin replied: 'Bill, I'm sorry, I can't let you do that. I've already offered that job to Joe.'" As Hillis pointed out: "Joe wasn't coming back for four years. He was going to the NIH and then a fellowship in genetics and he wasn't coming back till 1972."[38] It was more important to Seldin to honor his word and bet on Goldstein's long-term potential than to break his pledge in favor of the faster results with the already demonstrated success of Kelley. Seldin released Kelley from his commitment to return, and Kelley headed to Duke University instead, where within a year he was appointed chief of the Division of Rheumatic and Genetic Diseases. He went on to become chairman of medicine at the University of Michigan and later was appointed dean of the School of Medicine of the University of Pennsylvania and the head of its medical center.

Just as Seldin was fiercely loyal to Brown and Goldstein, they remained devoted to their mentor and supporter. Even after their high achievement, they continued to refer to him with deference as "Dr. Seldin." In their Nobel Prize address, they formally acknowledged their gratitude to him: "We express our deepest appreciation to D. W. Seldin, chairman of the Department of Internal Medicine at the University of Texas Southwestern Medical School for more than thirty years and creator of the intellectual environment that made our work possible."[39]

Three decades later, when the current chair of medicine at UT Southwestern, David Johnson, was tasked with preserving Seldin's files, he came across "an entire folder of letters that were sent to Don[ald Seldin] when Mike and Joe won the Nobel Prize. They were from many important figures throughout the world." Johnson described the recurrent theme: "Virtually every one of the letters had the same basic message: this is really your Nobel Prize, Don. You're the one who identified Joe as a medical student and sent him off and got him trained and brought him back. Fortunately, you brought Michael too. This is something over which you should be incredibly proud."[40]

CHAPTER 11

A UNIVERSITY WORTHY OF THE DEPARTMENT OF MEDICINE

Donald Seldin's major goal during his unprecedented thirty-six years as chairman of medicine at UT Southwestern was to build the department into an unrivaled community of clinical scholars. He managed to grow the core of a premier faculty by nurturing and retaining many of the best and brightest among his students. These home-grown physician-scientists were young, energetic, and very loyal to Seldin. In addition, he augmented the kids from Texas with established scientists that he handpicked from other institutions. The plan was working, and any other chair might have been satisfied with the progress within his own department. Seldin, however, had a bigger agenda and wanted to see the rest of UT Southwestern adopt the same high standards and expectations.

In most medical schools, the department of medicine is one of, if not the, largest and most powerful units. Almost without exception, departments of medicine set the scholarly pace at medical schools, especially at the academic stalwarts. At the same time, to emerge as a truly leading medical school, academic excellence must pervade the entire campus. Donald Seldin knew that his ambitions for the

Department of Medicine would never be fully realized unless the entire university was filled with brilliant and innovative investigators.

This issue came to the fore about a decade into Seldin's tenure as chairman. He had been offered jobs at other institutions, but one that really piqued his interest was the medicine chairmanship at the Harvard-affiliated Beth Israel Hospital. Seldin's recruitment was perhaps the worst-kept secret on campus, and many of the faculty in Dallas were concerned that their academic champion would be departing for Boston. As Seldin later confessed: "I tried to keep this as quiet as possible, but everybody became aware of the situation and I had a number of people come by to indicate how anxious they were that I would stay."[1] The leadership of the Board of Regents of the University of Texas System understood that Seldin's departure could be a major setback for the school.

As Seldin later recalled: "Harry Ransom at the time was chancellor of the University of Texas." Ransom, a dozen years older than Seldin, was a Galveston native who had obtained a doctorate in English at Yale and worked his way up the academic and administrative ranks at the University of Texas at Austin. At the time, the presidency of the Austin campus and the chancellorship of the UT System were jointly held positions. A half-century later, Seldin recalled Ransom's visit: "To this day I don't know who orchestrated that visit. Ransom came up to Dallas and talked to me about remaining here. We had a long discussion in which I highlighted the major weaknesses and strengths of the school as I saw them."[2] Elsewhere, Seldin noted a prominent theme of his analysis: "In conversations with him [Ransom] and with others, I argued the importance of having strong basic sciences and of providing money for those departments."[3] Seldin vividly remembered his guest's reaction: "Ransom listened attentively. He essentially told me that he wouldn't put financial resources into the school by way of a blank check. But if the school took the initiative to request well thought-out programs, appointments, and activities, he would support them in full."[4]

According to a junior medical student at the time who, a quarter-century later, went on to become president of UT Southwestern, Kern Wildenthal, the "others" that Seldin mentioned included Frank Erwin. Born the same year as Seldin in little Waxahachie, Texas, south of Dallas, Erwin earned a law degree from UT Austin. In the early 1960s, Erwin became a close confidant of both Governor John Connally and President Lyndon Johnson. With these powerful political connections, Erwin was appointed to the UT System Board of Regents in 1963 and was elected as its chairman in 1966. As Wildenthal noted: "He was, by far and away, the most powerful steerer of UT policy in those days."[5]

Because Seldin had the ear of both Ransom and Erwin, it might have been tempting for him to request additional resources for himself or for the Department of Medicine. Seldin resisted any such self-serving requests, however. He told the UT System leadership that the department could take care of its own needs. One former student and long-time colleague and friend, David Hillis, confirmed this: "I know for a fact that was the agreement if he stayed in Dallas—that major resources would be poured into the institution for the basic sciences—not for the Department of Medicine, but for the basic sciences." Hillis continued: "When he [Seldin] met with the faculty in Dallas to tell them that he was not going, but he was staying in Dallas, [there was] a huge celebration."[6]

The dividends of Seldin's negotiations became evident over the course of the next decade, as one after another new chairman was recruited to the basic science departments. Michael Brown, whom Seldin recruited and who later went on to win a Nobel Prize with faculty colleague Joe Goldstein, had an unusual vantage point from which to witness Seldin's recruitment strategy. According to Brown: "When I was in medical school at the University of Pennsylvania, there were three outstanding young professors [in the basic science departments]. . . . Samuel McCann, Ronald Estabrook, and Rupert Billingham. McCann was the physiologist, Estabrook was a biochemist, and Billingham was a cell biologist at Penn. They were considered rising stars at Penn." Brown continued: "So, I left Penn in 1966. By the time I got here [UT Southwestern] in 1971, all three of them were here."[7]

Samuel McCann was the first to arrive, becoming chairman of physiology around the time Brown was finishing medical school. A native of Houston, McCann was an endocrinologist who focused on the impact of hormones on the nervous system. McCann served as chairman for twenty years and remained a highly prolific investigator who published more than seven hundred papers during his career.

The next to arrive was Ronald "Ron" Estabrook, who was recruited to be chairman of biochemistry in 1968. A distinguished investigator, Estabrook was responsible for some of the key work on cytochrome p450, a family of important proteins that are involved in the metabolism of steroids and many pharmaceutical agents. Estabrook remained as chairman for fourteen years, also serving as the first dean of the graduate school at UT Southwestern.

Rupert "Bill" Billingham was the last of this trio to arrive in Dallas in 1971 as the chairman of cell biology and anatomy. An Englishman who earned his doctorate at Oxford, Billingham worked with Peter Medawar on the concept of immune tolerance in transplantation. "Immune tolerance" refers to the ability of the recipient of a transplanted tissue or organ to tolerate (i.e., not reject) the foreign material. In 1960, Medawar became the corecipient of the Nobel Prize in Physiology or Medicine for his work on immune tolerance. Arguably, Billingham might have been an appropriate corecipient, but the slight was mollified when Medawar acknowledged that their discoveries were a joint effort and divided the prize money with Billingham and Leslie Brent, a former graduate student who worked on immune tolerance.

Seldin recalled the apparent long odds of the Billingham recruitment: "Billingham was an immunologist of the highest order. Why would he want to come to Dallas to take over the Department of Anatomy, where there was no cell biology at all?" In discussion with faculty colleague Marvin Siperstein, however, Seldin indicated that the two thought "it was worth a try. What could we lose? Subsequently, I learned that Billingham and the chairman of the department at the University of Pennsylvania were at odds." When UT Southwestern approached Billingham, as Seldin recounted, "he accepted the job within a week or two. I was flabbergasted, because I regarded Billingham as a giant in basic science."[8]

Billingham remained chair at UT Southwestern for fifteen years. He later wrote with great affection for the environment that he found at UT Southwestern, where there was an "evident esprit de corps that paid no heed to departmental boundaries, of the usually more formidable ones that separate so-called basic sciences from clinical departments in most medical schools."[9]

Kern Wildenthal pointed out that Seldin's activism on behalf of the basic science departments was not embraced warmly by many of the other clinical department chairs of the institution: "Seldin, amongst the clinical chairs, was the one pushing to upgrade the basic science departments and was helping with the recruitment of basic science chairs." Two factions emerged on campus. In Wildenthal's words: "The dean of the day, a lovely man named [Atticus] James Gill, was the leader of the 'we never want to grow too big; we have our niche and we're filling it well'" bloc. Gill, a pathologist by training, joined the faculty when the school was first established and had served as its dean for thirteen years. Wildenthal contrasted the "old boys" perspective with that of the new guard who aspired to a different future: "There was a contingent of the faculty that wanted to grow in size and in excellence, with Seldin being the obvious leader of that [faction], and his recruits."[10]

The tension between these two camps came to a head in 1965 at a strategic planning retreat held in Salado, Texas. Located not quite 150 miles south of Dallas, Salado is a small village with a quiet and tranquil conference center. Apparently, this serene setting did little to calm the emotions of the UT Southwestern attendees. As Wildenthal recalled: "The report came back from the faculty leadership very strongly in favor of an aggressive expansion." Wildenthal added that Seldin "wasn't the chairman of the faculty committee that wrote that report, but as you might imagine, he was the power behind the throne."[11] This was consistent with the vision of Governor Connally, who was pushing to improve higher education in Texas.

Dean Gill was not prepared to lead such an effort. In Wildenthal's words, the dean said that "he was at a stage of his career that he could not devote the energy and time to fulfilling that, so he would submit his resignation."[12] A national search was launched for a new dean who would carry forward the mandate of the faculty. The successful candidate was at that time the dean of the Tulane University School of Medicine, Charles Sprague.

It was a return home for Sprague, who was born and raised in Dallas. He had excellent political skills, likely modeled after his father, George Sprague, a successful businessman who served as mayor of Dallas for two years. The younger Sprague graduated from Southern Methodist University, where (like two of his older brothers) he was captain of the football team. After completing medical school at the University of Texas Medical Branch in Galveston, he served as a naval officer in the Pacific during World War II and then returned for further training, first at Tulane University, then at Washington University in St. Louis, and finally at Oxford University. He was the first director of hematology at Tulane, where his principal research interest was sickle cell disease. In 1964, Sprague was appointed dean of the school, but when the opportunity arose at UT Southwestern three years later, Sprague was excited to join the up-and-coming school in his hometown.

Seldin found a kindred spirit in Sprague: "Charlie was an outstanding dean. Everybody loved him—with good reason. He possessed huge warmth and congeniality and was an effective spokesman for the school. He was never devious. He was never contrived." Seldin could not resist adding: "Charlie was the proverbial milk-drinking Texas boy. Even though his background and experience was in clinical medicine, he was very much in favor of developing the basic sciences and promoted them vigorously."[13]

Sprague and Seldin partnered on crafting a vision for the future of the campus. If the academic programs of the university were to grow, as both leaders desired, there was a need to greatly expand the physical plant of the campus. A campus master plan was developed, and Seldin chaired the committee that drew it up. A key decision was whether the campus would grow as a loose confederation of independent units or, alternatively, build strong connections across diverse programmatic areas. As Seldin later recalled: "There were forces beyond the committee that wanted to have separate buildings all over the campus for various functions, somewhat in the manner of the pavilion-style medical campuses in some European countries." The chairman of medicine took exception to this model: "It always seemed to me that the more important function was to integrate the campus."[14] Seldin's colleague, Floyd Rector, pointed out: "Almost single-handedly, he blocked that [independent building] plan, at great personal sacrifice and loss of goodwill among important individuals in the university and the community."[15]

At the time, the campus had only three buildings. The first two structures built were devoted to basic sciences and clinical sciences and opened in 1955 and 1958, respectively. As Robert Haley, a former student, resident physician, faculty member, and close friend of Seldin's, recalled: "There was a field of almost one hundred yards between the back door of the medical school and Parkland [Hospital]."[16] This was an unappealing walk, especially during the extremes of Dallas temperatures. Seldin argued for the construction of a building that would both add needed office and laboratory space while physically connecting the academic buildings to Parkland Hospital. As Haley described, Seldin "worked hard at getting it built,"[17] including soliciting support from the philanthropic community and hitting a home run when Dan Danciger, a Dallas philanthropist, made a hefty contribution. The Danciger Building opened in 1966, and according to Haley, Seldin "talked about it as one of the things that he was proudest of"[18] because it literally helped to cement the relationship between the medical school and Parkland Hospital.

The campus master plan that Seldin's committee produced built on the concept of connectivity. In his words: "I thought that it was very important that the campus, instead of being spread out and scattered, should be continuous. . . . This would encourage interactions among the various units so that people could talk and aggregate. Ultimately, that's what we did. We have a very integrated campus."[19] Decades before the concept of interdisciplinary collaboration became fashionable at American universities, Donald Seldin was envisioning how campus design could promote such cross-fertilization.

The master plan that emerged was innovative in design and bold in scale, with a million square feet of new space on the drawing board for a campus that less than two decades earlier was a collection of decaying shacks. The price tag for the expansion, at $40 million, also was an attention-grabber. Today, a single floor of a modern research building might cost that much, but in the late 1960s such a capital investment on a university campus was mind-boggling. Undaunted, Sprague reached out to community leaders to sell the plan. His deep roots in Dallas helped earn him the trust of civic leaders, and $8.5 million of philanthropic support was committed to the effort. During the two decades under Sprague's leadership, the campus expanded from the initial three buildings to twenty.[20]

But Seldin and Sprague did not win every battle. One potential opportunity that escaped them was the proposed location of the University of Texas at Dallas. The university traces its origins to a desire within the business community to grow the technology sector in Dallas. At the time, it was difficult to attract engineers to the region. Led by three founders of Texas Instruments (Cecil Green, Erik Jonsson, and Eugene McDermott), a private research institute—the Graduate Research Center of the Southwest—was launched in 1961 and housed initially at Southern Methodist University. Three years later, the first building was constructed on a new campus in North Dallas.

In 1968, the University of Texas System Board of Regents voted to create an urban research university in north-central Texas. The following year, the Texas legislature approved the establishment of the University of Texas at Dallas, which at the outset awarded only graduate degrees. For a brief time, the location of the new university was in question. As Wildenthal described: "Seldin argued that . . . UT Dallas would be greater and UT Southwestern would be greater if they were side-by-side and could enrich each other's faculty."[21] The founders of the Graduate Research Center of the Southwest, later renamed the Southwest Center for Advanced Studies, volunteered to transfer the private assets of the center to the state as a home for the new university. Their bid included the financial resources of the center and the 1,400 acres of associated land. The gift and the political clout of the three corporate titans won the day and UT Dallas was located at their preferred site, about twenty miles north of UT Southwestern. Some collaborations between faculty members of UT Dallas and UT Southwestern developed over the years, but Seldin's dream of an integrated community of scholars moving freely between sister institutions did not materialize.

When it came to faculty recruiting, Seldin not only played great offense in attracting stars to UT Southwestern; he was adept at defense when other institutions tried to lure away the best and brightest from Dallas. Franklin Epstein, head of nephrology at the Harvard-affiliated Beth Israel Hospital, conceded: "It is well known in academic circles that it has always been notoriously difficult to recruit a full-time faculty member of Seldin's department away from Dallas. Most chairmen have given up on it entirely and merely gaze enviously on his galaxy of stars."[22]

Perhaps the most legendary attempt to breach Seldin's fortress occurred in the 1970s when the newly established Gladstone Institutes in San Francisco set their sights on Joe Goldstein and Mike Brown. The Gladstone Institutes were named after J. David Gladstone, a successful real estate developer in California whose accidental death in 1971 led to the establishment of an $8 million trust. By the late 1970s, the trust had grown sufficiently to create a private research and training organization affiliated with the University of California, San Francisco and housed at San Francisco General Hospital. The initial focus of the Gladstone Institutes was on cardiovascular disease. Mike Brown and Joe Goldstein were the perfect targets for recruitment to lead the institution. Their landmark work on the cell surface receptor for low-density lipoprotein was opening doors for understanding the development of atherosclerotic heart disease—the leading cause of death in Western countries.

Seldin had advanced his young stars in lockstep to full professor status by 1976, which was lightning speed by academic standards. Nevertheless, when Lloyd Hollingsworth "Holly" Smith, chairman of medicine at UCSF, and William Rutter, chairman of biochemistry and biophysics at UCSF, came calling on behalf of the Gladstone Institutes the following year, the deal was almost too sweet to turn down. They tried to entice Brown and Goldstein with the promise of abundant laboratory space and financial support. For Brown, the siren song of San Francisco must have seemed like déjà vu all over again. When he was deciding where to begin his academic career, his leading alternative to UT Southwestern was UCSF.

For Seldin, the thought that his two brilliant faculty members might be headed to San Francisco also must have felt painfully familiar. After all, only three years earlier, Floyd Rector, who was like an intellectual son to Seldin, had packed his bags for UCSF to become director of nephrology. The possibility of also losing both Goldstein and Brown would have added insult to injury for Seldin and the department.

Wildenthal identified the challenge for Seldin and Sprague at this time: "Southwestern had no endowment virtually at that time and modest state resources."[23] Desperate for support from the community, "Sprague introduced them [Brown and Goldstein] to Erik Jonsson, who was one of the founders of Texas Instruments and a former mayor of Dallas."[24] Ironically, this is the same Erik Jonsson who was one of the three principals who successfully negotiated for UT Dallas to be located on donated land in North Dallas rather than adjacent to UT Southwestern. In this instance, Jonsson came to the aid of Sprague and Seldin. Mike Brown later described the meeting that Goldstein and he had with Jonsson: "He [Jonsson] shared a passionate vision of the city's future. He gave us his home phone number and said if we ever needed anything for our research we should call that number and the check would be on our desk the next morning. We left the meeting with tremendous confidence that the leaders of Dallas were behind us." Brown added: "We never called. We never had to. But the knowledge that the support was there if we needed it . . . gave us the courage to tackle difficult and challenging problems."[25]

Wildenthal described what Brown and Goldstein felt they needed to advance their work in Dallas, which was "their own research center with an autonomous budget and to be able to recruit."[26] Unfortunately at that time, there was no structure for creating such an independent entity. Wildenthal, who was then dean of the graduate school, had, in his words, "squirreled away some money" to create an already approved graduate program in biophysics.[27] He proposed that they creatively repurpose these funds to establish the Department of Medical Genetics, for which Goldstein would serve as chair. Both Brown and Goldstein also were awarded endowed chairs. The two chairs were named for Paul Thomas, a beloved internist in private practice in Dallas. Thomas had been one of the early supporters of Seldin's curricular reforms and taught UT Southwestern medical students at Parkland Hospital. The Center for Molecular Genetics was established and named in honor of Erik Jonsson and directed by Brown. So Brown and Goldstein, always balanced in their treatment by UT Southwestern, received matching endowed chairs, with Goldstein serving as a department chair and Brown appointed as a center director.

Eight years later, Brown and Goldstein were corecipients of the Nobel Prize in Physiology or Medicine at the remarkably young ages of forty-four and forty-five, respectively. Seldin was responsible for bringing Goldstein and Brown onto the faculty, nurturing their development, and retaining them when others came calling. Having made such a personal and departmental investment in their careers, other chairmen might have resisted the effort to establish a separate department for them. For Seldin, however, the greater good of the medical school was far more important than the parochial interests of the Department of Medicine.

Before long, UT Southwestern would claim more Nobel laureates. In 1988, the Department of Biochemistry was able to leverage funding from the Howard Hughes Medical Institute to recruit Johann Deisenhofer, a German scientist who studied the three-dimensional structure of biological molecules. Mere months after arriving at UT Southwestern, Deisenhofer, only forty-five years old, was announced as a corecipient of the 1988 Nobel Prize in Chemistry. Deisenhofer and his colleagues were recognized for groundbreaking studies on the structure of a complex reaction site for bacterial photosynthesis.

Next in line was Alfred Gilman, a physician-scientist who joined UT Southwestern as chairman of the Department of Pharmacology in 1981. Gilman became a corecipient of the Nobel Prize in Physiology or Medicine in 1994. The prize-winning work was on so-called G proteins, which transmit messages from outside of a cell into the cell's interior, where responsive biological actions are prompted.

Gilman's recruitment to UT Southwestern was initiated by none other than Joe Goldstein, who had met Gilman a decade earlier when they were fellows together in the Nirenberg lab at the NIH. Gilman turned down the initial invitation to Dallas because he was knee-deep in the G protein work while also revising the popular pharmacology textbook originally coedited by his father. The search committee then turned to Martin Rodbell (who, coincidentally, later shared the Nobel Prize with Gilman). Rodbell was wowed by what he saw in Dallas and accepted the job, only to decline it at the eleventh hour for personal reasons. With the chair still vacant, Seldin was assigned responsibility for trying to coax Gilman to reconsider.

Gilman later described the interaction: "I had never met Don, but I had certainly heard about him. . . . Don introduced himself very graciously, saying, 'Dr. Gilman, would you please give me just fifteen minutes of your time to describe the situation here.' . . . I don't think I got to say another word for about an hour!" According to Gilman, Seldin "had all his ducks lined up. Every inch of space, every nickel of funds was mentioned. He did a magnificent job of recruiting me."[28]

The fifth UT Southwestern Nobel laureate was Bruce Beutler, a physician-scientist who undertook his residency at Parkland Hospital. After three subsequent years at Rockefeller University, Beutler returned to Dallas in 1986 as a faculty member in the Department of Medicine, with an appointment in the Howard Hughes Medical Institute. After fourteen years at UT Southwestern, Beutler moved to the Scripps Research Institute in La Jolla, California, before returning to UT Southwestern in 2011. A few months later, Beutler was announced as a corecipient of the Nobel Prize in Physiology or Medicine for his studies of immunity that were launched at UT Southwestern. Two years after Beutler's recognition, Thomas Südhof, a physician-scientist, was likewise selected as a corecipient of the Nobel Prize in Physiology or Medicine. Although Südhof was on the faculty of Stanford University at the time of his selection, he had undertaken a postdoctoral fellowship under Brown and Goldstein and then served on the UT Southwestern faculty for more than two decades. His prize-winning studies, conducted in Dallas, relate to how connections are formed and operate between cells within the nervous system.

Even before Beutler and Südhof won their Nobel Prizes, the world of academic medicine had taken notice of the high quality reflected in the faculty and research at UT Southwestern. In 1996, the journal *Science* published an article titled "UT Southwestern: From Army Shacks to Research Elites."[29] The report chronicled the transformation that had occurred at the institution, giving abundant credit to Seldin. Included was a quote from Holly Smith, the chairman of medicine at UCSF who had built his own stellar department and nearly enticed Goldstein and Brown away from UT Southwestern. Smith admired Seldin's prowess in identifying and cultivating talent: "You would not have thought that the University of Texas would have as many outstanding young medical students come along as a Harvard or Yale, but [Seldin] identified those that were there and brought their achievements to fruition." Even with all the high praise and the excitement that the write-up in *Science* generated on campus, Seldin was displeased with it. Robert Alpern, whom Seldin had recruited from UCSF to serve as director of nephrology at UT Southwestern, described his boss's reaction: "Seldin came into my office, threw the issue of *Science* on my desk, and referred to it as a piece of trash. He said there was too much emphasis on the role of money: 'Everyone had money in those days; we had taste!'"[30]

Seldin, not known for compromising his beliefs, would yield to the will of his colleagues in another important domain. Seldin was firmly committed to Parkland Hospital and its mission. At Parkland, the faculty could pursue the Seldin model of a clinical scholar, where they taught students and residents, conducted research, and cared for patients concurrently. Parkland had such a high volume of patients, however, that it was hard to keep the three legs of the triple-threat stool equally balanced. It would be even more difficult if the clinical load was augmented by the addition of private-practice patients at another facility. As Seldin observed: "Ideally, the responsibility for patient care on the part of the clinical faculty should be somewhat limited by the requirements for teaching and research. Without this limitation, the faculty would have its energies dissipated in a whole set of different directions which, however socially valuable, would compromise the capacity to fulfill the academic functions."[31]

As Wildenthal described, Seldin "was worried that with the small size of the faculty, it would be detrimental to Parkland" if their attention was diverted by the demands of taking care of referred private patients. If the faculty admitted private patients in another facility, then "they would be distracted from teaching, they would be distracted from their research."[32] The surgeons at UT Southwestern, according to Wildenthal, "needed more variety of patients they were caring for and wanted to be more active in private practice." They recognized that Parkland Hospital could not be a site for this additional clinical activity "because it was just too crowded and there were too many emergencies."[33]

A first potential opportunity to develop the private-patient practice occurred in 1963 when the Catholic-affiliated St. Paul's Hospital built a new, nearly five-hundred-bed facility adjacent to UT Southwestern. The original idea was that the university would utilize St. Paul's for private patients, but in Wildenthal's words "neither the administration nor the doctors at St. Paul really were very eager for medical school people to be there, so that didn't work out."[34]

A second opportunity arose a few years later when Presbyterian Hospital was launched with the strong support of influential community leaders. The new, three-hundred-bed hospital was intended to be built close to UT Southwestern, and the founders looked to the medical school to provide experts in key specialty areas. After further evaluation, however, Presbyterian Hospital was sited in northeast Dallas, a location that was more convenient for the patient population that it was intended to serve. The new location was a twenty-minute commute from UT Southwestern, so only a few faculty members worked there after it opened in 1966.

After two failed attempts to establish a private-patient service, Chairman of Surgery Thomas Shires was ready to throw in the towel. Shires was raised in Dallas and knew the local politics well. A trauma surgeon, Shires graduated from UT Southwestern, trained at Parkland Hospital, and was appointed chairman of surgery at the tender age of thirty-five. After two failed attempts to build a private-patient service, Shires saw greener pastures at the University of Washington and in 1974 accepted the chairmanship of the surgery department in Seattle, taking a major contingent of the UT Southwestern surgeons with him.

Wildenthal was appointed to serve as dean of the medical school in 1980, and one of his first initiatives was to create a trio of strategic planning committees—one for education, another for research, and a third for patient care. All three groups came back with a recommendation that the top priority was to establish a private hospital. In addition to expanding the scope of care that faculty could provide, a private hospital was desired to expand clinical research and to provide students with a broader range of conditions to study than were seen at Parkland and the local VA hospital. As Wildenthal recalled: "Seldin bought into that. He was not opposed to the idea—he was just worried that it not replace our commitment to the three legs of the [triple-threat] stool and our commitment to Parkland." Wildenthal added: "A lot of people thought he opposed it. Having been in the thick of it at the time, I can vouch that he worried about it, but did not oppose it. He understood that it was necessary for the advancement of the institution overall."[35] Robert Alpern, Seldin's handpicked head of nephrology and later dean of the medical school, confirmed this assessment: "Once the medical school decided— disagreed with him and decided to build the hospital, he never mentioned it again. He wasn't somebody to perseverate on an issue."[36]

The obstacle this time was not in Dallas but in Austin. The UT System then owned two hospitals: one at the UT Medical Branch in Galveston, and one at UT's MD Anderson Cancer Center in Houston. Both were experiencing financial challenges, and the UT System

Board of Regents was unenthusiastic about adding a third hospital. As Wildenthal described the practical realities of the desired hospital: "There were no funds to build it, or staff it, or underwrite it," adding that there was "no land on which to put it, and no willingness of the Regents to assume UT responsibility."[37]

The situation seemed hopeless, but then an unexpected opportunity presented itself in 1982. At the suggestion of a private-practice physician named Robert Kramer, the Zale and Lipshy families came to Wildenthal and Sprague with a proposal. The two families were joined by blood and by business. The retail giant Zales began in 1924 as a jewelry store in Wichita Falls, Texas, founded by a poor Jewish immigrant from Russia named Morris Bernard "M. B." Zale along with his brother William and his brother-in-law Ben Lipshy. The company grew and prospered, going public in 1957 and becoming the nation's largest jewelry retailer, with more than 1,500 stores by the 1980s.[38] The Zale and Lipshy families wanted to honor the founders and settled on the idea of supporting a new private hospital at UT Southwestern.

Given the reluctance of the UT Board of Regents to own another hospital, a different proprietor was required. As Wildenthal described: "We were able to pull together a group of private citizens who also became donors to form University Medical Center, Inc., a 501(c)(3) [a private, nonprofit organization] that was totally independent of the University."[39] The purpose of this new independent entity, created in 1984, was to construct, own, and operate the new hospital dedicated for use of the UT Southwestern faculty and their private patients. A decision was made to locate the 160-bed facility adjacent to Parkland Hospital, and construction began three years later. The name "Zale-Lipshy Hospital" was announced in 1988, and the doors to the new facility opened in 1989, two years after Seldin stepped down as chairman of medicine.[40]

Over the subsequent decades, the private hospital presence at UT Southwestern continued to evolve. In 2000, UT Southwestern purchased St. Paul Hospital, and it was leased to the nonprofit running Zale-Lipshy, which operated both hospitals for several years.[41] In 2003, UT Southwestern took over the operation of both hospitals and, two years later, assumed ownership for both facilities.[42] In 2009, William P. Clements, a former Texas governor, made an unrestricted $100 million gift to UT Southwestern that served as the anchor for a campaign to build a state-of-the-art referral center and teaching hospital. In 2014, the 460-bed William P. Clements Jr. University Hospital was opened; a 290-bed expansion is scheduled to be completed in 2020.

Seldin's enormous contributions to the development of UT Southwestern were celebrated on several occasions. One was the dedication in honor of Donald Seldin and his wife, Muriel, of a twenty-seven-foot-long, seven-foot-tall mixed-media print titled "The Fountain," created by Frank Stella, one of Seldin's favorite artists. This artwork, a gift from Seldin's daughter, Donna, and her husband, Carroll Janis, was inspired by Herman Melville's novel *Moby-Dick*, in which a chapter titled "The Fountain" describes the spouting of white whales "sprinkling and mystifying the gardens of the deep."[43] Hung in a gathering place outside the lecture halls, Stella's masterpiece captures the magnificence of spouting whales. As Joe Goldstein asserted at the October 18, 1995, dedication ceremony, it was particularly fitting for "our own Don Seldin, who has been spouting knowledge, spraying wisdom and sprinkling and mystifying the gardens of Southwestern Medical School for almost one-half of a century."[44]

Another celebration of Seldin's contributions to UT Southwestern occurred on March 16, 2015, when a central plaza on campus was named in his honor. The plaza features a seven-foot bronze statue of Seldin, sculpted by the Philadelphia-based artist Zenos Frudakis. Seldin is depicted in a manner most familiar to generations of UT Southwestern medical students and resident physicians. The Master of Metabolic Rounds is shown lecturing in his shirtsleeves, chalk in hand, with a drawing of a nephron behind him on a blackboard. In Joe Goldstein's words, the statue captures "all of Dr. Seldin's wonderful qualities—his brilliance and intelligence, his energy and enthusiasm and his engaging and warm personality."[45]

When Gary Reed, former student, resident physician, division director, and personal physician to Seldin, learned about the plaza's naming, he couldn't resist ribbing his mentor about it. "Seldin and I were having lunch one day and I said: 'I hear they are going to put a statue of you out in the plaza.' He [Seldin] said: 'Yeah, that's no big deal.

Some people want to do that.'" Reed continued: "I said: 'Well, I heard it was going to be ten feet tall.' He [Seldin] thought for a minute, then he said: 'You don't think that's appropriate?'"[46] Seldin, the man whose outsized good taste in others helped to build a towering medical school, smiled at his old chum and laughed.

CHAPTER 12

A SOCIETY MAN

Professional societies devoted to research and clinical advancements in kidney disease were being launched around the same time that Donald Seldin arrived in Dallas. The first to be organized was the Société de Pathologie Rénale, which had its inaugural meeting in Paris in February 1949, with participants from the French-speaking countries of France, Belgium, and Switzerland. A year later, the British medical establishment followed suit, creating the Renal Association, with thirty attendees at its founding meeting in London in March 1950.

In the United States, there was considerably less enthusiasm among the American medical establishment for creating a freestanding organization dedicated to kidney disease. In the absence of a professional society, one of the early efforts to form a kidney-focused association grew out of patient advocacy. In November 1950, Ada and Harvey DeBold convened the Committee for Nephrosis Research. The DeBolds were motivated by the recent diagnosis of nephrosis in their two-year-old son, Bobby. At the time, there was no cure for nephrosis (known today as nephrotic syndrome), in which blood proteins inappropriately leak into the urine. Sadly, Bobby succumbed to his illness at four years of age, but the volunteer movement that his mother spawned would become the National Nephrosis Foundation, which in 1964 was renamed the National Kidney Foundation.[1] Established to support kidney patients and their families, the organization launched fund-raising campaigns, supported research, and advocated for federal support of kidney care. It included a scientific advisory board to ensure that it was connected to and supportive of the latest advances in the field.

Another outlet for American physicians interested in kidney disease was the Renal Section of the Council on Circulation of the American Heart Association. At the time, a relatively modest number of scientists and clinicians were focused on kidney disease, and most were content to be a small part of a much larger organization. Moreover, many in the field did not want to become disconnected from the breakthroughs in other areas of medicine.

The annual pilgrimage for sharing the latest and greatest advances across the full spectrum of medicine during the 1950s and 1960s was Atlantic City, New Jersey. During the first week in May, three societies would convene there simultaneously: the Association of Academic Physicians (popularly known as the "Old Turks" or, less tactfully, as the "Old Farts"); the American Society for Clinical Investigation (often described as the "Young Turks"); and the American Federation for Clinical Research (sometimes referred to as the "Young Squirts"). The major scientific talks were made at Chalfonte-Haddon Hall, a grand hotel, and to be selected as a presenter there was a high honor. The audience was filled with a who's who of academic medicine, including the movers and shakers of virtually every field of clinical investigation—including kidney research.[2]

While Americans hesitated to establish a national society for kidney specialists, Europeans forged ahead with their desire to create an integrating, global organization. The driving force behind that effort was the French physician Jean Hamburger. Working at Hôpital Necker in Paris, Hamburger led one of the first units dedicated to treating acute renal failure. He also created the Réanimation Médicale (Medical Resuscitation unit), which became a forerunner of the modern intensive care unit. Hamburger and his team were early adopters of kidney transplantation (1952), hemodialysis (1954), and renal biopsy (1954).[3]

In July 1957, Hamburger invited a select group of friends and colleagues to Paris to discuss the idea of convening an international meeting to focus on the latest advances in kidney research and care.

Mostly, the participants represented major European centers of medicine (France, Great Britain, Sweden, Germany, Italy, and Switzerland). Although some reservations were expressed about organizing a multinational conference, the group eventually endorsed the concept.[4]

The First International Congress of Nephrology convened in September 1960 in Geneva and across Lake Geneva at the French resort town of Évian-les-Bains. Attended by four hundred invited participants, including Donald Seldin, the First International Congress was deemed a success; a second meeting was scheduled for three years later in Prague. After much debate, it also was determined that an International Society of Nephrology (ISN) would be created; Hamburger was appointed as its founder and first president. Hamburger drafted a constitution for the new organization, and a society-sponsored journal, *Nephron*, was established. The 1963 meeting in Prague was followed by the Third International Congress of Nephrology in Washington, DC, in September 1966. Donald Seldin served on the organizing committee for the first stateside meeting of the ISN. The Washington meeting was sponsored by the Renal Section of the Council on Circulation of the American Heart Association. A number of other organizations served as cooperating societies, including the scientific advisory board of the National Kidney Foundation. The attendance swelled to 2,755, a nearly sixfold increase over the first meeting, with more than fifty countries being represented.[5] Seldin and his colleagues presented a paper on the physiology of diuretic medications.

At the Fifth Congress, held in Mexico in 1972, Donald Seldin was appointed to the ISN council, and a year later he attended a meeting of the executive committee in London. At the London session, Seldin was appointed to a group responsible for revising the ISN constitution and bylaws. It was not until November 1977 that the executive committee approved the revised constitution, which (among other changes) endorsed a more open ISN membership; linked dues to subscription to the society's new journal, *Kidney International*, which had replaced the prior affiliation with *Nephron*; and clarified the roles and selection process for the various ISN governing and operation groups. At the Seventh Congress, held in Montreal in June 1978, Seldin participated as a member of the ISN executive committee. He was elected as vice president of the ISN and was appointed to the management committee.[6]

Seldin became the ISN's president-elect at the Eighth Congress, held in Athens in June 1981. He succeeded in gaining support for a previously suggested annual continuing education course in developing countries. Seldin also was the first to implement the new ISN constitution's process for appointing a nominating committee for councilors and officers. Despite his many contributions on the international stage, some in his own backyard remained blissfully unaware of these outside accomplishments.

For example, Victor Schuster was a fellow training under Seldin in 1981. When he learned that joining the ISN would entitle him to a discounted subscription to *Kidney International*, Schuster filled out the one-page application form, but he needed the endorsement of two ISN members. As Schuster later described: "On a whim, I entered Seldin's office and held the application silently in my outstretched hand. He grabbed the page without inspecting it, scribbled a signature on it, and handed it back to me." Schuster was concerned that Seldin had not paid attention to what he was signing, so he asked his boss: "Dr. Seldin, you are a member of the International Society of Nephrology, aren't you?" Seldin looked up at the naive trainee and replied: "I'm the president-elect, you little squirt."[7] The little squirt in question grew up to become a treasurer of the ISN and senior vice dean at the Albert Einstein School of Medicine.

Seldin's presidency of the ISN began in September 1984 at a two-day meeting with the leaders of the upcoming Tenth Congress hosted in London. Three months later, the executive and management committees met, and among the topics discussed was the creation of one or more honorary lectures to be delivered at each Congress. Seldin was assigned the task of naming these lectures, and his recommendation was to create two. The first proposed award was for excellence in basic research and to be named in honor of Alfred Newton "A. N." Richards. A much-revered pharmacologist at the University of Pennsylvania, Richards developed the micropuncture technique that opened the door to studying how urine is formed within the various segments of the nephron. Many of the discoveries in the Seldin-Rector lab in

Dallas, as well as other renal physiology labs, were based on the micro-puncture technique pioneered by Richards. The first A. N. Richards Award was bestowed to Robert Berliner, one of the, if not *the*, principal rival to Seldin for supremacy in the field of renal physiology.

The second award was for excellence in clinical nephrology and was named in honor of the ISN's founding president, Jean Hamburger. The inaugural award was presented jointly to Willem Kolff, widely credited as the developer of the artificial kidney, and Belding Scrib-ner, who enabled long-term hemodialysis by creating a stable portal of vascular access. Eight years later, in 1995, Seldin himself was selected to receive the Jean Hamburger Award. Robert Alpern, Seldin's UT Southwestern colleague, made the presentation. Toward the end of his remarks, Alpern smiled and noted: "When I told Dr. Seldin I would be allowed only six minutes to discuss all of his accomplishments, he told me that would not be enough time." After the laughter in the room died down, Alpern resumed: "As always, he was correct."

Alpern concluded with a statement that resonated with the crowd: "It is perhaps his impact on future generations of researchers, many of whom are here today, that likely represents his greatest contribution to science."[8]

The July 1987 Congress in London was the capstone to Donald Seldin's term as president. It was a time of great progress for the ISN, with Seldin reporting on the launch of research conferences, the initi-ation of a fellowship program, and the formation of scientific commis-sions. The president's dinner was held in Middle Temple Hall located at the Inns of Court, home to the four ancient societies that promote legal education in England. Middle Temple Hall dates from the six-teenth century and is a premier example of Elizabethan architecture in London, having survived the 1666 Great Fire as well as the Nazi bom-bardments during World War II. In this hall, built when a powerful queen ruled England, Seldin was presented with a gift of appreciation for his service—a golden statue of another strong queen: Nefertiti, of ancient Egypt.[9]

Long before Nefertiti appeared in statue form at Middle Temple Hall in London, the ISN gave an even larger gift to American nephrology. During the run-up to the Third Congress in Washington in 1966, it was necessary to assemble an organizing committee. As there was no national association of nephrologists in the United States at the time, a group was constituted from two established sources: the Renal Section of the Council on Circulation of the American Heart Association and the scientific advisory board of the National Kidney Foundation. The eighteen members of this blue-ribbon group of physicians and scientists included the champions of the two main tributaries flowing into the new field of nephrology: the physiologists, like Seldin, who studied how the kidney functioned; and the dialyzers and transplanters who pursued treatments for failing kidneys.

Reflecting on these events many years later, Seldin recalled: "It was quite clear that one of the driving forces was the fact that [the United States] Congress was looking at the scene for advice on matters having to do with Nephrology."[10] Seldin was referring to a report commissioned by the Bureau of the Budget, the precursor agency to the Office of Management and Budget within the Department of Treasury. As hemodialysis was emerging as a treatment for chronic kidney failure, federal budget planners sought expert guidance on the use and financing of this new technology. To that end, the Committee on Chronic Kidney Disease was appointed, and Carl Gottschalk of the University of North Carolina was selected as its chair.

Gottschalk, like Seldin, was a renal physiologist, and though widely respected in the nephrology community he was not personally involved in hemodialysis. The advisory group, which became known simply as the "Gottschalk Committee," worked for nearly two years while discussions were being launched to form a national nephrology society in the United States. The Gottschalk Committee issued its report in November 1967, concluding that dialysis and transplantation were no longer experimental and that a national treatment program should be established and funded by the federal government.[11]

It would take another five years for the US Congress to act on this recommendation, even though the Gottschalk Committee's report made clear there was need for an organized body of kidney experts who could advise elected officials in an informed and impartial manner. In the absence of such a group, many feared that well-financed corporate interests might have undue sway over politicians. As Seldin later posed rhetorically: "Who would it [a policymaking group] find?

It would find various dialysis groups, very often dominated by people who weren't even physicians." Seldin added: "It would be very important . . . for an organizational structure to exist that represented the best work or the best minds in the country who could represent the needs of the nephrologic community."[12]

While the Gottschalk Committee was deliberating, leading proponents of the two camps—the renal physiologists and the dialysis/transplantation experts—convened to discuss the creation of an American nephrology learned society. Seldin came from the physiology school, as did Neal Bricker from Washington University in St. Louis and Robert Berliner, who was still at NIH. The dialysis community was well represented by heads of three of the premier programs: Belding Scribner from the University of Washington, John Merrill from the Harvard-affiliated Peter Bent Brigham Hospital, and George Schreiner from Georgetown University.

The group convened at New York City's Gramercy Park Hotel on June 26, 1966. This historic Renaissance Revival landmark, a gathering place for authors, artists, and musicians for decades, became the birthplace of the American Society of Nephrology (ASN). There were definite cultural and political differences between the two assembled factions. The physiologists tended to view hemodialysis as, in Seldin's words, "a crude, empirical enterprise, without any intellectual aspects."[13] In contrast, the hemodialysis advocates tended to view the physiologists as elitist scholars without a commitment to a new lifesaving technology. Despite these prejudices, which were slow to change, the bipartisan gang of eighteen drafted a constitution and bylaws, selected a first round of officers, and chose Los Angeles as the site for its debut meeting the following year.[14]

The momentum coming out of the Gramercy Park meeting was strong, and within the ASN's inaugural year more than a thousand kidney specialists joined. Attendance at the first meeting was 1,250, with nearly three hundred scientific abstracts submitted for consideration. The keynote address in renal physiology was delivered by Robert Berliner, whose competitive streak was evident when he repeatedly noted some disparate findings between his lab and the Seldin-Rector lab. Nevertheless, the respect for Seldin was undiminished, as evidenced by Seldin's election as the second president of the organization, succeeding Neal Bricker. Over the years, Seldin remained a very active participant in the ASN.

In 1983, Seldin was selected to receive the ASN's inaugural John P. Peters Award. This award, named in honor of Seldin's mentor at Yale, was designed to recognize those who had made major contributions to kidney research and who also advanced academic medicine through patient care, teaching, or administration. The Peters Award was presented by Franklin Epstein, who overlapped with Seldin as a trainee with Peters and later became chairman of medicine at the Harvard-affiliated Beth Israel Hospital. Epstein asserted: "We feel it uniquely appropriate, Dr. Seldin, that you receive the first John Punnett Peters Award of the American Society of Nephrology, for you have transmitted his tradition to our adolescent and expanding specialty." Epstein continued: "Your ability to communicate and to foster the excitement of science, your insistence on the highest intellectual and moral standards of excellence, your devotion—your *articulate* devotion—to precision and elegance, have helped to paint a new canvas through which the Peters style shines." Epstein concluded with words that only one disciple of Peters could address to another: "And I am sure, Don, that if the old man were with us today, he would be smiling."[15]

If there was an honor that could match the pride of receiving the first Peters Award, it came two years later when the ASN named its Young Investigator Award after Seldin. Cosponsored by the Council on the Kidney in Cardiovascular Disease of the American Heart Association, this prize recognizes excellence in either basic or applied research related to the functioning or diseases of the kidney. From the outset in 1985, ASN knew how to pick a winner: the first recipient was Peter Aronson. A couple years later, Aronson was appointed to head the nephrology section at Yale, a position that he held for fifteen years. Aronson would serve as president of ASN in 2008, and the following year he was elected to the prestigious American Academy of Arts and Sciences.

As one of the founding fathers of the ASN, Seldin followed its maturation with great pride: "The American Society of Nephrology has evolved in a very exciting way. . . . I think [the organization] has been very good in broadening its coverage and in insisting on high quality. And moreover, I think that it's been adventuresome in the way it's developed its programs."[16]

An inflection point for the ASN, and for American nephrology more broadly, came in October 1972 when the US Congress passed Section 2991 of Public Law 92-603 extending Medicare coverage to persons, regardless of age, who had chronic kidney failure. At the time, about 10,000 persons were on dialysis, and the estimated cost of their care was about $200 million per year. Just three years later, 63,000 patients were maintained on dialysis at an annual cost of $2.3 billion. Five years after that, nearly 160,000 patients were on dialysis at a cost of $6.7 billion.[17] This exponential growth continued unabated, giving rise to an entire industry to support the demand. Increasingly, representatives of the private sector were present at the ASN meetings to hawk their products and to build relationships with the nephrology community.

Academic departments, even those such as UT Southwestern, that initially resisted getting into dialysis and transplantation could no longer afford to do so. The need for kidney specialists continued to grow, in Seldin's words, "from the tremendous impact that dialysis and transplantation had on clinical medicine, and that, so to speak, constituted a necessary call for nephrology. . . . You couldn't have a nephrology program without a program in dialysis and transplantation."[18] Seldin continued: "It didn't matter whether you were interested or not interested or the like, you must have that. Otherwise, it's not a nephrology program. You are not addressing diseases of the kidney with therapeutic modalities. You could have it without renal physiology. . . . But it's hard for me to conceive a nephrology program in an academic center that didn't afford dialysis and transplantation. So, the force leading to the clear definition of this discipline [nephrology] was the development of dialysis and transplantation."[19]

Even the most visionary of the professoriate assembled at the Gramercy Park Hotel in June 1966, Donald Seldin among them, could not have predicted how dramatically nephrology would grow and evolve over the coming decades. And though the ASN organizers suspected that emerging treatments would give rise to unprecedented political, economic, educational, and scientific transformation, the scale of these changes was unimaginable then. Fortunately, Seldin and his seventeen colleagues had the wisdom to create a professional society that was inclusive, adaptable, and grounded in excellence. Generations of kidney specialists who know the founders, including Donald Seldin, only as historical figures can thank them for a job well done.

CHAPTER 13

GO FORTH AND PROSPER

Donald Seldin's formula for success was to identify talented young students and physicians and develop them at UT Southwestern and in other premier institutions. Out of inspiration and loyalty to Seldin, virtually all these rising stars returned to Dallas. With Seldin's guidance, they built their own reputations and, by reflection, burnished the patina of UT Southwestern.

It didn't take long for the rest of the academic medicine world to take notice. Any chairman of a department of medicine who was recruiting a nephrology division director was likely to pick up the telephone and call Seldin for advice. After all, Seldin was running one of the largest and most prestigious nephrology training programs in the world, and he was a frequent visitor to other leading institutions. Through these informal consultations, Seldin often knew about vacancies elsewhere before they became public; using this inside information he could help direct his own protégés to the best opportunities. UT Southwestern produced a veritable who's who of nephrology, with many individuals pursuing distinguished careers at other academic medical centers. Although these success stories are too numerous to catalogue in their entirety, a few examples are included here as exemplars of the larger group.

One of Seldin's earliest nephrology fellows was a gifted young physician from Lebanon named Wadi Suki. Having come to UT Southwestern in 1959 to conduct research with the high blood pressure guru Arthur Grollman, Suki, after his two-year appointment, applied for and was accepted into the medicine residency program. In 1963, when it was time to apply for a fellowship, Seldin invited Suki for a cup of coffee in the basement shop of Parkland Hospital. When Suki told his chairman that he was interested in a nephrology fellowship, Seldin asked where he was interested in applying. Suki named his top two institutions, but Seldin dismissed both quickly: Cornell, because it was too narrowly focused, and Cedars-Sinai in Los Angeles, because it might not be a friendly environment for a nice young man from Beirut. Beginning to feel that his options were limited, Suki asked Seldin where he should apply. Seldin's response was delivered in classic Brooklynese: "You stay here, you dope," punctuated by a swift jab of his index finger into Suki's chest.[1]

And so Suki remained in Dallas for his nephrology fellowship. Around this same time, the field was turned upside down by the introduction of a new type of diuretic. The medication now known as furosemide was approved for medical use, and it was found to be quick-acting and powerful at removing excess fluids from the body, but little was known about the mechanism by which it increased urine output. Seldin assigned Suki to study this issue, using dogs as the experimental animal. In an important paper published in 1965, Suki, Seldin, and Rector demonstrated that furosemide acted on a different part of the nephron than the other diuretics known at the time.[2] In an amazing piece of detective work, the team examined the fluid and electrolyte composition of the urine produced and from that inferred which part of the nephron was most likely the site at which furosemide operated. Their findings would be confirmed later when actual direct measurements could be made in various nephron segments.

Suki continued to impress Seldin, and when Suki's two-year fellowship ended in 1965 he was invited to join the division's faculty. After three more productive years in Dallas, a new opportunity became available for Suki down the road in Houston. At the Baylor University College of Medicine, plans were being developed to create a division of nephrology. By coincidence, the UT Southwestern senior investigator Marvin Siperstein was a visiting professor at Baylor at the time.

Knowing the strength of the program in Dallas, the Baylor leadership asked Siperstein if he could recommend anyone for the job. Although Suki was still very junior, Siperstein enthusiastically recommended him. When Suki was offered the job, Seldin provided him with encouragement to proceed. In Suki's words: "He understood the need to go and start my own show but was very supportive every inch of the way."[3]

Suki's first task was to recruit additional faculty members, as the division was responsible for covering the busy clinical services at the county public hospital, Ben Taub, and the Veterans Affairs medical center. Suki reached out to two friends and fellow UT Southwestern trainees—Manuel "Manny" Martinez Maldonado and Garabed "Gary" Eknoyan. Although a fan of all of these former trainees, Seldin was concerned that the three strong personalities might create a volatile mix. Suki recalled Seldin's caution to him: "You three are all driven, ambitious young people. You're going to fight and you're gonna kill one another. Do not do it."[4]

Turning a deaf ear to their mentor's admonition, the three intrepid colleagues set up shop together in Houston. The improbable and combustible mixture of three such disparate backgrounds turned out to be a real success story. Suki and Eknoyan remained in Houston throughout their decorated careers. Martinez Maldonado remained there for five highly productive years before moving on to a series of leadership positions in academic medicine elsewhere, including Emory University, Oregon Health Sciences University, Ponce School of Medicine, and the University of Louisville.

Suki and his compatriots benefited from Seldin's continuing stewardship of their careers. As Suki described the relationship: "If you were one of his children, he took great interest in you and your family life and your academic career." Suki continued: "He would say: 'Wadi, we have to get you into the Southern Society for Clinical Investigation.' So, there goes a proposal. I get in on the first ballot. Then, 'Wadi, we have to get you into the American Society for Clinical Investigation'— the ASCI—the Young Turks. So, there goes a proposal. I get in on the first vote. Then the AAP—the Association of American Physicians— same thing."[5] Although Seldin's protégés got in on their own merits, it was an advantage to have an insider who was their advocate.

In 1976, Suki returned to Dallas as a visiting professor to learn how to perform isolated tubule microperfusion from the new head of nephrology, Juha Kokko, who had arrived in Dallas three years earlier. Seldin welcomed Suki back home with open arms: "He was very gracious in having me back. . . . He was supportive every inch of the way, the whole time." Two decades later, when Suki was elected president of the American Society of Nephrology, Seldin was still "always there advising."[6]

Another early fellow was Neil Kurtzman, whose acceptance into the training program echoed Suki's experience. Kurtzman was a resident physician in medicine at William Beaumont General Hospital in El Paso. Seldin flew out once each month to teach the hospital's residents and grab an authentic Mexican meal across the border. On one such occasion, Kurtzman asked the visiting professor which nephrology fellowships he recommended. Seldin replied: "Why don't you come to our place?" Kurtzman, who knew Seldin only in his capacity as chairman of medicine, innocently asked: "Who is the chief [of nephrology]?"[7]

Seldin's response was a swift punch to Kurtzman's gut, both literally and figuratively. When Seldin identified himself as the head of nephrology, Kurtzman apologized, indicating that he thought that Seldin was the chairman of the entire department. When Seldin told him that both hats rested comfortably on his head, Kurtzman only made matters worse by inquiring: "Is the program any good?" Seldin, probably mulling over whether there was any hope for this impertinent trainee, offered no response. Instead, he picked up a telephone receiver and placed a call to a general at the Pentagon.[8]

Seldin had just completed a medical manpower assessment for the military, and he knew that they did not have any nephrology training programs. Seldin proceeded to negotiate a fellowship for Kurtzman at UT Southwestern, fully paid for by the Army, in exchange for payback service when the training was completed. So, at no cost to the university, Seldin had recruited another fellow to the program. When Kurtzman arrived in 1966, he opted for a research track and worked under Floyd Rector's supervision doing micropuncture studies.[9]

When the two-year fellowship neared its end, Seldin asked Kurtzman where he wanted to go next, given that he had an obligation to repay the military. Kurtzman presumed that the best option would be to try to get into the Army's main research hospital—Walter Reed Army Medical Center in Washington, DC. Seldin shook his head and said simply: "You don't want to go there." Now savvy to the expected response, Kurtzman asked: "Where do I want to go?" Seldin, who was moving chess pieces in his head, suggested that Kurtzman consider the burn unit at Brooke Army Medical Center in San Antonio. As before, Seldin placed a single telephone call to the Army brass at the Pentagon, and Kurtzman was on his way.[10]

Seldin's strategy soon became evident when, several months later, he recruited the head of the Brooke metabolic unit to the UT Southwestern faculty, leaving Kurtzman to fill the vacancy. Seldin maintained contact with Kurtzman through monthly visits to Brooke as a visiting professor. There, he saw Kurtzman establish the Army's first nephrology fellowship and chronic dialysis program.[11]

Four years later, at the tender age of thirty-five, Kurtzman was hired as chief of nephrology at the University of Illinois at Chicago. According to Kurtzman: "The reason I got it was the chairman of medicine at Illinois at that time decided the only person he was going to hire for chief of nephrology was someone who had been trained by Don Seldin. So, he was looking for a Seldin-trained fellow." Kurtzman continued: "I'm sure when my name came up that he called Dr. Seldin. I never asked him, but he'd be crazy not to." Seldin never mentioned such a call to Kurtzman, but the former trainee knew that he would not have received an offer without the blessing of his mentor.[12]

Later, Kurtzman accepted the offer of chairman of medicine at Texas Tech University, a position he held for thirteen years. During his tenure as chairman, Kurtzman was asked to consider a comparable position at another well-known medical school. He was uncertain about whether he should accept the offer, so he called Seldin, who invited him to UT Southwestern to review the situation. In Kurtzman's words: "I went to Dallas and spent the whole day. . . . We went through the entire offer. I had everything—budgets—everything. . . . At the end of the day, he says: 'I don't think you should take it,' and I didn't." Kurtzman elaborated: "This was a very dispassionate analysis on his part of what the pros and cons of taking that job were. I probably wouldn't have gotten the offer in the first place if he hadn't said that I had the requirements for the job. I'm sure they called him."[13]

Highly regarded among nephrologists, Kurtzman served a two-year term as president of the National Kidney Foundation and later received the David M. Hume Award, the organization's highest honor. He also received the Founder's Medal from the Southern Society for Clinical Investigation, in addition to many other honors. Kurtzman credits Seldin with opening the doors of opportunity for him: "Like so many other physicians, meeting Dr. Seldin and getting to work under him was the decisive event in my career. Whatever mean success I have had, none of it would have happened had I not met him."[14]

Another fellow from this period was Jay Stein. A graduate of the University of Tennessee's medical school in Memphis, he completed his residency in internal medicine at the University of Iowa. After a two-year stint studying the high rates of diabetes among Native Americans, Stein returned to Iowa, where he spent a year as chief resident and a year doing kidney micropuncture studies with Walter Kirkendall. As the fellowship in Iowa was coming to an end, Kirkendall called Seldin to recommend Stein for further training in nephrology. Arriving at the same time as Kurtzman, Stein was assigned immediately to the laboratory because of his experience with performing micropuncture. Stein described his fellowship in Dallas in glowing terms: "It was just a really wonderful two-year period from '67 to '69. I really loved every minute of it."[15] When it came time to secure a faculty position, Seldin encouraged Stein to remain in Dallas, with an appointment at the Department of Veterans Affairs Hospital. Stein opted instead to join the new nephrology division at Ohio State University.

After about five years, Stein was recruited to head the Division of Nephrology at the University of Texas Health Science Center in San Antonio. A couple years after that, the chairman of medicine in San Antonio departed for a similar job at the University of Pennsylvania. Following a national search, Stein was offered the position of chairman of medicine in San Antonio. As he later recalled: "I was somewhat shocked." So, he placed a call to Seldin and asked: "Should I do this?" Seldin invited Stein back to UT Southwestern to meet in his office the following morning to discuss the offer. Stein continued: "I took Southwest [Airlines] there, we met—he spent an hour and twenty minutes. I must say, at that point, I really didn't understand much about what the job was like." Seldin, who by that time had been a chairman for a quarter-century, provided a tutorial. "He just urged me to do it, and here I am, this little *schmekel* [Yiddish, meaning, among other things, a stupid or naive person] sitting in Don Seldin's office and he's telling me how to be a chairman of medicine. That was him; he'd just do anything for you."[16]

Stein accepted the chairmanship and remained there for fifteen years. He left to become senior vice president and provost of the University of Oklahoma Health Sciences Center, and three years after that he was appointed to a similar post at the University of Rochester. After eight years, Stein again moved, this time returning to Texas, where he became the vice president and dean for clinical affairs at Baylor College of Medicine. The one time self-described "little *schmekel*" had become what Seldin might have heard described on the streets of Brooklyn as a big *macher* ("big shot").

Another Seldin fellow, Thomas DuBose, arrived in Dallas in 1971 as an internal medicine resident. As he was completing his two years of clinical training, he consulted with Seldin about next steps. Seldin told him: "We always thought you would be a nephrologist." DuBose, who had been assigned to the nephrology service several times as a resident physician, had assumed that he was being asked to repeat the rotation until he got a satisfactory evaluation. So, Seldin's favorable assessment came as a surprise, and when a fellowship was offered for the coming year DuBose was forced to defer it while he fulfilled an obligation to the military.[17]

When DuBose returned two years later to undertake his nephrology fellowship, he performed so well that he was invited to join the faculty. DuBose states without any reservation that Seldin "taught me just about everything. Certainly, how to write a paper and how to present data. In some ways, how to lead. Not that I tried to be like him as a leader, but certainly, I learned a lot from him as a leader."[18]

After four years on the faculty, DuBose was ready to spread his wings. "I needed to be identified with my own area [of research] and be able to be identified as an independent investigator." DuBose accepted an offer from the University of Texas Medical Branch. Although the school in Galveston was the oldest medical school in the state, it was struggling financially and, at the time, did not have the kind of visionary leadership that had propelled UT Southwestern to success. "Dr. Seldin thought I'd lost my mind. He literally thought I was crazy to do that." Nevertheless, DuBose went to Galveston, where he became the head of nephrology before moving on to the sister University of Texas medical school forty-five miles away on the mainland in Houston. In Houston, DuBose's administrative skills were recognized, and he was appointed vice chairman of the internal medicine department.[19]

In 2000, DuBose left the state of Texas to become chairman of the Department of Medicine at the University of Kansas, and a few years later he assumed the comparable position at Wake Forest School of Medicine in Winston-Salem, North Carolina. DuBose remembered receiving a telephone call from Seldin when he was first appointed "chairman of medicine and he just talked to me about that. He gave me some helpful advice. It was very personal, very helpful."[20] Seldin remained a trusted adviser to DuBose over the years. "He kept in touch with me. . . . He was a mentor and he was a role model and he was a great man."[21]

DuBose noted that coming out of the Dallas training program gave him immediate cachet. "I was clearly identified as one of Seldin's 'boys' and that was a good thing." DuBose continued: "There's no doubt that a Seldin-trained fellow, particularly a research fellow, was given the benefit of the doubt until proven otherwise. . . . The assumption was they're going to be well trained; they're going to be well-informed. . . . They will likely succeed. . . . It was sort of a mark of approval—like a Good Housekeeping Seal."[22]

The fellows coming out of Seldin's shop naturally gravitated to leadership roles in academic medicine. At least twenty-five American medical schools had leaders who were products of the UT Southwestern nephrology fellowship during Seldin's chairmanship. In addition to those already mentioned, Fredric Coe was the long-time head of nephrology at the University of Chicago, Roland Blantz was chief of nephrology at the University of California, San Diego, Michael Bailie was chairman of pediatrics and vice dean at the University of Illinois, John Higgins was chairman of medicine at Texas Tech at Amarillo, Harry Jacobson was vice chancellor for health affairs at Vanderbilt

University, Lee Hamm was the senior vice president and dean at Tulane University, and Victor Schuster was senior vice dean at Albert Einstein College of Medicine.

The Seldin pipeline of leaders at American medical schools extended beyond former trainees to faculty that he had recruited and nurtured. Seldin's former student and long-time collaborator Floyd Rector departed UT Southwestern in 1973 to become director of nephrology at the University of California, San Francisco. After sixteen years in that position, Rector was appointed to chair the Department of Medicine there. When Rector left Dallas, Juha Kokko succeeded him as chief of nephrology and remained in that capacity for thirteen years. Kokko's research was garnering widespread attention, but he also knew that Seldin was working quietly behind the scenes to promote his young colleague. Kokko particularly appreciated the fact that Seldin "introduced me to the giants [of nephrology] in Europe. I got invited just about everywhere. . . . Don was behind many of these invitations."[23] When Kokko arrived in Berlin, for example, his hosts said: "Don Seldin has spoken highly of you and your work and that we ought to have you come here and give an invited lecture." Kokko added: "But he [Seldin] never told me about that. He's the one who opened those old-time, relatively closed doors."[24]

When the position of chairman of medicine became available at Emory University, Kokko's alma mater, the attraction to the Atlanta campus was irresistible. Emory was actually the fifth chairmanship that Kokko had been offered. As he described: "I had discussed all of those with Don. Don had helped me go through these."[25] Kokko freely admits that his interest in becoming a chairman was motivated, at least in part, by observing Seldin in the role. "I always wanted to be a chairman because I saw how much fun Don had, quite frankly, being a chairman."[26]

Kokko also credits Seldin with giving him valuable advice about how to approach the situation at Emory: "He gave me lots of hints as to how to handle various things. The main thing he told me is the job is too big for one person—you're going to have to divvy up various types of job descriptions." This may seem like strange advice coming from the person who was a one-man show at the start of his own service as chairman. In the intervening decades, however, departments of medicine had grown, finances had become much more complicated, and the bureaucratic environment of medical care and research had become far more onerous. Kokko pointed out that Seldin was adamant about retaining one key responsibility, however: "He said: 'One thing don't ever give up—don't give up being head of your house staff [resident physician] training program.'"[27]

When Juha Kokko left Dallas for Emory, Seldin needed to find a new chief of nephrology. There were two leading prospects in Seldin's mind: Peter Aronson, who was the newly appointed head of nephrology at Yale; and a young researcher named Robert Alpern in Floyd Rector's division at UCSF. According to Alpern, Seldin "discussed me with Floyd Rector and realized that Peter Aronson was not going to leave his new position at Yale." Alpern described Seldin's initial contact with him: "In the typical Seldin way, [he] said: 'I have decided that you should be the chief of nephrology here. I don't believe in search committees. You're basically not one of many candidates—you are the person I have decided to be the chief of nephrology and I'd like you to come out and visit, basically to close the deal.'"[28]

Alpern headed nephrology there for a decade, always believing that the "pinnacle of my career would be to become a chair of internal medicine, similar to Don Seldin."[29] That path did not develop for Alpern because, when Seldin stepped down in 1988, Daniel Foster, his former student and a highly respected senior diabetes researcher on the faculty, was next in line for the job. Seldin might have hoped that Alpern would wait his turn after Foster stepped down, but in the meantime the position of medical school dean at UT Southwestern became available and Alpern was selected. He confesses that he never imagined becoming a dean: "I had no role models who were deans, and I never had an aspiration to be a dean." Although Seldin may have been proud of Alpern's accomplishments, the protégé always felt that his mentor "was very disappointed when I became the dean. He was more disappointed when I moved to Yale" to assume the same responsibilities there. For Seldin, there was no higher calling than to be the chair of medicine.[30]

Other Seldin recruits went on to academic leadership positions as well. Fresh out of a nephrology fellowship at the University of Colorado, William Henrich arrived at UT Southwestern in 1978 as a young faculty member. Henrich spent seventeen years on the faculty in Dallas, moving up the ladder of academic ranks. Henrich credited Seldin with helping him to advance: "He took time to recruit me and then he took interest in my career. . . . He wanted to hear updates from me and he gave me advice during the entire time I was there. When I was nominated for honorific societies and so forth, he was the person who helped me."[31]

Henrich described Seldin's process for generating letters of support: "He would ask me to write a letter for myself and then he would spend an hour and a half correcting the letter." Henrich always felt that Seldin treated him with respect "and I'd even say in his way, affection, even though during those sessions he was dissecting my CV [curriculum vitae] or going over my letter, it didn't sound like he loved me."[32]

When Henrich was appointed chairman of internal medicine at the Medical College of Ohio in 1995, he continued to rely on Seldin for guidance: "He could not have been more gracious, and he was very helpful to me as a chairman of medicine. I had a couple of difficult circumstances I was going through with personnel, and he was, as always, the model of clear thinking in what I needed to do."[33] At Henrich's invitation, Seldin came to Ohio as a visiting professor and as a commencement speaker and was awarded an honorary degree. Subsequently, when Henrich was recruited to serve as chairman of the Department of Medicine at the University of Maryland, Seldin came to Baltimore to support him. As Henrich noted: "Once he [Seldin] had made up his mind that you were worth the effort, he would stay in touch and, in his way, mentor you. . . . He devoted himself to the cultivation of people he thought had the talent and ability and drive."[34]

In Henrich's case, the potential that Seldin nurtured came to full realization back in Texas. He was recruited first as the dean of the School of Medicine of the University of Texas Health Science Center in San Antonio and then was promoted to the institution's presidency. In summarizing his relationship with Seldin, Henrich acknowledged his mentor's role: "I'm grateful that I was exposed to a person of such enormous intellect and ability and honesty. I know I wouldn't have been shaped in the same way I am today without my exposure to him."[35]

Although the rise of Seldin's disciples was most evident in the United States, trainees were attracted from around the world and returned to their home countries in leadership roles. Early in its existence, the nephrology fellowship program at UT Southwestern was a magnet for international talent. The first foreign trainee, admitted in 1960, was E. P. M. Bhattathiri of Nigeria, who later was appointed to head the medical biochemistry department at the national university. The following year, Hiroshi Sakakida arrived from Japan and went on to become chairman of medicine at Kyoto Medical School. Four subsequent Japanese nephrology fellows trained in Dallas—more than from any other foreign country. Three Canadians crossed the border to study under Seldin. Two Spaniards came to the UT Southwestern program, including José Rodicio, who later was appointed chief of nephrology at the University of Madrid and also served as president of the Spanish Society of Nephrology. Other countries represented by at least one Seldin trainee were: Guatemala (J. Manuel Arias), Switzerland (Felix Brunner), Germany (Anslem Frick), Sweden (Anders Jonsson), Mexico (Jamie Herrera-Acosta), Italy (Vittorio Andreucci), Brazil (José Antonio Rocha Gontijo), and Finland (Christer Holberg). During the Seldin era, UT Southwestern became a virtual United Nations of Nephrology, with the globetrotting chairman of medicine serving as Secretary-General. Seldin built a multinational training program before it was fashionable to do so and thus left his personal imprint on academic medicine around the world.

CHAPTER 14

MORAL AUTHORITY

As a young physician serving in the United States Army in the 1940s, Donald Seldin came face to face with pure evil. As head of medical service at a large armed forces hospital in Munich, Germany, Seldin was summoned to nearby Dachau—the site of the notorious Nazi concentration camp. An American military tribunal was under way, and a former Nazi physician, Rudolf Brachtel, was on trial. He was accused of war crimes for conducting medical experiments on prisoners of war. Seldin testified that the physician performed dangerous procedures that were not medically necessary on subjects who had no ability to refuse the procedures. Other American medical consultants and organizations argued against conviction, because it might draw unwanted attention to the ethics of wartime malaria studies that had been conducted on civilian prisoners held in American penal institutions.[1] Brachtel was acquitted, with the court ruling that there was adequate consent and that the liver biopsies he performed could be justified clinically.

Separate trials of other Nazi doctors led to the so-called Nuremberg Code. In the wake of the verdicts resulting from the trials, ten principles were specified for the conduct of ethical research on human subjects. These requirements included, among others, voluntary subject participation and assurance that potential benefits exceeded risks. A later document, known as the Declaration of Helsinki, updated and refined the basic attributes of ethical research. Approved in 1964 by the World Medical Association, the Helsinki Declaration introduced, among other things, the forerunner of informed consent and concerns for protecting vulnerable populations. Examples of vulnerable populations include children, pregnant women, fetuses, prisoners, institutionalized persons, the elderly, ethnic minorities, refugees, physically and intellectually challenged persons, and the terminally ill.

As these codes of conduct emerged, compliance with ethical standards was treated as the responsibility of the investigator. That changed when more potentially abusive studies came to light in the United States. The studies in question included one conducted in 1962 by investigators from New York's Sloan-Kettering Hospital. In this research, twenty-two indigent elderly patients from Brooklyn's Jewish Chronic Disease Hospital were injected with live cancer cells to study the patients' immune responses.[2] Another investigation that drew criticism when it was exposed occurred between 1956 and 1972 and was undertaken by investigators from New York University and Yale University. In this research, institutionalized mentally impaired children and adolescents at Willowbrook State Hospital in Staten Island were injected with a hepatitis virus to study the spread of, and treatment for, the infection.[3]

The greatest public outrage by far occurred after the 1972 revelation that, for forty years, 399 black men with syphilis had been followed without treatment, even after penicillin was demonstrated to cure the disease. The study in Tuskegee, Alabama, was organized and funded by the US Public Health Service. The subjects were poor, minimally educated, and never informed of the true purpose of the study. They were encouraged to participate in "free treatments," which in fact were diagnostic procedures with no therapeutic benefit whatsoever and were designed only for purposes of research.[4]

Accounts of the Tuskegee Syphilis Study in the media prompted the federal Department of Health, Education, and Welfare (DHEW) to convene an external review panel. The advisers recommended immediately ending the study, providing appropriate care to the surviving subjects, and establishing a regulatory body for federally funded studies of human subjects. Public indignation over the abuse of these vulnerable populations led to congressional hearings convened by Senator Edward Kennedy of Massachusetts in February 1974. Following the hearings, Kennedy introduced legislation that became Public Law 93-348 (the National Research Act), which was approved on July 12, 1974. Title II within this act created the National Commission for the Protection of Human Subjects of Biomedical and Behavioral Research.[5]

The act stipulated that the Commission be composed of eleven members to be appointed by the secretary of DHEW. Five (but no more) members were to be active or former biomedical or behavioral researchers. The remaining members were to represent a variety of other disciplines including, among others, law, theology, and philosophy. The Commission was charged with developing a set of basic ethical principles that should underlie research on human subjects. The act further required the Commission to make recommendations to the secretary of DHEW on research related to several categories of vulnerable populations, including children, prisoners, and the institutionalized mentally "infirm." In addition, the act required the Commission to produce a report within four months on the hot-button political issue of research involving living human fetuses.[6] Less than eighteen months following the United States Supreme Court ruling in *Roe v. Wade* recognizing a woman's constitutional right to an abortion, opponents were concerned that fetal research might encourage more women to have abortions.

Given the high-stakes nature of the Commission's work, many organizations nominated potential members. After appropriate vetting, Caspar Weinberger, the secretary of DHEW, appointed the eleven members of the Commission. Three physicians were selected: Kenneth Ryan, Robert Cooke, and Donald Seldin. Ryan, an obstetrician-gynecologist, was chief of staff at the Harvard-affiliated Boston Hospital for Women, where he had recently launched the first abortion service in a university hospital. Cooke, a pediatrician, had been a year behind Donald Seldin at the Yale School of Medicine. He later served as chairman of pediatrics at Johns Hopkins before departing to head the health science center at the University of Wisconsin in Madison. In

1960, Cooke had proposed to President John F. Kennedy the establishment of a research institute devoted to children, which subsequently
became the National Institute for Child Health and Development. Five
years later, Cooke chaired an advisory committee that recommended
the creation of the Head Start program.

Given that the Commission was asked to review research on
fetuses and children, it was not surprising that the membership
included a distinguished obstetrician and a prominent pediatrician.
Seldin's appointment was perhaps less driven by his specialized expertise in kidney disease and more related to his reputation as a thought
leader in academic medicine. The two remaining researchers were the
behavioral scientist Joseph Brady of Johns Hopkins University and the
physiological psychologist Eliot Stellar, provost of the University of
Pennsylvania.

The Commission included two ethicists, both from fields of religious studies: Albert Jonsen from the University of California, San
Francisco, and Karen Lebacqz from the Pacific School of Religion. The
legal profession was represented by Patricia King from Georgetown
University, David Louisell from the University of California, Berke-
ley, and Robert Turtle from a Washington law firm. Finally, Dorothy
Height from the National Council of Negro Women was appointed as a
public representative because of her prominent role as an advocate for
minority and women's rights.

The Commission was convened initially on December 3, 1974,
at which time the members were administered their oaths of office
by Secretary Weinberger. Although originally authorized for just two
years, the Commission required almost four years to complete its
assignments. On the Commission's second day of operation, Kenneth
Ryan was elected by its members to serve as chair, and he proved to
be a wise and popular choice. As the commissioner Patricia King later
recalled: "The chairman of the Commission was an extraordinary man
and he kept an often fractious and unwieldy group all marching in
the same direction." King elaborated further: "He didn't really crack a
whip, but he was firm," adding, "he set the tone. He was respectful. . . .
He listened to everybody's views. He kept his own inclinations firmly
in check as long as he was acting as chair."[7]

Coming from such disparate backgrounds, the commissioners

reflected cross-cultural divides. As Karen Lebacqz recalled: "I have several early memories that are very strong. One was how difficult it was for us to talk to each other in those first meetings." Lebacqz added: "I remember that it took us almost four months to develop a common language so that, when the scientists talked, the rest of us understood what they were saying. And when the lawyers talked, the ethicists understood what they were saying."[8]

The commissioners were learning to communicate with each other while also honoring the mandate that their meetings must be conducted in public. In the words of Commissioner King: "If I remember the most daunting thing, it was to discuss issues like fetal research and abortion in public in the sense that you had to deliberate in public." She added that the "consensus had to be hashed out in front of an audience, and that was quite unnerving at the time."[9]

The commissioners reflected a broad range of professional backgrounds, as well as ideological perspectives, although the reasons for selecting individual members were not disclosed and remain confidential. Patricia King described the ideological divide: "We had both pro-choice and pro-life—avowedly pro-choice and pro-life—members of the National Commission. Certainly, in the beginning, it seemed that we would never—could never—reach agreement about fetal research."[10]

One of the avowedly pro-choice commissioners was the activist Dorothy Height. Not a person who was easily intimidated by the titles and degrees of the other commissioners, Height felt that the group developed an esprit de corps: "That's what I liked about being in the group. I could be who I am and speak up at any moment on any issue . . . each of us had respect for the other."[11]

Although the eleven commissioners were dealing with divisive issues, personal relationships developed among them and between the commissioners and staff members. Donald Seldin and Patricia King found an easy rapport, and he also established strong connections with the staff members Tom Beauchamp and Robert Levine. Commissioner Robert Cooke characterized the experience this way: "It hit all the things you like to have in experiences in life. It was intellectually exciting. It was socially great. And you felt as though you were doing something that was important for the world."[12]

During their otherwise very serious deliberations, the commissioners found tension-breaking moments of levity. One such example occurred at the twenty-seventh meeting (February 11–13, 1977). Seldin had just finished a long-winded monologue on a philosophical point. Chairman Ryan then called on Robert Cooke, who turned to Seldin and asked as a courtesy: "Are you through?" When Seldin responded in the affirmative, Cooke added: "That will be the day." The group dissolved into laughter, and after a well-timed pause Seldin added wryly: "I got caught a little short because I am used to longer speeches." Once again, the meeting was interrupted with peals of laughter.[13]

The Commission did not have the luxury of a scholarly pace of activity because the National Research Act established a four-month deadline for generating the mandated report on fetal research. The Commission quickly immersed itself in background materials and lively debate. As Commissioner Albert Jonsen recalled: "We had lots of good arguments." He described the typical writing process as follows: "People were assigned sections to draft, and then they were criticized and redrafted. So, I remember times when I sat with maybe one or another commissioner in the hall, in Building 10 at NIH and pounded things out on the typewriter so they could go back to the commission."[14] Much of the actual drafting of reports through many iterations was handled by the professional staff.

On July 25, 1975, the Commission delivered its first report.[15] Although the Commission was unable to satisfy the originally intended and probably unrealistic schedule, its members met eight times to work their way through one of the most contentious issues: research on the fetus. The National Research Act contained a provision that imposed a temporary moratorium on federally funded research involving fetal tissues. In its report, the Commission recommended lifting the moratorium immediately. Additionally, the Commission endorsed fetal research in a variety of contexts.[16]

One of the procedural issues that arose in this first report was how to deal with differences of opinion on a given topic. To the extent possible, the commissioners attempted to reach a consensus, but they also accommodated areas of disagreement. As Commissioner Lebacqz recalled: "One of the things that we did there and elsewhere was to reach a point where we said: 'We are not going to agree on this. Let's make sure that minority voices can be heard,' and to put out a report that included the majority report and then several different minority voices."[17] For example, in the fetal research report, Commissioner Louisell took exception to two recommendations that related to nontherapeutic research on the fetus in anticipation of abortion and during an abortion, as well as on a nonviable fetus after abortion.[18]

Unlike a typical federal advisory group whose recommendations could be received and filed away, the enabling legislation required that the secretary of DHEW must respond within 180 days to a Commission report and its recommendations. As described by Commissioner Lebacqz: "If the secretary departed from what we recommended, the secretary had to explain why."[19]

The Commission continued to work through its mandated assignments, producing a report on research involving prisoners on October 1, 1976. The following year, three additional reports were published, including a highly visible one on research involving children (September 6, 1977). On February 2, 1978, the Commission produced a report on research involving institutionalized persons who were mentally "infirm" (using terminology designated in the National Research Act).

As the Commission was beginning to hit its stride on the various mandated reports, it held a retreat between February 13 and 16, 1976. The purpose of the retreat was to tackle another required assignment from the enabling legislation: "To identify the basic ethical principles which should underlie the conduct of biomedical and behavioral research involving human subjects."[20] It was decided that the meeting should take place in a relaxed setting but not one that would appear too luxurious. The venue selected was the Belmont Conference Center in Elkridge, Maryland, about ten miles south of Baltimore. Then owned by the Smithsonian Institution, the conference center included a Georgian manor house originally constructed in 1738, along with various subsequent additions. An irony of this chosen location is that during the antebellum period the surrounding plantation operated with nearly one hundred slaves.[21] Thus, in a setting where involuntary labor was compelled a century earlier, the commissioners discussed the core principles of protecting human beings who were vulnerable subjects of biomedical research.

When the commissioners arrived at Belmont it was midwinter, and there were patches of snow on the ground under a gray sky.[22] The dreary weather did not deter the commissioners from their appointed task, which in many ways was an extension of the work that they had already undertaken in the individual reports. The animated discussions at Belmont pared down the number of basic ethical principles from an initial half-dozen or more to just three. These core principles were codified as *respect for persons, beneficence,* and *justice.*

The concept of *respect for persons* relates to honoring the right of people to make decisions for themselves when properly informed about the benefits and risks of participation. It also acknowledges that persons who have diminished capacity, such as children or those with mental incompetence, who make such self-determining decisions are entitled to respect for their personhood and for protection. An important implication of the respect-for-persons criterion is the requirement to inform potential subjects about the purpose of the research and possible outcomes that might occur and to obtain their, or their legal representative's, voluntary consent to participate.[23]

The principle of *beneficence* embraces the dictate to "do no harm," which is enshrined in the Hippocratic Oath physicians have sworn to for millennia. Additionally, beneficence requires the investigator to maximize the benefits to research subjects while minimizing any potential adverse effects. This principle requires that proposed research be examined by a group separate from the investigator to ensure that potential risks and benefits are balanced appropriately.[24]

The third and final principle is *justice,* which relates to the just and fair distribution of rewards and benefits of participating in research. In other words, research populations should not preferentially include persons because of their social or economic standing. Factors such as race, impoverishment, or institutionalization may unduly influence access to and participation of vulnerable populations.[25]

These three principles were discussed without assigning primacy to any of them. Commissioner Albert Jonsen made an analogy to the Bill of Rights—the first ten amendments to the United States Constitution. Just as there is no prioritized ordering of these constitutional rights, one above the other, the Commission made no rank ordering of the ethical principles.

The task of translating the Commission's deliberations at the Belmont Conference Center into a document fell squarely on the shoulders of a staff member hired after the retreat. Tom L. Beauchamp was an assistant professor of philosophy at the time, and as he recalled later: "Seldin did not crave a youthful philosopher six years out of graduate school. He would have preferred John Rawls [a Harvard ethicist and author of the landmark *A Theory of Justice*], or at least someone of an international reputation."[26] Seldin and Beauchamp would become close friends over the following years, but at the outset Seldin played more of an avuncular role: "Seldin encouraged me with as much vigor as he could muster (which was and remains today—considerable) to make my drafts as philosophical as possible. Seldin wanted some Mills here, some Kant there, and the signature of in-depth philosophical argument sprinkled throughout the document. I tried this style, but the other Commissioners wanted a minimalist statement relatively free of the style of academic philosophy."[27]

Beauchamp's early drafts were lengthy and somewhat dense with scholarly content, but successive iterations shortened and simplified the content. As Commissioner Dorothy Height recalled: "It was a hard task, but I think there was a kind of group determination, and the chairman kept pushing us in that direction to make this something that could be useful, but also something that could be understood."[28] As an advocate for civil and gender rights, Height wanted the report to be comprehensible to diverse audiences: "You don't have to have four dictionaries to read it. You can bring it within the mass of people so that they can understand it and can use it, and then that begins to build confidence neighbor to neighbor, community to community."[29]

The finished product was named in a most unusual way for a government report. It was titled after the conference center where the Commission met to discuss their assignment. *The Belmont Report: Ethical Principles and Guidelines for the Protection of Human Subjects of Research*[30] was submitted on September 30, 1978, as the Commission was wrapping up its activities. The twenty-page report included a section on the distinction between clinical research and clinical practice that was drafted in part by a subcommittee chaired by Seldin and in part by Robert Levine, a staff member and consultant. The boundary between clinical research and patient care can be indistinct, as they often occur together. Nevertheless, "practice" was defined as relating to interventions intended to benefit an individual, whereas "research" was characterized as organized activity designed to develop generalizable knowledge.[31]

The initial reaction to the ethical principles was not uniformly positive. As Seldin recalled: "In general [the Belmont Report] was very favorably received. . . . There were, to be sure[,] considerable criticisms." Seldin elaborated: "The principles were very broad. They very often conflicted with one another. They were hard to translate back to patients."[32] Despite these and other criticisms, the Belmont Report became the chief document enshrining basic moral principles governing clinical research by the federal government and remains so today. Although it was not written in a regulatory style, some of its ideas found their way into federal requirements concerning the protection of human participants in research. These regulations are now known as the "Common Rule" because they have been adopted by nearly twenty federal agencies.

The process of working on the National Commission served to reinforce for Seldin the importance of the emerging field of biomedical ethics. He became convinced that leading-edge academic health centers should have experts in biomedical ethics on their faculties. He advocated for the creation of a Department of Humanistic Medicine within the Graduate School at UT Southwestern, which would include a focus on biomedical ethics. In an internal proposal that Seldin prepared shortly after the National Commission completed its work, he wrote:

> At present the Medical School has advanced in striking fashion along scientific lines. However, we have not developed any program in the area of Humanistic Medicine. As a consequence, students are not educated in this domain in the best possible manner; there is very little expert presence of individuals concerned primarily with medical ethics in the wards and clinics of our hospitals; we do not contribute to the agonizing national debate over the health care system, the moral issues implicit in cost containment, the legitimate

application of scientific knowledge to individual patients, or the formulation of policies dealing with fertilization, gene therapy, definition of dying, termination of suffering.[33]

Seldin specified five domains that he felt should be covered: *biomedical ethics, philosophy of law, medical economics, logic of biomedical science,* and *medical history.* He even identified the National Commission staff member Tom Beauchamp, then on the faculty of Georgetown University, as a potential leader for the proposed center. Seldin and campus president Charles Sprague approached Hans Mark, the UT System chancellor at the time, about the need for such a center, and Mark agreed but was not able to provide financial support. Next, Seldin turned to private fund-raising, but given the many other priorities on campus the center was never developed—one of the few initiatives that Seldin was unable to deliver during his thirty-six years as chairman.

Even if Seldin's institutional ambitions in biomedical ethics were not realized, the work of the National Commission left an indelible mark on the field of biomedical ethics. One observer has characterized the National Commission as "probably the single most influential body in the United States involved with the protection of human research subjects."[34] For Donald Seldin, who thirty years earlier faced down the evil of Nazi medical experiments, it was particularly rewarding to help set standards that would protect countless other vulnerable populations for decades to come.

CHAPTER 15

LIFE PARTNERS

DURING HIS COLLEGE YEARS AT NEW YORK University, Donald Seldin met a music student named Muriel Goldberg, and they fell in love. Muriel was a year older than Seldin, having been born in New York City on March 17, 1919. She was a striking woman with long black hair, and despite her youth she displayed an almost aristocratic elegance. Seldin was attracted to her physical beauty but equally to her intellect and confident manner. They began dating, which continued after he graduated from NYU and headed off to Yale School of Medicine. On weekends, he would travel by train back to New York City or she would visit New Haven so that they could spend time together. They married on April 1, 1943, eight months before Seldin graduated from medical school.[1]

While Seldin continued his clinical training, the newlyweds enjoyed the intellectual climate of Yale. Their sojourn in New Haven was interrupted in 1946 when Seldin was called to active duty as a US Army physician stationed in Munich. For the initial part of his tour of duty, Seldin was unaccompanied by Muriel. He used every spare minute of leave to explore the art and history of Europe, especially France and Italy. When Muriel arrived later, all of their free time was spent luxuriating in the Old World culture. The diversion of art, architecture, music, and cuisine was particularly healing during the difficult months after the couple lost their firstborn child to a bloodstream bacterial infection.[2]

In 1948, Seldin was discharged from the Army and the couple returned to New Haven, where Seldin was offered a faculty position by his mentor, John Peters. The Seldins' neighbors at Yale included faculty members ranging from philosophers, to historians, to economists, to political scientists. Muriel took piano lessons (she was an accomplished pianist), and the couple befriended several faculty members in Yale's music department.[3] It was an almost idyllic environment, and the Seldins joyously welcomed a new baby daughter, Leslie, into the world on October 18, 1949.

The candles on Leslie's first birthday cake barely were blown out when Donald Seldin accepted a new job at the Southwestern Medical School of the University of Texas. The Seldin family moved to Dallas, only to discover that the school was in a state of physical and intellectual shambles. After debating whether to return to Yale, they decided to settle down in Dallas with the happy news that Muriel was pregnant again. Their son, Craig, was born on August 9, 1952.

In 1954, Muriel became the first French and art history teacher at Greenhill School, a four-year-old private coeducational day school. Just like her husband, Muriel had a reputation for maintaining high expectations for her students. Seldin's nephrology colleague Michael Emmett affirmed this assessment: "I know she was a pretty tough teacher—I hear that from people who had kids in her class."[4]

Muriel gave birth to the Seldins' youngest child, their daughter Donna, on January 9, 1955. Given the demands of her husband's work and travel schedules, Muriel took the lead in raising their three children. In addition to her parenting responsibilities, Muriel continued to teach at Greenhill School, remaining on the faculty for twenty-eight years. As long-time UT Southwestern faculty colleague Eugene Frenkel noted: "Muriel was very, very good with the children."[5] She also served on the board of the Dallas Chamber Music Society.

Beyond her classroom, civic, and household obligations, Muriel often was called upon to help host faculty recruits, visiting professors, and the department's annual New Year's Eve bash. Mike Brown described the holiday festivities: "At midnight, Seldin would make omelets. Everybody would line up to get their omelet from Dr. Seldin." Brown continued: "As the department grew, there were too many for just one omelet-maker. So, another one of our faculty, Jere Mitchell, also took a pan and started making omelets. I would never go on Jere Mitchell's line. I only got in Seldin's line because I figured that's what brought me luck every year."[6]

Although she could be demanding in the classroom, Muriel had a soft spot in her heart for any child in need. That dimension of Muriel was well illustrated by the attention she directed to the daughter of faculty colleague John Fordtran. Josephine "Joey" Fordtran was diagnosed with an inherited kidney disease, and as her father described: "Muriel comes and starts taking my daughter, Joey, on art trips. I mean all the time. She'd pick her up on weekends and take her to one museum. The next weekend they'd go to another museum. Next week, they'd go to Fort Worth, and she taught art history to my daughter."[7] Fordtran noted that such kindnesses from the Seldins were offered graciously and discretely. In his opinion, "That was just a side of them I don't think many people saw."[8]

Others noted that Muriel was every bit the match for her husband. Frenkel averred that "Muriel was just the perfect, perfect individual to mate with Don at every level. . . . They just functioned together in a beautiful way."[9] As the nephrologist Richard Glassock noted: "She herself was a formidable person and an intellect that would be equally comparable to Don's. She knew a lot of stuff and she was a great conversationalist." Glassock added: "She was gentle and soft-spoken. I found her to be an engaging person whom I always looked forward to the opportunity to meet."[10]

One former trainee and future academic health science center leader, Jay Stein, agreed: "We loved her [Muriel]. She was just like him in a way. She was really something—also very opinionated."[11] Helen Hobbs, whom Seldin nurtured from chief resident to research dynamo, described the aura that surrounded Muriel: "She would smoke cigarettes with a long, red cigarette holder. She was very dramatic." Hobbs and her late husband, Dennis Stone, also a UT Southwestern faculty member, often dined with the Seldins. Hobbs noted that Muriel "was a great cook. She was a very cultured woman, and stylish, and I always thought she was fun to be with." Hobbs found Muriel to be a "self-actualized, spirited lady."[12]

In Muriel, Mike Brown saw characteristics reminiscent of one of his aunts. "She was a very sophisticated woman and very formal. . . . When we went to that aunt's house, we had to be on our best behavior. You keep your elbows off the table, chew with your mouth closed—all those things. That was the way you felt around her [Muriel]." Brown paused and then observed: "Through this sort of austere exterior, she was actually a very warm person."[13]

The three Seldin children chose different career pathways, although none pursued medicine or science. Leslie, the eldest, moved to New York and was employed by the Associated Press and then Reuters. Craig became a lawyer and practiced in Dallas and Houston. Donna, the youngest, moved to New York and worked as a curator in an art gallery. She later married Carroll Janis, director of the Sidney Janis Gallery, a fixture in the New York art scene. Founded by Carroll's father, it was renowned for its exhibitions of works by the leading Abstract Expressionists. Together, Donna and Carroll raised two children.

In her early sixties, Muriel developed a rare condition—cerebral amyloid angiitis—in which blood vessels within the central nervous system become inflamed, often resulting in bleeding episodes. Over a period of a decade or more, Muriel experienced a number of these hemorrhages, with a progressive impairment of her cognition. As her illness advanced and she became more incapacitated, Donald assumed greater responsibility for her day-to-day care. As his former faculty colleague and close friend David Hillis described: "A couple of times we went to small dinners with them; dinners to celebrate a chair or something like that. It was obvious that, at that point, she was in pretty bad shape." Hillis continued: "I don't think she knew where she was, but he never left her side. . . . He was her caretaker, her nurse—whatever she needed, and [he] did so with great patience and calmness."[14]

Neil Kurtzman, the former trainee and later a medicine department chair, provided similar perspective: "He was tough on her sometimes when they were younger and healthy, but when she was sick, he took great care of her." Kurtzman paused and added: "That really,

I think, showed the fineness of his character."[15] Juha Kokko, the former director of nephrology who also went on to chair a department
of medicine, described the transformation in his mentor: "When she
[Muriel] became ill . . . Don became the most attentive person in the
world to her. We saw a side of Don that I had never really seen, and
it was pure respect and love for Muriel when she got sick."[16] Hobbs
noted that Muriel "was really impaired and he was amazing. I would
never have anticipated that he would be such a phenomenal partner.
She would go to the bathroom and he'd go with her. He just took care
of her every time. At the dinner table when she was having trouble eating, he would feed her." Hobbs added that Seldin was quick to deflect
any praise for his caregiving: "When I would comment to him [on his
attentiveness to Muriel's needs], he would roll his eyes."[17]

Muriel passed away on September 13, 1994, from a massive brain
hemorrhage, leaving her husband of fifty-one years devastated. As Juha
Kokko described: "When she died, he became incredibly depressed.
He lost all kinds of weight . . . and he was so weak that I had to lift
him into the taxi . . . because he couldn't get in there himself."[18] Helen
Hobbs elaborated further: "After Muriel died, he'd been so depressed,
lonely . . . he lost the quick in his step. I mean, he just wasn't the same
guy. Dr. Seldin is meant to be married. That's just the way it is. He really
likes women and he needs to be with a woman." Hobbs, one of the few
women who made it into the Seldins' inner circle of faculty colleagues,
noted that Seldin had an eye for what he phrased a "well-turned heel."
She added: "He definitely really enjoyed good-looking women and
well-dressed women."[19]

The turning point for Seldin's recovery from the loss of Muriel came a
year later from a surprising source—a former student. Ellen Taylor had
enrolled at UT Southwestern in 1966 at the age of twenty-seven. Her
route to Dallas had been anything but direct. The second-oldest of five
siblings born to an Annapolis-trained Navy officer and his wife, Ellen
was born in China on July 28, 1939, while her father was stationed
there. Her family moved around the world as the father was appointed
to a succession of posts. Eventually, Ellen completed a nursing program
at Massachusetts General Hospital. She then obtained a baccalaureate
degree in nursing from Boston University, spending her junior year

in Paris on an exchange program. After completing her degree, she decided to pursue medical education, completing the necessary prerequisites at the University of Texas at Austin. She was admitted to UT Southwestern in 1966 and, while attending school, worked as a nurse on the weekends to support herself.[20]

Ellen Taylor initially encountered Donald Seldin the following year in a physical diagnosis course. She later recalled her first impressions of Seldin as a "handsome, well-dressed, energetic man," thinking to herself: "Oh, my God. He is the handsomest man I've ever seen." It was another year before she saw Seldin in action again, when she attended Department of Medicine conferences while conducting research in John Fordtran's laboratory. She later confessed to having developed a crush on Seldin; exercising discretion, she kept such feelings to herself. When it came time to choose a clinical domain for further training, Ellen selected surgery and matched into the program at the University of Colorado—only the third woman to be appointed to the surgery residency in Denver.[21]

After her training, Ellen entered private practice in Denver, maintaining a teaching appointment at the university. She married a urologist on the faculty of the medical school, but in 1985 the marriage ended in an amicable divorce. Four years later, Ellen moved to Seattle, where she joined a busy surgical group. She subsequently developed a disabling respiratory condition and decided to switch to part-time work as an emergency physician. She then moved to Greenville, Kentucky, believing that the slower pace in a rural setting would facilitate her recovery. In her spare time, Ellen played piano for the Unitarian church that she joined.[22]

Over the quarter-century since she graduated from medical school, Ellen had periodically written to Seldin to give him updates on her life. She also attended the party to celebrate his retirement as chairman in 1987. When she learned of Muriel's passing in 1994, she sent him a note and indicated that she would be attending a music conference the following year in Houston. He replied by inviting her to make a side trip to Dallas. In the interim, she sent him a manuscript that she had written on Johann Sebastian Bach for her part-time coursework in music. When she did not hear back from him, she asked him to return the paper (she had sent him the original copy). He wrote back apologizing for not responding sooner, as he had been hospitalized with pneumonia that had turned into a serious blood infection. He provided detailed comments on her paper, which she found very insightful.[23]

Ellen arrived in Dallas on August 6, 1996, during a typical summer heat wave, with the high temperature exceeding 100 degrees. She reserved a room at a local Unitarian bed-and-breakfast, which must have seemed a modest backdrop when Seldin arrived to pick her up in a sporty, black, two-door Lincoln sedan. He drove them to the Riviera restaurant, which as the name suggests featured French-Mediterranean cuisine. Midway through the meal, as they sat side by side at the restaurant, Seldin leaned over and said to her: "You rekindle something in me I haven't felt in years." To her surprise, he followed up that declaration with a kiss and—true to form—proceeded to recite for her a poem by William Butler Yeats titled "Politics:"[24]

> How can I, that girl standing there,
> My attention fix
> On Roman or on Russian
> Or on Spanish politics?
> Yet here's a travelled man that knows
> What he talks about,
> And there's a politician
> That has read and thought,
> And maybe what they say is true
> Of war and war's alarms,
> But O that I were young again
> And held her in my arms.[25]

With the recitation complete, Seldin asked: "Are you ready to leave?" Ellen—still stunned by the unanticipated overt expression of affection, kiss, and poetry—could hardly think of food and responded affirmatively. Seldin then invited her back to his house for a brandy before returning her to her Unitarian lodgings.[26]

Seldin's courtship of Ellen continued with biweekly visits to Texas or New York City until Ellen relocated to Dallas the following year. When asked about which aspects of Ellen most appealed to him, Seldin responded: "She's very lively, full of pep and verve."[27] Others noticed the salutary effect that Ellen had on Donald's physical and emotional well-being. As Juha Kokko described: "Ellen completely revived him to the point of his old cantankerous fighting self. He became just like he was in the old days." Kokko elaborated: "I have never seen somebody at old age come out from a deep depression to the absolute top of the world again. And Ellen deserves all the credit for that."[28]

Donald and Ellen were married on May 4, 1998. Among the old habits that Ellen revived in her husband was his desire to shop for her and pick out her jewelry and clothing. As fellow nephrologist and friend Barry Brenner observed: "He would dress her as he did Muriel."[29] Brenner added that, when the couples were traveling together, his own wife, Jane, occasionally joined the shopping excursions, "and he [Seldin] picked out all the clothes. They were going to the jewelry store—the three of them—and he would pick out the jewelry."[30]

Dallas nephrologist Michael Emmett provided his own color commentary about Seldin's sense of style: "He loved to shop. He'd go shopping with them [initially Muriel and later Ellen], he'd pick their clothes. He insisted that they wear their hair in a certain way. . . . He insisted that they dress in a certain way and carry themselves in a certain way."[31]

Ellen affirmed her husband's strong opinions on fashion: "He is exacting about everything. It is easier, for example, if I present the outfit I am thinking of wearing ahead of time." She then described a typical exchange about her attire, which she would initiate by asking: "'Do you agree that this goes with this and this goes with that?' He may say, 'That's ridiculous. Why would you want to take that purse with this outfit? You've got much better purses. I'll find one.' And he does."[32]

Brenner noted that Seldin was equally controlling when it came to what and how much his spouses ate. "He wouldn't let either Muriel or Ellen ever finish the food on their plate. He was so concerned with keeping them slender, as he was concerned about staying slender [himself]."[33]

Although Donald was the leading expert on couture in the Seldin household, Ellen ruled in other domains. According to Barry Brenner, Seldin "had a magazine subscription to *Vogue* and she [Ellen] had a magazine subscription to *Popular Mechanics*."[34] Ellen was quick to correct Brenner—she did not subscribe to *Popular Mechanics*—it was a subscription to [*Family*] *Handyman* magazine![35] She did point out that Brenner and his wife did choose wisely for a wedding gift, purchasing a new set of tools for Ellen. As a former surgeon, Ellen was mechanically inclined, and she demonstrated her talents by personally repairing some of the plumbing at the Seldin abode. She also loved gardening, and she once described a scene in which she was fertilizing newly planted cherry laurels in their yard: "I was working away trying to get a fish emulsion just right, and I was covered with dirt. He [Donald Seldin] walked out, saw me, and just shook his head, 'You are in your element. You love every bit of this. I know it.'"[36] Noting that her husband was not much of an outdoorsman, Ellen observed: "When he sees me out in the rain and the cold, he comes outside to stand and watch."[37] When she did not have her hands immersed in soil, Ellen enjoyed playing the piano. She described a typical evening early in their marriage spent quietly at home with Donald: "If we have a free evening at home, I usually practice the piano and he reads."[38]

Ellen's love of music led her to undertake formal coursework at Southern Methodist University in Dallas. She proudly notes that she was the oldest student admitted to the bachelor of arts in music program. After graduation, she was accepted into the master of composition program, which she completed in 2015.[39] In her years as a student, Ellen would immerse herself in composition studies during the evenings, with a curtain call around ten o'clock when Donald would invite her to share a nightcap with him before retiring. Beyond her student years, Ellen has continued to work on composition with her former professor and is collaborating with a librettist on writing an opera.[40]

Donald Seldin was a fortunate man to enjoy two long and happy marriages. He found love in his youth and rediscovered it again half a century later. Seldin, the very epitome of self-sufficiency, was lost during the few years that he spent without a female companion. Both of his life partners were strong and talented women who enriched his life in unique ways. The mysteries of love, so beautifully captured by Yeats in *The Young Man's Song*, speak eloquently to Seldin's happy marriages:

> O love is the crooked thing,
> There is nobody wise enough
> To find out all that is in it,

For he would be thinking of love
Till the stars had run away
And the shadows eaten the moon.
Ah, penny brown penny, brown penny
One cannot begin too soon.[41]

CHAPTER 16

JOIE DE VIVRE

Despite—or perhaps because of—his all-consuming enthusiasm for work, Donald Seldin managed to find time to enjoy life outside medicine. Being an enthusiastic gourmand, Seldin took special pleasure in haute cuisine. One might even say he applied the same exacting standards to the preparation of a meal that he demanded in patient care. One former trainee, Neil Kurtzman, who subsequently was appointed as the head of nephrology at the University of Illinois in Chicago, recounted one such episode. Seldin had come to Chicago for a visit, and Kurtzman took his former boss to one of the finest French restaurants in the Windy City. One of the items on the menu was veal Orloff, the dish created for Prince Orloff, a nineteenth-century Russian ambassador to France, by his French chef Urbain Dubois.

Seldin asked Kurtzman: "Is this real veal Orloff?" Kurtzman didn't know what he meant, so Seldin clarified: "Does it have *soubise* in it?" Kurtzman recalled: "I didn't even know what *soubise* was" (a sauce made predominantly from onions), "so I called the waiter over and Seldin said: 'Is this real veal Orloff?'" The waiter responded: "Of course." So, Seldin inquired further: "Does it have *soubise* in it?" The waiter admitted that he did not know, so he called over the maître d', to whom Seldin posed the same questions: "Is this real veal Orloff?" When the response again came back in the affirmative, Seldin inquired about the *soubise* and the maître d' was forced to confess that he did not know either. Finally, the chef was summoned to the table, and the same questions were posed again. After claiming that it was real veal Orloff, the chef admitted that it did not contain *soubise*, to which Seldin replied: "Well then, it is not real veal Orloff." Kurtzman continued: "So, the waiter comes back and says: 'Well, what'll you have?' He [Seldin] says: 'I'll have the veal Orloff.'"[1]

When John Warner and James de Lemos were co–chief residents (both later became UT Southwestern faculty members), they would dine at least once every couple of months with Seldin. On these occasions, Seldin would educate his two junior colleagues on the finer points of dining. As Warner described: "We would go to the Mansion on Turtle Creek, which was by far the most expensive and nicest restaurant in town. Dean Fearing was the chef there."[2] Warner continued: Seldin "would put him [Fearing] through the same thing he would put our internal medicine residents through—just asking questions, exchanging information, a little bit of harassment."[3]

When Seldin selected a different restaurant, the same ritual was performed, the chef would come to the table, and Seldin "would often order off the menu. He wanted something different than what was on the menu. He wanted to know what ingredients were available."[4] Warner added: "Then there would be a critique of the food toward the end of the evening that either left the chef feeling good about himself or not so good about himself . . . but they all loved him. They were glad to see him there."[5]

The dessert after dinner with the chief residents was an extended evening of conversation at Seldin's home. As Warner described: "We would go back to his house and drink wine or cognac or Armagnac or something and stay up late. . . . The first night we were there . . . it was about two in the morning, thereabouts, and we're both thinking it's time for us to go. We talked to each other and we had responsibilities early the next morning, and he [Seldin] said: 'Don't be weak. Sit down. I'll tell you when it's time to go. We have things left to cover.'"[6] And so, the life lessons continued while the sleep-deprived chief residents struggled to stay awake.

For many years, Seldin, a passionate oenophile, carried in his pocket a card with a listing of the best vintages for various regions and types of grapes. He had a wine cellar[7] that was constructed for him in secrecy by his loyal and creative faculty and fellows. To gain access to the Seldin residence, the coconspirators treated Seldin and his first wife, Muriel, to an all-expense-paid vacation. While the couple was away, a former Cold War–era, brick-walled bomb shelter in the garage was converted into a wood-lined wine cellar and filled with several hundred bottles of wine.

Seldin delighted in maintaining a full cellar with his favorite vintages, and he would entertain the faculty and residents with periodic wine tastings. As the former head of nephrology Robert Alpern characterized it, Seldin "would have the same commitment to wine tasting that he had to understanding the kidney and medicine."[8] For the residents, this was just another lesson delivered by the master teacher. "We would have these events in his house in which his goal was to teach the residents about wine," John Warner said.[9] "I remember being just as anxious getting quizzed about the wine as . . . presenting to him at [a] nephrology conference. . . . He had the same level of expectations. . . . 'I taught you that last time and you don't remember what this region of France produces in terms of grapes. I told you that last time. How could you forget that?'"[10]

When pressed to identify a personal favorite wine, Seldin selected Montrachet. A French dry white wine, Montrachet is produced from Chardonnay grapes in the Côte de Beaune region of Burgundy. Among red wines, Seldin was partial to cabernet sauvignon.[11] If he disapproved of the choices on a wine menu, Seldin would prefer to switch to his favorite mixed drink—a gin and tonic, which was Tanqueray gin and ice, without any diluting tonic.

Food and wine were only two of Seldin's passions. He was a sponge soaking up information in almost any field of human endeavor. As Robert Alpern described: "He'd go home and he'd have a double espresso after dinner . . . and read a book. He never forgot anything. He was so committed to knowledge."[12] Seldin once described his reading predilections this way: "I read in rather broad areas, and I like to read in depth, with a certain density. I'm interested in philosophy and logic, art, paintings, architecture, literature, poetry, and in problems of history and political science. I get involved with a subject and then

penetrate more or less deeply into it before I leave it and go on to something else."[13]

A former trainee and later head of nephrology at the University
of Chicago, Fred Coe, described Seldin's home library: "I pulled books
out at random and looked at them to see what he was reading. I did
note that he had written marginalia in every book I took down. . . .
At the end of every chapter, he had written summaries of the books I
happened to take down. I have a feeling he did that everywhere."[14]

Coe continued: "When all is said and done, Seldin was artistic."
This cultured sensibility, although self-taught, was so ingrained in Seldin that he often trusted his own judgment over those of professionals
in the field. One such event occurred at a dinner gathering organized
by his nephrology colleague Barry Brenner. The dinner was held at the
Jockey Club restaurant in the Fairfax Hotel in Washington, DC. Seldin was the honoree, and knowing of his passion for the arts, Brenner
invited Leo Steinberg, the Benjamin Franklin Professor of the History
of Art at the University of Pennsylvania, to be the guest speaker. Prior
to the talk, Brenner played a little game to warm up the speaker and
the guest of honor.[15]

Brenner had brought a series of postcards of famous works of
art; using them as flashcards, he asked Steinberg about his opinion on
each of them. Invariably, whatever Steinberg responded, Seldin would
offer a contradictory point of view. As Brenner recalled: "Seldin was as
knowledgeable, it seemed to me, as was Steinberg in all of this. It was,
again, an example of Seldin's extraordinary erudition—his appreciation for things way outside of his professional realm."[16]

Steinberg, one of the country's leading art historians, entertained
the group of nephrologists with an after-dinner talk about Michelan-
gelo's Sistine Chapel ceiling. Robert Alpern, also at the dinner, picked
up the description of the fresco that was the focus of the talk: it was
"the one where God and Adam are reaching out to each other. And
he [Steinberg] spoke for . . . thirty minutes on the panel. After he
spoke, he . . . sat down next to Seldin. . . . Seldin proceeded to explain
to him why he disagreed with him on his interpretation. This was
classic Seldin."[17]

For Alpern, Seldin's after-dinner critique must have brought back
memories of his very first meeting with Seldin. When Alpern was

being recruited by Seldin to head nephrology at UT Southwestern, the visit began with the customary scientific presentation. Afterward, Seldin drove Alpern to the Dallas Museum of Art, and in Alpern's words: Seldin "took me piece by piece through the museum telling me the history of each piece; what the artist was doing when he painted it. We spent like three hours in the museum."[18] Alpern continued: "Then he drove me to the top restaurant in Dallas, the Mansion at Turtle Creek, and I still remember, ordered a Barbaresco from the wine list and explained to me the beauties of Barbaresco and why that's such a great wine. And then we spoke for two or three hours over an unbelievable dinner with just the two of us."[19] Alpern concluded: "He was the smoothest recruiter I've ever met, and I was sold. I went back the next day and knew I was going to Dallas."[20]

Brenner described a similar episode when he came to Dallas as an invited visiting professor. Seldin took Brenner and Alpern to the home of the banker and real estate developer Raymond Nasher. An avid art collector, Nasher had amassed a very large sculpture collection that included works by, among others, Henry Moore, Alexander Calder, Joan Miró, and Willem de Kooning. At the time, Nasher maintained the sculptures at his home, but later he created a public sculpture garden in a park adjacent to the Dallas Museum of Art. As Brenner described, Seldin "took me to Nasher's home and walked me from piece to piece to piece with Bob [Alpern] and Ray [Nasher]. Ray didn't have a chance to get a word in with him [Seldin]."[21] Brenner continued: "Then, when I was in his [Seldin's] home . . . he took me from item to item and lectured me about each of these things."[22]

The former trainee and later faculty colleague Helen Hobbs had a similar experience in art appreciation at the Seldin home: "He has beautiful art at his house. Every single piece has . . . a story behind it of why this piece. Why did he pick this piece and not another?"[23] Seldin's personal art collection included several works by Frank Stella, a George Segal sculpture, and some Picasso ceramics and drawings. For Hobbs, a trip to an art exhibition with Seldin was a special treat: "I loved going to museums with him. He just has a beautiful eye. He has a fantastic eye. I would see things that I wouldn't have seen by myself." Hobbs noted that "by the time he goes to a show, he has an encyclopedic knowledge of the painter."[24]

Seldin's love of the visual arts grew, in his words, from an early interest in "the Renaissance and classical art and architecture, but I'd never seen anything. I'd studied art and architecture and I knew, for example, the classical work of Arthur Kingsley Porter, Meyer Shapiro, C. P. Morley, and other scholars."[25] His first exposure to the great masters occurred when he served in Europe after World War II. As he described: "That's when I became acquainted firsthand with European art and architecture. When I was stationed in Munich for two years, we [his first wife, Muriel, and he] spent our leave time in France and Italy. That was a major experience. I studied in advance and planned out the trips so as to be knowledgeable."[26]

When asked whether he had a favorite style of art, Seldin responded: "I wouldn't say any one thing. I'm very attracted to modern art (abstract expressionists). I like the classical modern painters (Picasso, Matisse, Mondrian, and the like). Also, I like very much classical art—Renaissance art."[27] In addition, Seldin developed an enthusiasm for architecture, which grew, as he described, as "part and parcel of my general interest in art. I always thought that some of the modern architects were really transforming the scene. I was very interested in Mies van de Rohe, Frank Lloyd Wright, and others. I enjoy Greek and Renaissance architecture as well."[28]

Seldin's home was located in a quiet, leafy North Dallas neighborhood and was designed by a student of Frank Lloyd Wright. The large Midcentury Modern structure was built mainly of wood and stone, echoing the natural elements of its surrounding environment. It was configured in a U shape. One wing was the dominion of the three children, and the other wing—the scene of many dinners and parties—included a small study, living and dining rooms, and the master suite. On quiet nights at home, Seldin could be found enjoying a cognac or an Armagnac, reading on the couch in the living room next to the fireplace, embraced by his prized Frank Stella paintings.

Seldin's love of the arts extended to the written word and especially to poetry. Friends and colleagues noted Seldin's special affinity for the work of the Irish Nobel Prize winner William Butler Yeats. Within Yeats's oeuvre, Seldin was particularly fond of the latter works in which the poet reflected on his life and impending death. In one such poem,

"Under Ben Bulben," Yeats foresees his own demise and concludes with his desired epitaph, later inscribed on his headstone:

> Cast a cold eye,
> On life, on death.
> Horseman, pass by![29]

According to the former trainee Neil Kurtzman, Seldin "would begin a recitation of "Under Ben Bulben" often without the hint of an excuse. He was particularly fond of the poem's last stanza and its concluding three lines. . . . They would get a very dramatic flourish."[30]

Another former trainee, Thomas Parker, similarly recalled Seldin's affection for the work of Yeats.[31] "Vacillation," also published late in the poet's life, contained a verse that Seldin found particularly poignant:

> Things said or done long years ago,
> Or things I did not do or say
> But thought that I might say or do,
> Weigh me down, and not a day
> But something is recalled,
> My conscience or my vanity appalled.[32]

Yet another former trainee, Fredric Coe, shared Seldin's enthusiasm for poetry. Coe[33] recalled his mentor being captivated by lines from Yeats's "An Acre of Grass," in which the aging poet confided:

> My temptation is quiet.
> Here at life's end
> Neither loose imagination
> Nor the mill of the mind
> Consuming its rag and bone,
> Can make the truth known.[34]

The line "My temptation is quiet" spoke to Seldin. As Coe remembered: "He saw in that what great art is. He was right. It's really a great line."[35] Coe added: "He understood that in that line was a deep mystery—a profound mystery that was worth every imaginable intention."[36] In pursuit of his study of this line, Seldin traveled to Ireland to meet with Yeats scholars to discuss the poet's phraseology and other aspects of Yeats's work.

When asked about the reasons for his ardor for poetry, Seldin replied: "Not all of human experience is embraced in the principles of rationality. There are moving experiences outside of the rational calculus. Poetry is very moving to me because of the feelings it incorporates. The beauty of the language, the style of the poet—all of these have the effect of charging experience with emotional intensity."[37]

When searching for readings in the domain that Seldin described as "rational calculus," he was likely to be found reading philosophy or economics. One of his preferred philosophers was John Dewey, a Columbia University professor who wrote on a wide range of topics, from the theory of learning to political, social, and educational reforms. Dewey was a leading advocate of the philosophical movement known as pragmatism, in which the value of a theory is judged according to its ability to be put into practical action.

Seldin's interest in philosophy was not confined to the celebrated works of progressive thinkers. The former trainee Jay Stein recalled: "I used to think that I knew a little bit about the great philosopher Spinoza, and I somehow mentioned that."[38] Stein was referring to the seventeenth-century Jewish Dutch philosopher Baruch Spinoza, famous for his role in the rationalist movement, in which intellectual reasoning is proposed as the sole source of knowledge. Stein continued: "Next thing I know, I'm getting a thirty-five-minute lecture from him [Seldin] about Spinoza, and that was just extraordinary. He was like this on innumerable subjects. He really was one of the most well-read, broad-based people, certainly that I've ever met."[39]

Seldin's nonfiction reading extended to economic analysis, and he observed that "the entire issue of economics is pertinent for intelligent interpretation of various political problems that beset the nation. . . . I've read and try to study a whole variety of different economists. These days, the people who impress me a good deal are Robert Solow, James Tobin, Paul Krugman, [and] Lawrence Summers."[40]

The Seldin household was enlivened with frequent musical performances. Although encouraged by his father to take violin lessons,

Seldin never practiced or learned how to play. It was only later that he developed an appreciation for orchestral work, particularly pieces by his favorite composers, Bach and Beethoven. Both of Seldin's spouses, Muriel and Ellen, were pianists, and in Seldin's words: "We had an active musical life. . . . We knew many of the musicians in the symphony, and they would come over to the house and play in ensembles."[41] As Plack Carr of the Southwestern Medical Foundation noted of Seldin: "He's very interested in all sorts of music—primarily classical music and opera. On one occasion, I heard an aria and I asked him: 'I heard this so-and-so aria. Do you know that?' He looked at me in all seriousness and said: 'Oh, yes. Do you want to hear it in German or Italian?'"[42] This was a typically bold statement for a man who could not read sheet music and whose singing voice was marked more by enthusiasm than euphony. As in most matters, Seldin had strong opinions about the quality of musical pieces. As his former student (and later president of UT Southwestern) Kern Wildenthal recalled, Seldin "had his own opinions about which symphonies were the best and whether opera was as high an art form as a string quartet. . . . It was never dull to be around Don Seldin."[43]

Neil Kurtzman trained in nephrology under Seldin but was not bashful about contesting Seldin's critical acumen when it came to opera. As Kurtzman wrote about Seldin: "He knew more about anything than I did except for opera. And even here he would not have conceded the point." Kurtzman continued: "He was up to speed on three Mozart operas (*Figaro, Don Giovanni,* and *The Magic Flute*), didn't care for Wagner, and only liked three Verdi operas—*Rigoletto, Otello,* and *Falstaff.* His taste appeared too fastidious for the rest of the Italian master's oeuvre." Kurtzman added: "Over the years, he's broadened his Italian horizon a bit and would probably allow that [*Un*] *Ballo* [*in Maschera*] is a great opera. *Traviata* is still too much of a stretch for him. Puccini is beyond the pale."[44]

Kurtzman enjoyed every opportunity to pull Seldin's operatic string. "A few years ago, I said that audience (over the long haul) is the only critic that counts," Kurtzman recalled. Seldin replied, "Oh yeah, what about Puccini?" "A genius," Kurtzman answered and "walked away before he could respond. By then I had learned that a riposte followed by an exit drove him nuts."[45]

Although he may not have been a fan of Italian opera, Seldin had a love affair with Italy and Italians. His introduction to the place and to the people came when he was stationed in Munich after World War II. Venice became one of his favorite cities, and one of his most beloved haunts there was Harry's Bar, made popular by the frequent visitor Ernest Hemingway and many other literati. Seldin befriended the founder and proprietor, Giuseppe Cipriani, and was welcomed back as a regular customer. Seldin and wife, Ellen, chose to ring in the twenty-first century at Harry's Bar and had such a good time that they started a tradition of returning there for annual celebrations of New Year's Eve. They also enjoyed visiting Venice during Carnival, festooned in finery with elaborate party masks.[46]

Perhaps influenced by his frequent trips to Italy, Seldin developed a sense of style in his personal clothing, as well as the dresses that he selected and purchased for his first wife, Muriel, and later for his second wife, Ellen. The Armani store in Rome was one of his favorite shopping venues, but he also shopped for suits at Domenico Vacca, Stanley Korshak, Neiman Marcus, and Bergdorf Goodman. Seldin adored fine fabrics, and he wore suits that complemented his tall, lean frame, favoring a little stylish flair when possible. His collection of neckties was large enough to allow him to select a different one every day for the better part of a year.[47]

The Seldins often traveled to Europe with friends and family. Among their frequent traveling companions were his former trainee and later faculty colleague David Hillis and his wife, Nancy. According to Hillis, "These were trips that, almost inevitably, ended up somewhere in Italy." In Venice, occasionally Hillis and Seldin would venture off on their own, leaving their spouses to enjoy some relaxing private time. As Hillis recalled: "Dr. Seldin and I would go off for two or three hours and head to a church or just go walking the streets of Venice." Hillis added that Seldin "and I would hop on a water taxi and go out to [the church of] San Giorgio [Maggiore] and see the Tintorettos [two masterworks, *The Last Supper* and *The Fall of Manna*, by the sixteenth-century painter Jacopo Comin, known as Tintoretto] out there, or whatever else he was interested in doing. He was a terrific traveling companion."[48]

From Hillis's perspective, the most memorable trip with Seldin occurred in May 2005. The journey was a redux of a trip that Seldin had made almost sixty years earlier when he was stationed with the Army in Munich along with Muriel. The newlyweds had traveled a pilgrimage road from southern France to Spain, retracing the well-trodden footsteps of centuries of religious pilgrims. The original trip was inspired by Seldin's library reading of the Harvard art historian Arthur Kingsley Porter's *Romanesque Sculpture of the Pilgrimage Roads*. At Hillis's invitation, Seldin and Gerhard Giebisch, a close friend and nephrology textbook coeditor, headed for their own pilgrimage trip. As Hillis recalled, the trio flew into Paris: "We spent the night there and then flew down to Marseille, started in Avignon, and then drove all across the south of France to various cultural spots."[49] From there, the group entered Spain and journeyed "all the way to Santiago de Compostela. It was a two-week trip—just the three of us and it was marvelous."[50]

Travel had opened new worlds of enrichment for Seldin, so he was quick to recommend it to others. As the UT Southwestern executive John Warner remembered: "He really felt that travel was important to everyone . . . so, he would encourage you to travel. If you had traveled, he'd want to hear about it. He wanted to know things that you did. He would critique your use of time . . . the wine, the food. He wanted to make sure your time outside of medicine was being spent in a useful way."[51]

Among Donald Seldin's many diversions, perhaps most surprising was his passion for professional football, especially for the hometown Dallas Cowboys. The original expansion team of the National Football League (NFL), the Cowboys first played in a winless 1960 season. Gradually, the team built a competitive roster starring, among others, defensive tackle Bob Lilly, quarterback Don Meredith, linebacker Lee Ray Jordan, cornerback Mel Renfro, and running back Dan Reeves. After the 1966 and 1967 regular seasons Dallas played the Green Bay Packers for the NFL title, losing both games.

The Cowboys made it to Super Bowl V after winning their conference for the 1970 season, only to lose the franchise's third NFL title game, this time to the Baltimore Colts. And then after the 1971 season, Dallas beat the Miami Dolphins in Super Bowl VI behind the leadership of quarterback Roger Staubach. They made three more Super Bowl appearances in the 1970s, winning one and earning the reputation as "America's Team" in 1978.

From the early days of the Cowboys franchise, Donald Seldin was a confirmed fan. His former trainee and later faculty colleague John Fordtran fondly recalled attending home games with his mentor. The outings were undertaken as a diversion when Fordtran's son, Bill, was diagnosed with renal failure. Seldin organized father-son outings to Cowboys games, bringing his own son, Craig, who had himself survived a battle with spinal cancer. "Craig had been through an illness too. . . . He was very ill for a while, but he had fully recovered," Fordtran noted. "Don began to arrange for us to go to Dallas football games together."[52]

A couple of years later, Seldin trainee (and later a medical center leader) Jay Stein arrived in Dallas and became a devoted Cowboys season ticket holder. As Stein recalled: "Don Meredith was the quarterback and that's how one of Seldin's many nicknames was 'Dandy Don.' Seldin learned quickly that I loved football and he would come in on Mondays . . . and we'd talk about what happened to the Cowboys." The NFL Championship Game that year was played in Green Bay, Wisconsin, in record cold weather, with the Cowboys losing on the last play of the game. The game became known as the classic "Ice Bowl," and Stein still remembered the raw emotions of the evening: "They had a party at Seldin's house that night, and it was like a wake. One of his kids said, 'Well, now it's time to make my dad coach. This guy [Tom] Landry can't do it.'"[53] Contrary to the opinion of some in the Seldin household, Landry's job was safe, as he went on to coach the Cowboys for another two decades, leading to his induction into the NFL Hall of Fame. Still, the theory that Seldin could have done a better job was never really tested.

Other colleagues were equally entertained by Seldin's mastery of the art of football. Robert Alpern, the former head of nephrology and later dean of the medical schools in Dallas and Yale, commented: "Following every Dallas Cowboys game it is not uncommon to see Seldin presenting a lecture in the hallway on the strategic errors of the game."[54]

John Warner reminisced about the days that he and co–chief resident James de Lemos attended impromptu seminars by Seldin on the Cowboys' performance. "James de Lemos and I are big Cowboys fans, so we would come in on Monday morning and he [Seldin] would dissect the Cowboys game play-by-play, possession-by-possession, . . . position-by-position. We could talk for a long time—often hours—about the game." Warner pointed out that Seldin would analyze "all the successes and failures. . . . The content of thought was amazing . . . what they did wrong and how they didn't respond to this series of plays and they should have gone back and adjusted at that point." Warner observed that "it was the same intellectual firepower that he could use to discover things could be used to explain what offense the Cowboys were lined up in at the third quarter."[55]

Warner saw Seldin's absorption with the Cowboys as completely compatible with what energized him in his work life. "He likes anything with competition. . . . He loved the strategy of the game and the utilization of players. These were not . . . trivial conversations of what transpired. And it was week-to-week." Warner cited some of Seldin's football assessments that sounded strikingly like his evaluation of patient care: "'They should have learned this from last week and they didn't. They did it again.'"[56]

Donald Seldin was the embodiment of a true Renaissance man. Although medicine was his vocation, his avocations were as diverse as human experience—ranging from fine dining and wine to art and architecture, to music, to haute couture, to poetry, to economics and philosophy, to travel, and even to professional football. There was almost no aspect of human achievement and refinement that was uninteresting to him. As Joe Goldstein described: "One of my fondest memories of Dr. Seldin is when I would slip into his book-strewn office, where he would tell me about the latest things on his mind. That's where I learned about the marbles [sculptures] of Caravaggio, Romanesque sculpture, Don Giovanni, and Harry's Bar in Venice."[57]

The broad sweep of Seldin's humanistic pursuits appealed to his former trainee Frederic Coe, who believed that Seldin "understood high culture deeply. He knew what it was and he understood excellence in terms of high culture." Coe continued: "He understood human life for what it was and he understood transcendence as coming from the expression of self in a perfected form. He fully grasped that . . . and he lived it."[58]

CHAPTER 17

THE FINAL CLASS

Donald Seldin spent a lifetime caring for the health of others, but he was not overly attentive to his own personal wellness except when it came to caloric intake. He was a strong advocate for weight control, and at six feet tall he weighed a lean 155 pounds. He achieved this ideal body mass by carefully controlling what he ate. In his words: "I refrain from eating anything that I don't like, eat about half of what I do like, and then partake of everything."[1] When it came to exercise, however, Seldin was a bit of a conscientious objector. He did acknowledge the benefits of physical activity, declaring that "exercise is very valuable in and of itself. It leads to conditioning such that muscle tone is better, the circulation is improved, and various reflex functions are more active and precise."[2] Still, when it came to anything other than a brisk walk, Seldin demurred. He rarely used the stairs at Parkland Hospital, preferring to wait for the sluggish elevators to transport him to the internal medicine patients on the sixth floor.

As was common among men of his generation, Seldin was a heavy smoker. After about twenty years of the habit, his cigarette consumption hit a crescendo in 1966 when he was under pressure from the simultaneous combination of writing, hosting a visiting professor, and preparing for a trip to Europe himself. After smoking three packs a day and getting hardly any sleep for nearly two weeks,

Seldin lost his voice. He decided then and there to quit smoking, and as might be expected of a man with such iron willpower, he was never tempted to resume.

A chronic insomniac, Seldin survived on four to five hours of sleep per night. He didn't complain about his lack of sleep—in fact, it simply gave him more time to read and study in privacy. For most of his long life, Seldin worked hard, played hard, and enjoyed generally good health. Nevertheless, he did have to face several bouts of potentially life-threatening illnesses. One such episode involved a cancer of the urinary bladder, and he underwent a surgical procedure to remove the tumor. Following the operation, Seldin bled profusely and required replacement of a considerable amount of blood and body fluids. Gary Reed, head of the Division of General Internal Medicine and Seldin's personal physician, successfully oversaw the resuscitation. The following day, Seldin told Reed: "I noticed what you did yesterday— you used Ringer's lactate." Seldin was referring to the fluid solution, named after the nineteenth-century British physician and physiologist Sydney Ringer, that was modified later and used to restore blood volume in patients who had sustained bleeding. Along with the blood transfusion, it worked well in Seldin's case, but the former chairman of medicine—an expert on fluids and electrolytes—preferred volume restoration with normal saline. Containing just salt and sterile water, saline lacks the potassium and lactate found in Ringer's lactate. Even after being successfully resuscitated by his former student, Seldin was not about to let a teachable moment pass without comment, repeating: "I just want you to know that I noticed you used Ringer's lactate."[3]

After further treatment of the cancer with immunotherapy injected into the bladder, the malignancy went into remission. Seldin had an earlier bout of cancer in 1997, first noticed as a lump under his arm. When a sample of the mass was surgically removed and examined, it was discovered to be a low-grade lymphoma—that is, a slow-growing and indolent malignancy of lymph tissue. The founding head of medical hematology-oncology, Eugene Frenkel, earlier had cared for Seldin's son, Craig, when he had a spinal cord tumor. Craig's aggressive form of cancer was beaten back successfully with a frontal assault involving surgery, radiation, and chemotherapy. In contrast, with the typically slow-motion course of low-grade lymphomas,

Seldin and Frenkel had the luxury to watch and wait to see if the malignancy progressed.[4]

Seldin passed his eightieth birthday and the lymphoma remained in check. Whether related to the malignancy or as a separate problem, Seldin developed an immunodeficiency syndrome, with reduced white blood cell counts and low levels of circulating antibodies. With his immune system thus compromised, he became susceptible to infections and had multiple separate bouts of pneumonia. One of these episodes occurred at a meeting in Banff in Alberta, Canada. The illness progressed to a systemic blood infection, and Seldin had to be transported urgently to the nearest teaching hospital eighty miles away at the University of Calgary. His former trainee Thomas Parker, the meeting's organizer, recalled that the resident physicians, in their eagerness to treat him, inadvertently administered too much sodium in Seldin's intravenous fluids. Parker remembered his boss explaining to the resident physicians that he was headed for an overload of sodium, saying: "You gotta give me more free water, you gotta give me more free water." Fortunately, either his counsel or a quick check of blood chemistries caused a reassessment of the fluid administration and Seldin survived yet another teachable moment.[5]

Seldin experienced a reoccurrence of debilitating pneumonia on a later trip to Europe, but remarkably none of these illnesses discouraged the indefatigable traveler. Periodically, his count of platelets (blood cell fragments involved in clotting) would drop, but these were treated successfully as well. In late 2017, as he was approaching ninety-seven years of age, an enlarged lymph node was detected in his right groin. By February 2018, the lymph node had become inflamed and he had an associated painful swelling and infection of the skin of his right leg. He suffered a fall and was admitted to the hospital on February 15; he was treated with intravenous antibiotics and discharged two days later.

Over the course of the next month Seldin lost weight and became increasingly frail, so he was readmitted to the hospital and a biopsy of the lymph node in his groin was performed. The removed tissue revealed an aggressive, diffuse large B-cell lymphoma, likely a further transformation of the lymphoma that had been his silent companion for two decades. Imaging of his abdomen revealed a grapefruit-sized tumor mass in his pelvis. Even in his diminished state, Seldin was still hoping to attend the upcoming annual black-tie Ball for Eye Research, a fund-raiser for the Department of Ophthalmology that he supported regularly.

Within a few days, however, the lymphoma mass had swelled to the point that it was obstructing his small bowel and Seldin was readmitted to the hospital. Reed remembers the sinking feeling he experienced when he had to review the current situation with Seldin: "I was about to suffer the Parkland resident's worst nightmare. I was about to have to go tell Dr. Seldin that he had acute kidney injury from volume depletion from, of all things, vomiting." With Seldin's lectures from decades earlier playing in his head, Reed decided "the only way to do this was that I was going to go in and tell him without studying for it."[6]

Reed continued: "So, when I told him . . . his response to it was 'Well, you know the serum creatinine is not that great a measurement of GFR [glomerular filtration rate—an indicator of kidney function] in people with acute kidney injury.' And he started telling me that I didn't have a clue what his catabolism [the breakdown of fuel to generate energy] was. I had not measured his twenty-four-hour urinary creatinine excretion." Reed sighed and noted: "Finally, when he came to a little break, I said: 'Dr. Seldin, I've heard this a thousand times.' And his comment was: 'Yes, but I didn't want you to forget it.'"[7]

As a VIP patient, Seldin could have been treated privately by his physicians, but he wanted to be on the teaching service so that he would be surrounded by medical students and resident physicians. Seldin—who remained the institution's best talent scout—told Reed to pay attention to one special medical student, saying: "She's going to be good."[8]

John Warner, the former trainee and later hospital chief executive officer, described Seldin's attitude during his hospitalization: "There was never any sort of sympathy or anything that he was looking for. He was just thinking about ways to get better. How his own internal biology might be improved by some treatment or care."[9]

Understandably, as Warner noted, the staff stayed on high alert: "The entire hospital was just terrified of him. You're nervous about taking care of him and everybody's adrenaline levels are as high as they could possibly go." Warner added: "Everybody loved taking care of him. He's an interesting, smart person who's engaged with everybody. People really enjoyed being a part of his life and [felt] privileged to take care of him." Then, Warner laughed and observed: "They just weren't standing in line to do it!"[10]

Seldin remained in the hospital for a week, and Robert Collins, a medical oncologist, advised on the treatment options for the lymphoma. Seldin was seen a week later as an outpatient. He was not able to eat much, and consequently he continued to lose weight and became weaker and quite frail. Seldin declined any pain medications, but he expressed a desire to receive treatment for the lymphoma, avoiding any excessive drug toxicities. His goal was to be able to travel to James Madison High School in Brooklyn a few weeks later, where he was scheduled to be honored by inclusion on the "Wall of Fame" of distinguished alumni. For a man who held six honorary degrees including one from Yale, his medical school alma mater, recognition from his high school still meant the world to him. Even after nearly seven decades in Texas, at his core Donald Seldin remained the inquisitive boy from Brooklyn.

He was treated with a single dose of rituximab, an antibody treatment for lymphoma.[11] Seldin walked into the clinic for treatment but needed a wheelchair to depart. The lingering effects of the treatment kept him in bed for the next two days, where he declined all offers of food and drink. According to his wife, Ellen, in typical Seldin fashion he still hoped to make the trip back to Brooklyn.

Ellen invited Robert Collins to the house to discuss the treatment and likely course of events. Collins sat with his patient on the couch next to the fireplace. For Seldin, this was one of his most favored seats—the site where he had spent tens of thousands of hours reading late into the night. Now, however, the conversation was about the future and not about the past. Without emotion or reservation, Seldin asked Collins how much time he had left. Collins responded that Seldin was entering the final stages of his illness and probably had only a few weeks remaining. Seldin wanted his last days to be meaningful for himself and for others, so he decided to decline any further medical treatment and opted to spend his last days quietly at home in hospice care.[12] With the end now in sight, all three of his children returned to Dallas to spend a few final days with their father.

Through this ordeal, Collins noted that Seldin remained brave and almost "matter-of-fact" about his pending mortality. He was gracious and kind to his caregivers and even managed to keep his doctors laughing. Ellen attended to his every need, including taking down dictated messages to a host of friends that she subsequently mailed electronically on his behalf. One such message addressed to two long-time friends, the husband-and-wife biomedical ethicists Tom Beauchamp and Ruth Faden, reads as follows:

> Saturday, April 14, 2018
> Dear Tom and Ruthie,
> Just a short note to tell you that Ellen and I have been planning to join you on Martha's Vineyard, but the intervention of an aggressive lymphoma has interrupted these plans.
>
> I want you to know that it has been one of the pleasures of my academic life to have interacted with you both on a personal and professional level.
>
> I still feel that there is a serious discontinuity between seemingly related events which requires some sort of logical bridge so that influences from the first event can be justifiably linked to the second. When I was on the [National] Commission [for the Protection of Human Subjects of Biomedical and Behavioral Research], I tried to introduce the notion of "generalizability." Nothing much came of this, but I still think that it is a critical issue which allows one event to function as a causal successor to another.
>
> Be that as it may, it was always a pleasure . . . perhaps there is still time for us to get together to solve the problems of mankind.
>
> Ellen joins me in sending this note and in wishing you a rich life ahead.
>
> Don[13]

As this letter illustrates, even during the last days of his life Seldin remained intellectually fine-tuned and still engaged with ethical issues that he first confronted four decades earlier. Whereas others in his situation might find themselves self-absorbed with pain and suffering, Seldin was focused on reaching out to those whose lives he had touched and had touched his. Tom Beauchamp, who first met Seldin when they worked together on the Belmont Report and became a close friend in the process, noted that Seldin's reference to "generalizability" understated the true impact of Seldin's contribution. As Beauchamp indicated: "The concept of generalizability became, through the Belmont Report, a critical anchor of US federal regulations."[14] As evidence, Beauchamp cited the current official federal definition of research: "A systematic investigation, including research development, testing and evaluation, designed to develop or contribute to *generalizable knowledge* [emphasis added]."[15]

As Ellen Seldin was working on getting these personal notes processed, she began to cry. Helen Hobbs later described the scene: "Dr. Seldin asked her sharply, 'What are you crying for?' She [Ellen] replied: 'No one wants to lose you.' He then told her: 'Go and cry somewhere else. I've got work to do.'"[16]

Although sapped of energy, Seldin wanted to say goodbye in person to a few close friends and associates. John Fordtran, a former trainee and head of gastroenterology, and Michael Emmett, a nephrology colleague, were on the shortlist of invitees. Fordtran later described their farewell: "He's in a bed that's real big, in a room that's dark, but his mind is perfect." Seldin, who was partially deaf, could hear perfectly in that quiet room. Fordtran continued: "He was in bed, skinny, and just absolutely looked like he was out of a prison camp or something. We talked for about an hour and it was real fun—I mean, enjoyable reminiscing about everything."[17]

"As we were about to leave," Fordtran said, "Seldin had my hand in one hand and Mike's hand in the other." Then Seldin delivered his final evaluation of Fordtran: "He said, 'John, you did OK.' And I thought it was the correct grade. Absolutely I did because he has all these Nobel prize people who are in there, he had Floyd Rector, he had Marvin Siperstein, and all these geniuses." Fordtran continued: "I think it was the right grade—the correct grade—and it wasn't inflated or deflated . . . I think he meant it as a compliment. . . . He was telling me that I'd done a good job—not an A, but a B."[18]

According to Fordtran, Seldin then turned to Emmett, who had been complaining about how the practice of medicine was being undermined by hospitals. He blamed hospital administrators for focusing too much on procedures that bring in revenue, simultaneously acting tight-fisted when it came to spending money on needed equipment and facilities. Seldin was not a fan of hospital administrators, but he left Emmett with a message of hope: "Mike, don't be a prophet of doom."[19]

Among the other visitors during Seldin's final days were four former chief residents, all of whom were subsequently appointed to the faculty. The quartet included the first pair of female co–chief residents, Carol Croft and Gail Peterson, as well as the co–chief residents John Warner and James de Lemos. Warner described the occasion: "His wife called and said that he wants to see the four of you soon. So, we came either that day or the next day, and it was like nothing was any different than it had been before." Warner continued: "We talked about wine, poetry, the state of the world, travel. He had things he wanted us to think about and even do. He was concerned about the future and wanted to make sure that we had thought through it." Toward the end of the visit, according to Warner, "he let most of us have it at the same time. Here are things you've done right. Here are things you've done wrong. So, don't repeat the wrong things."[20] It was as if Seldin was still in the classroom, chalk in hand, lecturing his four former trainees on how to be better clinicians and human beings.

Another former chief resident who had gone on to a distinguished research career at UT Southwestern was Helen Hobbs. She was traveling in France when she received an urgent message from Ellen Seldin: "Dr. Seldin is dying. Hurry home, he says he won't die until he sees you and Joe [Goldstein]." Hobbs immediately flew back to Dallas, thinking the entire time of what she wanted to say to her mentor, and it occurred to her that she had "never really told him what he means to me and how much I care about him." So, when she arrived at the Seldin house, she tearfully started to share with him her deepest feelings of admiration and devotion. "At the end, I say all this and he says: 'Helen, I'm tired.'" Hobbs departed, and as she recalled, "I realize immediately, *oh, my gosh*, I've done completely the wrong thing. For him, this is just so boring and beside the point."[21]

From Ellen Seldin, Hobbs hears about Joe Goldstein's last visit with Seldin. As Hobbs described: "Joe has brought him a book from an art museum that he has gone to. The two of them sit on the bed and go through the book." As Goldstein prepares to leave, Seldin instructed Ellen to "ask Joe to pick a book that he wants from the room. Take any book you want. Joe looks around and he grabs a book and leaves."[22]

Hobbs quickly realized why Goldstein's visit had energized Seldin and hers had exhausted him. She asked if she could drop by a couple days later, and Seldin, who had rallied slightly, invited her back. For the first time in days, Seldin's appetite returned. He got out of bed and, according to Hobbs, demonstrated some of his trademark feistiness: "This is the last time he gets up. We go to the table and he begins to quiz Ellen on whether she has gotten the right ingredients for the pasta sauce." If this was going to be his last meal, he wanted it prepared to his customary high standards.[23]

"Then the two of us start talking," Hobbs said. "We're looking for a dean at the medical school at this time and I'm on the committee. . . . We had this really long talk about what to look for in a dean. . . . As usual, he's very perceptive and he really comes up with points that I hadn't thought about." After this detailed conversation "he is just smiling on his way back to bed," Hobbs recalled with a catch in her voice. "I was engaging him in life, which is what he needed. Not to be crying about his death, but to be feeling that he was still part of it all and connected."[24]

One of the most difficult farewells for Seldin was to his wife and caretaker, Ellen. On Tuesday, April 17, Donald told Ellen: "I want you to go right now to Neiman [Marcus] and pick out whatever you would like. Find something special—something extravagant. I want to give something to you, right now, today." Ellen responded: "Leave you while you are in bed, in this shape? No, I won't do that." Seldin replied: "Don't be silly. I want you to have something from me . . . don't you understand?"[25]

Respecting his resolve, Ellen agreed: "Alright, why don't I have your favorite cufflinks made into a pendant and a ring for me?" This idea appealed to Seldin, and he asked Ellen to contact their jeweler at Neiman Marcus. As it turned out, Tuesday was the jeweler's day off, but he made a house call within an hour to his loyal customers. The price was negotiated, Seldin wrote a check, and the cufflinks were transformed into a ring and pendant. As Ellen observed: "This was his [Seldin's] way of honoring me—I later understood." She wears the pendant often "because it shows the heart and ability to love and think of others of this man, even though he knew he was dying."[26]

A week after presenting Ellen with his final gift, Donald Wayne Seldin died peacefully, drawing his last breath at 1:25 A.M. on Wednesday, April 25, 2018. A few minutes later, his former student and personal physician, Gary Reed, arrived to make the pronouncement official. Seldin's passing had faint echoes of the death of his favorite poet, William Butler Yeats. Suffering from repeated heart attacks, the seventy-three-year-old Yeats had rented an apartment for the winter on the French Riviera. There, he continued to write as his health deteriorated, publishing three final poems in *The Atlantic* in January 1939. He passed away on January 28, 1939, attended by his wife, Georgie Hyde-Lees. One of the trio of parting poems, "Man and the Echo," finds the poet reflecting on his life and work, just as Seldin may have done eight decades later:

> Then stands in judgment on his soul,
> And, all work done, dismisses all
> Out of intellect and sight
> And sinks at last into the night.[27]

Chapter 1: Welcome to Big D

1. W. Allison, "How Dallas Became Big D," *D Magazine*, September 2008, dmagazine.com/publications/d-magazine/2008/september/how-dallas-became-big-d.

2. D. W. Seldin, quoted in E. C. Friedberg, *From Rags to Riches: The Phenomenal Rise of the University of Texas Southwestern Medical Center at Dallas* (Durham, NC: Carolina Academic Press, 2007), 54–55.

3. D. W. Seldin, quoted in W. C. Roberts, "Donald Wayne Seldin, MD: A Conversation with the Editor," *Proceedings of the Baylor University Medical Center* 16 (2003): 193–220.

4. J. S. Chapman, *The University of Texas Southwestern Medical School: Medical Education in Dallas, 1900–1975* (Dallas: Southern Methodist University Press, 1976), 58.

5. D. W. Seldin, quoted in M. J. Mooney, "The Father of Dallas Medicine," *D Magazine*, October 2013, dmagazine.com/publications/d-magazine/2013/october/dr-donald-seldin-of-ut-southwestern-father-of-dallas-medicine.

6. D. W. Seldin, quoted in Roberts, "Donald Seldin: A Conversation."

7. J. D. Wilson, personal interview by Raymond S. Greenberg, November 13, 2018, University of Texas Southwestern Medical Center, Dallas.

8. R. C. Jones, "History of the Department of Surgery at Baylor University Medical Center," *Baylor University Medical Center Proceedings* 17 (2004): 130–167.

9. Jones.

10. J. S. Fordtran, "Medicine in Dallas 100 Years Ago," *Baylor University Medical Center Proceedings* 12 (2000): 34–44.

11. Jones, "History of the Department."

12. Jones.

13. Fordtran, "Medicine in Dallas."

14. Fordtran.

15. Jones, "History of the Department."

16. Jones.

17. Jones.

18. Jones.

19. Jones.

20. UT Southwestern Medical Center, *Mission and History: 1943–1959* (section titled "The Years of Organization"), utsouthwestern.edu/about-us/mission-history/1943-1959.html.

21. J. S. Chapman, *The University of Texas Southwestern Medical School: Medical Education in Dallas, 1900–1975* (Dallas: Southern Methodist University Press, 1976), 37.

22. P. Wascovich, "Last of the First," UT Southwestern Medical Center, March 7, 2018, utsouthwestern.edu/newsroom/articles/year-2018/claxton-wilson.html.

23. D. W. Seldin, quoted in Roberts, "Donald Seldin: A Conversation."

24. D. W. Seldin, quoted in Roberts.

25. D. W. Seldin, quoted in Roberts.

26. D. W. Seldin, quoted in Roberts.

27. Anonymous, "75 Years of Vision: The Lasting Gift of the Southwestern Medical Foundation," *Southwestern Medical Perspectives*, Spring 2014, 35.

28. D. W. Seldin, quoted in Roberts, "Donald Seldin: A Conversation."

29. M. S. Brown, personal interview by Raymond S. Greenberg, November 13, 2018, University of Texas Southwestern Medical Center, Dallas.

Chapter 2: The Nickel Empire

1. M. Immerso, *Coney Island: The People's Playground* (New Brunswick, NJ: Rutgers University Press, 2002).

2. Immerso.

3. D. W. Seldin, quoted in W. C. Roberts, "Donald Wayne Seldin, MD: A Conversation with the Editor," *Baylor University Medical Center Proceedings* 16 (2003): 193–220.

4. D. W. Seldin, quoted in Roberts.

5. D. W. Seldin, quoted in Roberts.

6. D. W. Seldin, quoted in Roberts.

7. D. W. Seldin, quoted in Roberts.

8. M. Cooper, "Neighborhood Report: Flatbush/Midwood; James Madison High: The View from the Loyal Class of '35," *New York Times*, November 19, 1995, nytimes.com/1995/11/19/nyregion/neighborhood-report-flatbush-midwood-james-madison-high-view-loyal-class-35.html.

9. Cooper.

10. Cooper.

11. N. A. Kurtzman, "Donald Seldin—An Interview," *Medicine and Opera: Comments and Reviews of Opera, Music, and Medicine*, medicine-opera.com/2012/08/donald-seldin-an-interview.

12. A. K. Porter, *Romanesque Sculpture of the Pilgrimage Roads* (Boston: Marshall Jones Company, 1923).

13. L. D. Hillis, telephone interview by Raymond S. Greenberg, January 18, 2019.

14. C. Gray, "Streetscapes: The Weyhe Book Store and Gallery; From Books to Baked Goods," *New York Times*, September 29, 1991, nytimes.com/1991/09/29/realestate/streetscapes-the-weyhe-book-store-and-gallery-from-books-to-baked-goods.html.

15. D. W. Seldin, quoted in Roberts, "Donald Seldin: A Conversation."

16. J. J. Warner, personal interview by Raymond S. Greenberg, December 12, 2018, University of Texas Southwestern Medical Center, Dallas.

17. D. W. Seldin, quoted in Roberts, "Donald Seldin: A Conversation."

18. New York University, *Museum of Living Art, A. E. Gallatin Collection, New York University* (New York: G. Grady Press, 1940).

19. D. W. Seldin, quoted in Roberts, "Donald Seldin: A Conversation."

20. D. W. Seldin, quoted in Roberts.

21. D. W. Seldin, quoted in Roberts.

22. D. W. Seldin, quoted in Roberts.

23. D. W. Seldin, quoted in Roberts.

24. D. W. Seldin, quoted in Roberts.

25. J. R. Angell, "Address Delivered at the Dedication of the Institute of Human Relations, Yale University, May 9, 1931," *Angell Papers* 108:1103, 1–2.

26. D. W. Seldin, quoted in Roberts, "Donald Seldin: A Conversation."

27. D. W. Seldin, quoted in Roberts.

28. D. W. Seldin, quoted in Roberts.

Chapter 3: Perfect Chemistry

1. J. R. Paul and C. N. H. Long, "John Punnett Peters, 1887–1955," *Biographical Memoirs* (Washington, DC: National Academy of Sciences, 1958), 347–375.

2. Paul and Long.

3. Paul and Long.

4. Paul and Long.

5. Paul and Long.

6. A. B. Hastings, "Donald Dexter Van Slyke, 1883–1971," *Biographical Memoirs* (Washington, DC: National Academy of Sciences, 1976), 309–360.

7. J. R. Paul, "Francis Gilman Blake, 1887–1952," *Biographical Memoirs* (Washington, DC: National Academy of Sciences, 1954), 1–29.

8. J. M. Prutkin, "Abraham Flexner and the Development of the Yale School of Medicine," *Yale Journal of Biology and Medicine* 83 (2010): 151–159.

9. Prutkin.

10. Paul and Long, "John Punnett Peters, 1887–1955."

11. F. H. Epstein, "John P. Peters and Nephrology," *Yale Journal of Biology and Medicine* 75 (2002): 3–11.

12. U. C. Brewster, "Miss Pauline M. Hald: A Pioneer Clinical Chemist," *Clinical Chemistry* 63 (2017): 1781–1782.

13. Epstein, "Peters and Nephrology."

14. Epstein, "Peters and Nephrology."

15. J. Peters and D. Van Slyke, *Quantitative Clinical Chemistry, Volume I: Interpretations* (Baltimore: Williams and Wilkins Company, 1931).

16. J. Peters and D. Van Slyke, *Quantitative Clinical Chemistry, Volume II: Methods* (Baltimore: Williams and Wilkins Company, 1932).

17. L. Rosenfeld, interview by P. D. Olch in "Donald Dexter Van Slyke (1883–1971): An Oral Biography," *Clinical Chemistry* 45 (1999): 703–713.

18. A. H. Sanford, "A Collective Review of Recent Books on Clinical Pathology," *Archives of Pathology* 12 (1931): 857–867.

19. A. Butler, "American Medicine: Expert Testimony out of Court," *New England Journal of Medicine* 217 (1937): 459–462.

20. J. Peters, "The Story of the Principles and Proposals for the Improvement of Medical Care," *New England Journal of Medicine* 217 (1937): 459–462.

21. Anonymous, "The American Foundation Proposals for the Improvement of Medical Care," *Journal of the American Medical Association* 109 (1937): 1280–1281.

22. J. Peters, "Improvement of Medical Care," *Journal of the Association of Medical Students* 11 (1937): 28–30.

23. J. Peters, "The Social Responsibilities of Medicine," *Annals of Internal Medicine* 12 (1938): 536–543.

24. Anonymous, "The Rev. J. P. Peters Flays the Church," *New York Times*, June 7, 1911, 2.

25. B. Furman, "Taft Health Bill Is Called 'a Sop,'" *New York Times*, July 3, 1947, 13.

26. L. A. Huston, "High Court Voids Dr. Peters' Ouster by Loyalty Board," *New York Times*, June 7, 1955, 1.

27. D. W. Seldin, quoted in W. C. Roberts, "Donald Wayne Seldin, MD: A Conversation with the Editor," *Baylor University Medical Center Proceedings* 16 (2003): 193–220.

28. D. W. Seldin, "Special Issue Dedicated to Dr. Robert F. Pitts: Introduction," *Nephron* 6 (1969): 161–163.

29. D. W. Seldin, interview by Drs. Leon Fine and Robert Alpern, 1997, from the Video Legacy Project of the International Society of Nephrology, youtube.com/watch?v=2cuIxx-hBOg.

30. D. W. Seldin, interview by Drs. Leon Fine and Robert Alpern.

31. L. G. Welt, D. W. Seldin, W. P. Nelson, III, W. J. German, and J. P. Peters, "Role of the Central Nervous System in Metabolism of Electrolytes and Water," *A.M.A. Archives of Internal Medicine* 90 (1952): 355–378.

32. Epstein, "Peters and Nephrology."

33. D. W. Seldin, "The Moral Dignity of John P. Peters," *Yale Journal of Biology and Medicine* 75 (2002): 19–22.

Chapter 4: War and Peace

1. P. Christakis, "The Birth of Chemotherapy at Yale," *Yale Journal of Biology and Medicine* 84 (2011): 169–172.

2. S. J. Peitzman, "The Flame Photometer as Engine of Nephrology: A Biography," *American Journal of Kidney Diseases* 56 (2010): 379–386.

3. A. A. Liebow, "Medical Research at Yale in the Twentieth Century," *Yale Journal of Biology and Medicine* 33 (1960): 193–211.

4. D. W. Seldin, quoted in W. C. Roberts, "Donald Wayne Seldin, MD: A Conversation with the Editor," *Baylor University Medical Center Proceedings* 16 (2003): 193–220.

5. D. W. Seldin, quoted in Roberts.

6. R. J. Alpern, telephone interview by Raymond S. Greenberg, November 18, 2018.

7. D. W. Seldin, quoted in Roberts, "Donald Seldin: A Conversation."

8. Office of Theater Chief Surgeon, "98th General Hospital, Munich, Germany," *Medical Bulletin*, September 1946.

9. D. W. Seldin, quoted in Roberts, "Donald Seldin: A Conversation."

10. D. W. Seldin, quoted in Roberts.

11. D. deLeeuw, *In the Name of Humanity: Nazi Doctors and Human Experiments in German Concentration Camps, 1939–1945*, master's thesis (Department of History, University of Amsterdam, November 13, 2013), niod.nl/sites/niod.nl/files/Scriptie%20Daan%20de%20Leeuw%20-%20In%20the%20Name%20of%20Humanity.pdf.

12. deLeeuw.

13. Judge Advocate General (Army), War Crimes Branch, Entry 149, *Records of Concentration Camp Trials*, Case No. 000-50-2-103 (College Park, MD: National Archives).

14. Judge Advocate General.

15. United States v. Rudolf Adalbert Brachtel, Headquarters, 7708 War Crimes Group, European Command, Case No. 000-50-2-103, February 26, 1948, jewishvirtuallibrary.org/jsource/Holocaust/dachautrial/d104.pdf.

16. A. S. Alving, B. Craige, and T. N. Pullman et al., "Procedures Used at Stateville Penitentiary for the Testing of Potential Antimalarial Agents," *Journal of Clinical Investigation* 27 (1948): 2–5.

17. E. Shuster, "Fifty Years Later: The Significance of the Nuremberg Code," *New England Journal of Medicine* 337 (1997): 1436–1440.

18. deLeeuw, *In the Name of Humanity.*

19. deLeeuw.

20. D. W. Seldin, quoted in Roberts, "Donald Seldin: A Conversation."

21. D. W. Seldin, quoted in Roberts.

22. D. W. Seldin, quoted in L. Pembrook, "A University Should Be an Institution of Learning, Not a Public Utility," *Modern Medicine* (March 15, 1975): 92–104.

23. D. W. Seldin and R. Tarail, "Effect of Hypertonic Solutions on Metabolism and Excretion of Electrolytes," *American Journal of Physiology* 159 (1949): 160–174.

24. D. W. Seldin and R. Tarail, "The Metabolism of Glucose and Electrolytes in Diabetic Acidosis," *Journal of Clinical Investigation* 29 (1950): 552–565.

25. D. W. Seldin, quoted in Roberts, "Donald Seldin: A Conversation."

26. C. H. Burnett, R. R. Commons, and F. Albright et al., "Hypercalcemia Without Hypercalcuria or Hypophosphatemia, Calcinosis and Renal Insufficiency—A Syndrome Following Prolonged Intake of Milk and Alkali," *New England Journal of Medicine* 240 (1949): 787–794.

Chapter 5: A New Sheriff in Town

1. D. W. Seldin, interview in *Donald W. Seldin: The Lengthened Shadow of One Man*, October 10, 2013, University of Texas Southwestern Medical Center, Dallas, youtube.com/watch?v=wA74-SKeWng.

2. G. Curtis, "The Right Way to Build Something out of Nothing," Behind the Lines, *Texas Monthly*, December 1985, 5–6.

3. R. J. Alpern, "Presentation of the 1985 Jean Hamburger Award to Donald W. Seldin," *Kidney International* 48 (1995): 2036–2038.

4. D. W. Seldin, quoted in W. C. Roberts, "Donald Wayne Seldin, MD: A Conversation with the Editor," *Baylor University Medical Center Proceedings* 16 (2003): 193–200.

5. D. W. Seldin, quoted in Roberts.

6. D. W. Seldin, quoted in Roberts.

7. D. W. Seldin, quoted in Roberts.

8. W. M. Armstrong, M. Emmett, and J. S. Fordtran, "History of Internal Medicine at Baylor University Medical Center, Part 2," *Baylor University Medical Center Proceedings* 17 (2004): 116–119.

9. J. S. Fordtran, W. M. Armstrong, and M. Emmett et al., "The History of Internal Medicine at Baylor University Medical Center, Part 1," *Baylor University Medical Center Proceedings* 17 (2004): 9–22.

10. E. R. Hayes, "Elmer Russell Hayes, MD: A Conversation with the Editor," *Baylor University Medical Center Proceedings* 18 (2005): 165–172.

11. J. S. Fordtran, personal interview by Raymond S. Greenberg, December 12, 2018, University of Texas Southwestern Medical Center, Dallas.

12. Fordtran, personal interview.

13. R. W. Haley, telephone interview by Raymond S. Greenberg, March 1, 2019.

14. Haley, telephone interview.

15. Haley, telephone interview.

16. J. J. Warner, personal interview by Raymond S. Greenberg, December 12, 2018, University of Texas Southwestern Medical Center, Dallas.

17. N. A. Kurtzman, telephone interview by Raymond S. Greenberg, December 2, 2018.

18. J. S. Chapman, *The University of Texas Southwestern Medical School: Medical Education in Dallas, 1900–1975* (Dallas: Southern Methodist University Press, 1976), 57–58.

19. Warner, personal interview.

20. F. C. Rector, telephone interview by Raymond S. Greenberg, November 28–29, 2018.

21. D. W. Foster, interview in *Lengthened Shadow of One Man*.

Chapter 6: Talent Scout

1. R. A. Cooper, "Medical Schools and Their Applicants: An Analysis," *Health Affairs* 22 (2003): 71–84.

2. Association of American Medical Colleges, AAMC Data Book, Table B1: *U.S. Medical School Applicants, Matriculants, Enrollment, and Graduates* (Washington, DC: Association of American Medical Colleges, 2017), 16.

3. D. Kaiser, "History: Shut Up and Calculate!" *Nature* 505 (2014): 153–155.

4. V. Bush, *Science: The Endless Frontier* (Washington, DC: US Government Printing Office, 1945).

5. E. M. Allen, "Early Years of NIH Research Grants," *NIH Alumni Association Newsletter* 2, no. 2 (April 1980): 6–8, history.nih.gov/research/downloads/Allen-GrantsHistory.pdf.

6. D. W. Seldin, interview in *Donald W. Seldin: The Lengthened Shadow of One Man*, University of Texas Southwestern Medical Center, Dallas, October 10, 2013, youtube.com/watch?v=wA74-SKeWng.

7. M. J. Mooney, "The Father of Dallas Medicine," *D Magazine*, October 2013, dmagazine.com/publications/d-magazine/2013/october/dr-donald-seldin-of-ut-southwestern-father-of-dallas-medicine.

8. K. Wildenthal, interview in *Lengthened Shadow of One Man*.

9. D. W. Seldin, interview by U. S. Neill, "A Conversation with Donald Seldin," *Journal of Clinical Investigation* 122 (2012): 2707–2708.

10. W. C. Roberts, "Norman Mayer Kaplan, MD: A Conversation with the Editor," *American Journal of Cardiology* 82 (1998): 490–504.

11. Roberts.

12. J. H. Mitchell, interview by Marc Kaufman, September 8, 2016, Dallas, for the Living History Project of the American Physiological Society, youtube.com/watch?v=ST4DnMwLRSE&list=PLW3R7lwluzvfywUFg9LZ9y9K0l_EVBgZd&index-=31&t=0s.

13. F. C. Rector, telephone interview by Raymond S. Greenberg, November 29, 2018.

14. Rector, telephone interview.

15. Rector, telephone interview.

16. National Institutes of Health, *NIH Almanac*, "Robert W. Berliner, M.D.: Deputy Director for Science, February 23, 1969–September 1, 1973," nih.gov/about-nih/what-we-do/nih-almanac/robert-w-berliner-md.

17. J. Wilson, interview by U. S. Neill, "A Conversation with Jean Wilson," *Journal of Clinical Investigation* 122 (2012): 3027–3028.

18. D. W. Seldin, "Special Issue Dedicated to Dr. Robert F. Pitts: Introduction," *Nephron* 6 (1969): 161–163.

19. J. D. Wilson, *The Memoir of a Fortunate Man* (Charleston, SC: CreateSpace Independent Publishing Platform, 2016).

20. J. D. Wilson and D. W. Seldin, "Effect of Adrenalectomy on Production and Excretion of Ammonia by the Kidneys," *American Journal of Physiology* 188 (1957): 524–528.

21. J. D. Wilson, "A Double Life: Academic Physician and Androgen Physiologist," *Annual Reviews of Physiology* 65 (2003): 1–21.

22. J. D. Wilson, personal interview by Raymond S. Greenberg, November 13, 2018, University of Texas Southwestern Medical Center, Dallas.

23. Wilson, "A Double Life."

24. D. W. Foster, interview in *Lengthened Shadow of One Man*.

25. E. Braunwald, interview in *Lengthened Shadow of One Man*.

26. E. Braunwald, telephone interview by Raymond S. Greenberg on January 18, 2019.

27. N. A. Kurtzman, telephone interview by Raymond S. Greenberg on December 2, 2018.

28. Kurtzman, telephone interview.

29. L. D. Hillis, telephone interview by Raymond S. Greenberg on January 18, 2019.

30. Braunwald, telephone interview.

31. Hillis, personal interview.

32. Hillis, personal interview.

33. M. S. Brown, personal interview by Raymond S. Greenberg, November 13, 2018, University of Texas Southwestern Medical Center, Dallas.

Chapter 7: Here's a Dime

1. H. H. Hobbs, telephone interview by Raymond S. Greenberg, March 5, 2019.

2. D. H. Johnson, telephone interview by Raymond S. Greenberg, March 5, 2019.

3. Hobbs, telephone interview.

4. R. W. Haley, telephone interview by Raymond S. Greenberg, March 1, 2019.

5. Haley, telephone interview.

6. L. D. Hillis, telephone interview by Raymond S. Greenberg, January 8, 2019.

7. Hillis, telephone interview.

8. J. J. Warner, personal interview by Raymond S. Greenberg, December 12, 2018, University of Texas Southwestern Medical Center, Dallas.

9. J. P. Kokko, telephone interview by Raymond S. Greenberg, November 28, 2018.

10. Warner, personal interview.

11. F. L. Coe, telephone interview by Raymond S. Greenberg, January 21, 2019.

12. Hillis, telephone interview.

13. Coe, telephone interview.

14. Coe, telephone interview.

15. H. H. Hobbs, interview by Ushma S. Neill on October 1, 2015, for the *Journal of Clinical Investigation* ("JCI's Conversations with Giants in Medicine: Helen Hobbs"), University of Texas Southwestern Medical Center, Dallas, youtube.com/watch?v=ZiM50rOsm5E.

16. Hobbs, interview by Neill.

17. H. H. Hobbs, interview in *Donald W. Seldin: The Lengthened Shadow of One Man*, October 10, 2013, University of Texas Southwestern Medical Center, Dallas, youtube.com/watch?v=wA74-SKeWng.

18. D. W. Seldin, quoted in W. C. Roberts, "Donald Wayne Seldin, MD: A

Conversation with the Editor," *Baylor University Medical Center Proceedings* 16 (2003): 193–200.

19. W. L. Henrich, personal interview by Raymond S. Greenberg, January 17, 2019, University of Texas System, Austin.

20. Haley, telephone interview.

21. Henrich, personal interview.

22. Warner, personal interview.

23. Henrich, personal interview.

24. Warner, personal interview.

25. Warner, personal interview.

26. Kokko, telephone interview.

27. J. D. Wilson, interview in *Lengthened Shadow of One Man.*

28. Henrich, personal interview.

29. R. J. Alpern, telephone interview by Raymond S. Greenberg, November 18, 2018.

30. T. D. DuBose, telephone interview by Raymond S. Greenberg, December 7, 2018.

31. O. W. Moe, personal interview by Raymond S. Greenberg, December 12, 2018, University of Texas Southwestern Medical Center, Dallas.

32. Moe, personal interview.

33. Alpern, telephone interview.

34. Coe, telephone interview.

35. Coe, telephone interview.

36. Coe, telephone interview.

37. Coe, telephone interview.

38. Coe, telephone interview.

39. Coe, telephone interview.

40. D. W. Seldin, "Acceptance of the George M. Kober Medal for 1985," *Transactions of the Association of American Physicians* 98 (1985): cxlviii–cl.

41. Kokko, telephone interview.

42. Wilson, interview in *Lengthened Shadow of One Man.*

43. J. D. Wilson, quoted in S. Shinneman, "Friends and Mentees Reflect on the Legacy of Dr. Donald Seldin, the Intellectual Father of UTSW," *D CEO Healthcare,* April 26, 2018, healthcare.dmagazine.com/2018/04/26/friends-and-mentees-reflect-on-the-legacy-of-dr-donald-seldin-the-intellectual-father-of-utsw.

44. Wilson, interview in *Lengthened Shadow of One Man.*

45. J. D. Wilson, personal interview by Raymond S. Greenberg, November 13, 2018, University of Texas Southwestern Medical Center, Dallas.

46. M. S. Brown, interview in *Lengthened Shadow of One Man.*

47. Brown, interview in *Lengthened Shadow of One Man.*

48. Alpern, telephone interview.

49. F. C. Rector Jr., "Presentation of the George M. Kober Medal to Donald W. Seldin," *Transactions of the Association of American Physicians* 98 (1985): cxxxii–cl.

Chapter 8: The Triple Threat

1. J. P. Geyman, "The Oslerian Tradition and Changing Medical Education. A Reappraisal," *Western Journal of Medicine* 138 (1983): 884–888.

2. W. Osler, *The Principles and Practice of Medicine* (New York: D. Appleton and Company, 1893), 1079.

3. W. Osler, "Remarks," *Boston Medical and Surgical Journal* 144 (1901): 60–61.

4. W. Osler, "The Student Life," *Modern Essays*, ed. C. Morley (New York: Harcourt, Brace and Co., 1921), 128–133.

5. W. Osler, *Aequanimitas: With Other Addresses to Medical Students, Nurses, and Practitioners of Medicine*, 2nd ed. (Philadelphia: P. Blakiston's Son & Co., 1910), 407.

6. E. Braunwald, telephone interview by Raymond S. Greenberg, January 18, 2019.

7. D. W. Seldin, interview by Drs. Leon Fine and Robert Alpern for the ISN Video Legacy Project of the International Society of Nephrology, 1997, cybernephrology .ualberta.ca/ISN/VLP/Trans/Seldin.htm.

8. D. W. Seldin, interview by Fine and Alpern.

9. D. W. Seldin, interview by Fine and Alpern.

10. D. W. Seldin, interview by Fine and Alpern.

11. D. W. Seldin, interview by Fine and Alpern.

12. D. W. Seldin, "Some Reflections on the Role of Basic Research and Service in Clinical Departments," *Journal of Clinical Investigation* 45 (1966): 976–979.

13. D. W. Seldin, "Some Reflections."

14. D. W. Seldin, "B. The Clinical Teacher: Scholarship as the Heart of the Educational Process," *Journal of Medical Education* 34 (1959): 81–85.

15. D. W. Seldin, "Some Reflections."

16. D. W. Seldin, "Some Reflections."

17. D. W. Seldin, "Clinical Teacher."

18. D. W. Seldin, interview by Fine and Alpern.

19. J. D. Wilson, personal interview by Raymond S. Greenberg, November 13, 2018, University of Texas Southwestern Medical Center, Dallas.

20. W. L. Henrich, personal interview by Raymond S. Greenberg, January 17, 2019.

21. D. H. Johnson, telephone interview by Raymond S. Greenberg, March 5, 2019.

22. L. D. Hillis, telephone interview by Raymond S. Greenberg, January 18, 2019.

23. D. W. Seldin, "Clinical Teacher."

24. D. W. Seldin, "Clinical Teacher."

25. R. J. Alpern, telephone interview by Raymond S. Greenberg, November 18, 2018.

26. Alpern, telephone interview.

27. D. W. Seldin, "Some Reflections."

28. D. W. Seldin, interview by Fine and Alpern.

29. D. W. Seldin, "Some Reflections."

30. D. W. Seldin, "Some Reflections."

31. Alpern, telephone interview.

32. Alpern, telephone interview.

33. D. W. Seldin, interview by Fine and Alpern.

34. D. W. Seldin, interview by Fine and Alpern.

35. B. M. Brenner, as quoted by Ivan Oransky and Adam Marcus, "Obituary," *The Lancet* 391 (2018): 2410.

36. Braunwald, telephone interview.

37. J. H. Dirks, telephone interview by Raymond S. Greenberg, December 19, 2018.

38. Braunwald, telephone interview.

39. D. W. Seldin, quoted in W. C. Roberts, "Donald Wayne Seldin, MD: A Conversation with the Editor," *Baylor University Medical Center Proceedings* 16 (2003): 193–220.

40. J. L. Goldstein, remarks at "Seldin: A Celebration of Life," University of Texas Southwestern Medical Center, Dallas, June 16, 2018, vimeo.com/275851709 /56f3109c4e.

41. F. C. Rector, "Presentation of the George M. Kober Medal to Donald W. Seldin," *Transactions of the Association of American Physicians* 98 (1985): cxxxii–cl.

42. Goldstein, remarks at "Seldin: A Celebration of Life."

43. J. L. Goldstein and M. S. Brown, "Acceptance of the Kober Medal," *Journal of Clinical Investigation* 110 (2002): S11–S13.

44. Goldstein and Brown.

45. Braunwald, telephone interview.

46. E. Braunwald, quoted in T. H. Lee, *Eugene Braunwald and the Rise of Modern Medicine* (Cambridge, MA: Harvard University Press, 2013), 180.

47. Braunwald, quoted in Lee.

48. Braunwald, telephone interview.

49. E. Braunwald, remarks at "Seldin: A Celebration of Life," University of Texas Southwestern Medical Center, Dallas, June 16, 2018, vimeo.com/275851709 /56f3109c4e.

50. Braunwald, telephone interview.

51. Braunwald, quoted in Lee, *Braunwald and the Rise of Modern Medicine*.

52. Braunwald, telephone interview.

53. M. S. Brown, remarks at "Seldin: A Celebration of Life," University of Texas Southwestern Medical Center, Dallas, June 16, 2018, vimeo.com/275851709 /56f3109c4e.

Chapter 9: Lab Partners

1. D. W. Seldin, "Scientific Achievements of John P. Peters," *American Journal of Nephrology* 22 (2002): 192–196.

2. D. W. Seldin and R. Tarail, "The Metabolism and Excretion of Electrolytes and Glucose in Diabetic Acidosis," *Journal of Clinical Investigation* 28 (1949): 810.

3. L. G. Welt, D. W. Seldin, and J. H. Cort, "The Effects of Pituitary and Adrenal Hormones on the Metabolism and Excretion of Sodium and Water," *Journal of Clinical Investigation* 30 (1951): 682.

4. D. W. Seldin, "Presentation of the 2001 A. N. Richards Award to Floyd C. Rector, Jr.," *Kidney International* 64 (2003): 379–386.

5. R. J. Alpern, telephone interview by Raymond S. Greenberg, November 18, 2018.

6. O. W. Moe, personal interview by Raymond S. Greenberg, December 12, 2018, University of Texas Southwestern Medical Center, Dallas.

7. J. T. Wearn and A. N. Richards, "Observations on the Composition of Glomerular Urine, with Particular Reference to the Problem of Reabsorption in the Renal Tubules," *American Journal of Physiology* 71 (1924): 209–227.

8. F. C. Rector and J. R. Clapp, "Evidence for Active Chloride Reabsorption in the Distal Renal Tubule of the Rat," *Journal of Clinical Investigation* 41 (1962): 101–107.

9. N. A. Kurtzman, telephone interview by Raymond S. Greenberg, December 2, 2018.

10. F. L. Coe, telephone interview by Raymond S. Greenberg, January 21, 2019.

11. J. H. Dirks, telephone interview by Raymond S. Greenberg, December 19, 2018.

12. B. M. Brenner, telephone interview by Raymond S. Greenberg, January 16, 2019.

13. F. C. Rector, F. P. Brunner, and D. W. Seldin, "Mechanism of Glomerular Balance. I. Effect of Aortic Constriction and Elevated Ureteropelvic Pressure on Glomerular Filtration Rate, Fractional Reabsorption, Transit Time, and Tubular Size in the Proximal Tubule of the Rat," *Journal of Clinical Investigation* 45 (1966): 590–602.

14. Brenner, telephone interview.

15. Brenner, telephone interview.

16. B. M. Brenner, C. M. Bennett, and R. W. Berliner, "The Relationship Between Glomerular Filtration Rate and Sodium Reabsorption by the Proximal Tubule of the Rat Nephron," *Journal of Clinical Investigation* 47 (1968): 1358–1374.

17. Brenner, telephone interview.

18. Brenner, telephone interview.

19. H. E. de Wardener, I. H. Mills, and W. F. Clapham et al., "Studies on the Efferent Mechanism of the Sodium Diuresis Which Follows the Administration of Intravenous Saline in the Dog," *Clinical Science* 21 (1961): 249–258.

20. F. C. Rector Jr., M. Martinez-Maldonado, and N. A. Kurtzman et al., "Demonstration of a Hormonal Inhibitor of Proximal Tubular Reabsorption During Expansion of Extracellular Volume with Isotonic Saline," *Journal of Clinical Investigation* 47 (1968): 761–773.

21. F. S. Wright, B. M. Brenner, and C. M. Bennett et al., "Failure to Demonstrate a Hormonal Inhibitor of Proximal Sodium Reabsorption," *Journal of Clinical Investigation* 48 (1969): 1107–1113.

22. Coe, telephone interview.

23. Brenner, telephone interview.

24. Brenner, telephone interview.

25. A. J. de Bold, H. B. Borenstein, and A. T. Veress et al., "A Rapid and Potent Natriuretic Response to Intravenous Injection of Atrial Extract in Rats," *Life Sciences* 28 (1981): 89–94.

26. L. R. Potter, A. R. Yoder, and D. R. Flora et al., "Natriuretic Peptides: Their Structures, Receptors, Physiologic Functions, and Therapeutic Applications," *Handbook of Experimental Pharmacology* 191 (2009): 341–366.

27. Moe, personal interview.

28. H. A. Bloomer, F. C. Rector Jr., and D. W. Seldin, "The Mechanism of Potassium Reabsorption in the Proximal Tubule of the Rat," *Journal of Clinical Investigation* 1963 (42): 277–285.

29. F. C. Rector Jr., N. W. Carter, and D. W. Seldin, "The Mechanism of Bicarbonate Reabsorption in the Proximal and Distal Tubules of the Kidney," *Journal of Clinical Investigation* 44 (1965): 278–290.

30. W. Suki, F. C. Rector Jr., and D. W. Seldin, "The Site of Action of Furosemide and Other Sulfonamide Diuretics in the Dog," *Journal of Clinical Investigation* 44 (1965): 1458–1469.

31. N. W. Carter, F. C. Rector Jr., and D. S. Campion et al., "Measurement of Intracellular pH of Skeletal Muscle with pH-Sensitive Glass Microelectrodes," *Journal of Clinical Investigation* 46 (1967): 920–933.

32. Dirks, telephone interview.

33. F. C. Rector Jr., N. W. Carter, and D. W. Seldin, "The Mechanism of Bicarbonate Reabsorption in the Proximal and Distal Tubules of the Kidney," *Journal of Clinical Investigation* 44 (1965): 278–290.

34. F. C. Rector Jr., telephone interview by Raymond S. Greenberg, November 28, 29, 2018.

35. Rector, telephone interview.

36. Rector, telephone interview.

37. Rector, telephone interview.

38. Brenner, telephone interview.

39. Coe, telephone interview.

40. Coe, telephone interview.

41. T. D. DuBose, telephone interview by Raymond S. Greenberg, December 7, 2018.

42. Kurtzman, telephone interview.

43. DuBose, telephone interview.

44. Rector, telephone interview.

45. Kurtzman, telephone interview.

46. Rector, telephone interview.

47. Rector, telephone interview.

48. L. D. Hillis, telephone interview by Raymond S. Greenberg, January 18, 2019.

49. J. H. Stein, telephone interview by Raymond S. Greenberg, January 15, 2019.

50. Rector, telephone interview.

51. Rector, telephone interview.

52. Rector, telephone interview.

53. Rector, telephone interview.

54. R. J. Alpern, telephone interview.

Chapter 10: The Road to Stockholm

1. L. Madison, quoted in J. G. Hanna, "A Nobel Prize: Dr. Joseph Goldstein, '63, Honored for Medical Research," *Alumni Magazine of Washington and Lee* 60 (1985): 2–7.

2. J. Goldstein, quoted in S. Schenker, "In Memoriam: Burton Combes, M.D.," *Hepatology* 59 (2014): 1655–1656.

3. M. Brown, quoted in U. S. Neill and H. A. Rockman, "A Conversation with Robert Lefkowitz, Joseph Goldstein, and Michael Brown," *Journal of Clinical Investigation* 122 (2012): 1586–1587.

4. J. G. Goldstein, personal interview by Raymond S. Greenberg, June 5, 2017, University of Texas Southwestern Medical Center, Dallas.

5. M. S. Brown and J. L. Goldstein, interview by Adam Smith, December 10, 2012, for The Nobel Foundation, Stockholm, nobelprize.org/prizes/medicine/1985/goldstein/interview.

6. M. S. Brown, personal interview by Raymond S. Greenberg, November 13, 2018, University of Texas Southwestern Medical Center, Dallas.

7. M. S. Brown, personal interview by Raymond S. Greenberg, July 27, 2017, University of Texas Southwestern Medical Center, Dallas.

8. Brown, personal interview.

9. Brown, personal interview.

10. Brown, personal interview.

11. Brown, personal interview.

12. J. L. Goldstein, H. G. Schrott, W. R. Hazzard, E. L. Bierman, and A. G. Motulsky, "Hyperlipidemia in Coronary Heart Disease. II. Genetic Analysis of Lipid Levels in 176 Families and Delineation of a New Inherited Disorder, Combined Hyperlipidemia," *Journal of Clinical Investigation* 52 (1973): 1544–1568.

13. Goldstein, personal interview.

14. Brown, personal interview.

15. Brown, personal interview.

16. Brown, personal interview.

17. J. Goldstein, quoted in R. Williams, "Joseph Goldstein and Michael Brown: Demoting Egos, Promoting Success," *Circulation Research* 106 (2010): 1006–1010.

18. Brown and Goldstein, interview by Smith.

19. Brown, personal interview.

20. Brown, personal interview.

21. Brown, personal interview.

22. S. Dana, interview in "Cholesterol Metabolism: The Work of Drs. Brown and Goldstein," Southwestern Research Foundation, Dallas, May 4, 2012, vimeo.com/38781944.

23. J. L. Goldstein, interview in "Cholesterol Metabolism: The Work of Drs. Brown and Goldstein," Southwestern Research Foundation, Dallas, May 4, 2012, vimeo.com/38781944.

24. M. S. Brown, interview in "Cholesterol Metabolism: The Work of Drs. Brown and Goldstein," Southwestern Research Foundation, Dallas, May 4, 2012, vimeo.com/38781944.

25. J. L. Goldstein and M. S. Brown, "Familial Hypercholesterolemia: Identification of a Defect in the Regulation of 3-Hydroxy-3-Methylglutaryl Coenzyme A Reductase Activity Associated with Overproduction of Cholesterol," *Proceedings of the National Academy of Sciences* 70 (1973): 2804–2808.

26. M. S. Brown, S. E. Dana, and J. L. Goldstein, "Regulation of 3-Hydroxy-3-Methylglutaryl Coenzyme A Reductase Activity in Cultured Human Fibroblasts: Comparison of Cells from a Normal Subject and from a Patient with Homozygous Familial Hypercholesterolemia," *Journal of Biological Chemistry* 249 (1974): 789–796.

27. M. S. Brown and J. L. Goldstein, "Familial Hypercholesterolemia: Defective Binding of Lipoproteins to Cultured Fibroblasts Associated with Impaired Regulation of 3-Hydroxy-3-Methylglutaryl Coenzyme A Reductase Activity," *Proceedings of the National Academy of Sciences* 71 (1974): 788–792.

28. J. L. Goldstein and M. S. Brown, "Binding and Degradation of Low Density Lipoproteins by Cultured Human Fibroblasts," *Journal of Biological Chemistry* 249 (1974): 5153–5162.

29. J. L. Goldstein, S. K. Basu, G. Y. Brunschede, and M. S. Brown, "Release of Low Density Lipoprotein from Its Cell Surface Receptor by Sulfated Glycosaminoglycans," *Cell* 7 (1976): 85–95.

30. M. S. Brown, S. E. Dana, and J. L. Goldstein, "Receptor-dependent Hydrolysis of Cholesteryl Esters Contained in Plasma Low Density Lipoprotein," *Proceedings of the National Academy of Sciences* 72 (1975): 2925–2929.

31. R. G. W. Anderson, M. S. Brown, and J. L. Goldstein, "Role of the Coated Endocytic Vesicle in the Uptake of Receptor-Bound Low Density Lipoprotein in Human Fibroblasts," *Cell* 10 (1977): 351–364.

32. W. J. Schneider, U. Beisiegel, J. L. Goldstein, and M. S. Brown, "Purification of the Low Density Lipoprotein Receptor, an Acidic Glycoprotein of 164,000 Molecular Weight," *Journal of Biological Chemistry* 257 (1982): 2664–2673.

33. T. Yamamoto, C. G. Davis, M. S. Brown, W. J. Schneider, M. L. Casey, J. L. Goldstein, and D. W. Russell, "The Human LDL Receptor: A Cysteine-Rich Protein with Multiple Alu Sequences in Its mRNA," *Cell* 39 (1984): 27–38.

34. P. T. Kovanen, D. W. Bilheimer, J. L. Goldstein, J. J. Jaramillo, and M. S. Brown, "Regulatory Role for Hepatic Low Density Lipoprotein Receptors *in vivo* in the Dog," *Proceedings of the National Academy of Sciences* 78 (1981): 1194–1198.

35. Brown, interview in "Cholesterol Metabolism."

36. Goldstein, interview in "Cholesterol Metabolism."

37. L. D. Hillis, telephone interview by Raymond S. Greenberg, January 18, 2019.

38. Hillis, telephone interview.

39. M. S. Brown and J. L. Goldstein, "A Receptor-Mediated Pathway for Cholesterol Homeostasis," *Science* 232 (1986): 34–47.

40. D. H. Johnson, telephone interview by Raymond S. Greenberg, March 5, 2019.

Chapter 11: A University Worthy of the Department of Medicine

1. D. W. Seldin, quoted in E. C. Friedberg, *From Rags to Riches: The Phenomenal Rise of the University of Texas Southwestern Medical Center at Dallas* (Durham, NC: Carolina Academic Press, 2007), 73–75.

2. D. W. Seldin, quoted in Friedberg.

3. D. W. Seldin, quoted in W. C. Roberts, "Donald Wayne Seldin, MD: A Conversation with the Editor," *Baylor University Medical Center Proceedings* 16 (2003): 193–220.

4. D. W. Seldin, quoted in Friedberg, *From Rags to Riches*, at 73–75.

5. K. Wildenthal, telephone interview by Raymond S. Greenberg, March 4, 2019.

6. L. D. Hillis, telephone interview by Raymond S. Greenberg, January 18, 2019.

7. M. S. Brown, personal interview by Raymond S. Greenberg, November 13, 2018, University of Texas Southwestern Medical Center, Dallas.

8. D. W. Seldin, quoted in E. C. Friedberg, *From Rags to Riches*, 84–85.

9. R. E. Billingham, "Reminiscences of a 'Transplanter,'" *Transplantation Proceedings* 6 (4 Supplement 1) (1974): 5–17.

10. Wildenthal, telephone interview.

11. Wildenthal, telephone interview.

12. Wildenthal, telephone interview.

13. D. W. Seldin, quoted in E. C. Friedberg, *From Rags to Riches*, 78.

14. D. W. Seldin, quoted in Roberts, "Donald Seldin: A Conversation."

15. F. C. Rector, "Presentation of the George M. Kober Medal to Donald W. Seldin," *Transactions of the Association of American Physicians* 98 (1985): cxxxii–cl.

16. R. W. Haley, telephone interview by Raymond S. Greenberg, March 1, 2019.

17. Haley, telephone interview.

18. Haley, telephone interview.

19. D. W. Seldin, quoted in Roberts, "Donald Seldin: A Conversation."

20. M. V. Hazel and T. Peeler, "The Best Doctors in Dallas," *D Magazine*, October 2005, dmagazine.com/publications/d-magazine/2005/october/the-best-doctors-in-dallas.

21. Wildenthal, telephone interview.

22. F. H. Epstein, "Recollections of Nephrology: Peters and Seldin. Presentation of the First John P. Peters Award to Donald W. Seldin, 1983," *Seminars in Nephrology* 4 (1984): 107–112.

23. Wildenthal, telephone interview.

24. Wildenthal, telephone interview.

25. M. S. Brown, quoted in Anonymous, "75 Years of Vision: The Lasting Gift of the Southwest Medical Foundation," *Southwestern Medical Perspectives*, Spring 2014, 51.

26. Wildenthal, telephone interview.

27. Wildenthal, telephone interview.

28. A. G. Gilman, quoted in Friedberg, *From Rags to Riches*, at 89.

29. J. Kling, "UT Southwestern: From Army Shacks to Research Elites," *Science* 274 (1996): 1459–1461.

30. R. Alpern and G. Giebisch, "Donald Seldin: A Transformative Leader in Medicine and Nephrology," *Journal of the American Society of Nephrology* 29 (2018): 2029–2030.

31. D. W. Seldin, quoted in Roberts, "Donald Seldin: A Conversation."

32. Wildenthal, telephone interview.

33. Wildenthal, telephone interview.

34. Wildenthal, telephone interview.

35. Wildenthal, telephone interview.

36. R. J. Alpern, telephone interview by Raymond S. Greenberg, November 18, 2018.

37. Wildenthal, telephone interview.

38. T. W. Stinger, *The Zale Corporation*, Ph.D. diss. (Fort Worth: North Texas State University, 1984).

39. Wildenthal, telephone interview.

40. W. Maina, "Zale Lipshy University Hospital Historical Timeline," University of Texas Southwestern Medical Center Archives, Dallas, library.utsouthwestern.edu/speccol/archives/ZLHistTimeline.pdf.

41. W. Maina, "St. Paul Hospital Historical Timeline," University of Texas Southwestern Medical Center Archives, Dallas, library.utsouthwestern.edu/speccol/archives/SPHistTimeline.pdf.

42. K. Wildenthal, personal communication to Raymond S. Greenberg, March 4, 2019.

43. H. Melville, *Moby-Dick* (Boston: C. H. Simonds Company, 1926), 348.

44. J. L. Goldstein, Remarks at the Dedication Ceremony for "The Fountain," October 18, 1995, University of Texas Southwestern Medical Center, Dallas.

45. J. G. Goldstein, Remarks at the Announcement of the Seldin Statue and New Plaza Dedication, May 13, 2014, University of Texas Southwestern Medical Center, Dallas.

46. W. G. Reed, telephone interview by Raymond S. Greenberg, March 6, 2019.

Chapter 12: A Society Man

1. N. Brochu, "How One Mom's Loss Saved Countless Others from Kidney Disease," *South Florida Sun Sentinel*, March 20, 2011, sun-sentinel.com/health/fl-xpm-2011-03-20-fl-nbcol-kidney-disease-brochu-column20110320-story.html.

2. F. H. Epstein, "Atlantic City Memories," *Journal of Clinical Investigation* 118 (2008): 1222–1223.

3. G. Richet, "Jean Hamburger, 1909–1992," *Kidney International* 42 (1992): 810–812.

4. R. R. Robinson and G. Richet, "The First Decade: 1960–1969: Crucible for the Birth of an Idea," *Kidney International* 79 (2001): S2–S18.

5. Robinson and Richet, "First Decade."

6. R. R. Robinson and G. Richet, "The Second Decade: 1970s," *Kidney International* 79 (2001): S19–S48.

7. V. L. Schuster, "Donald W. Seldin, MD (1920–2018)," *Kidney International* 94 (2018): 438–439.

8. R. J. Alpern, "Presentation of the 1995 Jean Hamburger Award to Donald W. Seldin," *Kidney International* 48 (1995): 2036–2038.

9. R. R. Robinson and G. Richet, "The Third Decade: 1980s," *Kidney International* 79 (2001): S34–S48.

10. D. W. Seldin, interview by Drs. Leon Fine and Robert Alpern, 1997, for the Video Legacy Project of the International Society of Nephrology, cybernephrology. ualberta.ca/ISN/VLP/Trans/Seldin.htm.

11. US Bureau of the Budget, *Report of the Committee on Chronic Kidney Disease* (Washington, DC: Department of the Treasury, 1967).

12. D. W. Seldin, interview by Fine and Alpern.

13. D. W. Seldin, interview by Fine and Alpern.

14. R. C. Harris, T. Ibrahim, and K. A. Nath, "Celebrating the ASN at 50," *Journal of the American Society of Nephrology* 27 (2016): 1575–1576.

15. F. H. Epstein, "Recollections of Nephrology: Peters and Seldin. Presentation of the First John P. Peters Award to Donald W. Seldin, 1983," *Seminars in Nephrology* 4 (1984): 107–112.

16. D. W. Seldin, interview by Fine and Alpern.

17. M. J. Lysaght, "Maintenance Dialysis Population Dynamics: Current Trends and Long-Term Implications," *Journal of the American Society of Nephrology* 13 (2002): S37–S40.

18. D. W. Seldin, interview by Fine and Alpern.

19. D. W. Seldin, interview by Fine and Alpern.

Chapter 13: Go Forth and Prosper

1. W. N. Suki, personal communication to Raymond S. Greenberg, February 18, 2019.

2. W. N. Suki, F. C. Rector Jr., and D. W. Seldin, "The Site of Action of Furosemide and Other Sulfonamide Diuretics in Dogs," *Journal of Clinical Investigation* 44 (1965): 1458–1469.

3. W. N. Suki, telephone interview by Raymond S. Greenberg, March 5, 2019.

4. Suki, telephone interview.

5. Suki, telephone interview.

6. Suki, telephone interview.

7. N. A. Kurtzman, "Donald Seldin—An Interview," in *Medicine and Opera: Comments and Reviews of Opera, Music, and Medicine*, August 6, 2012, medicine-opera. com/2012/08/donald-seldin-an-interview.

8. Kurtzman, "Donald Seldin—An Interview."

9. Kurtzman, "Donald Seldin—An Interview."

10. Kurtzman, "Donald Seldin—An Interview."

11. Kurtzman, "Donald Seldin—An Interview."

12. N. A. Kurtzman, telephone interview by Raymond S. Greenberg, December 2, 2018.

13. Kurtzman, telephone interview.

14. Kurtzman, "Donald Seldin—An Interview."

15. J. H. Stein, telephone interview by Raymond S. Greenberg, January 15, 2019.

16. Stein, telephone interview.

17. T. D. DuBose, telephone interview by Raymond S. Greenberg, December 7, 2018.

18. DuBose, telephone interview.

19. DuBose, telephone interview.

20. DuBose, telephone interview.

21. DuBose, telephone interview.

22. DuBose, telephone interview.

23. J. P. Kokko, telephone interview by Raymond S. Greenberg, November 28, 2018.

24. Kokko, telephone interview.

25. Kokko, telephone interview.

26. Kokko, telephone interview.

27. Kokko, telephone interview.

28. R. J. Alpern, telephone interview by Raymond S. Greenberg, November 18, 2018.

29. Alpern, telephone interview.

30. Alpern, telephone interview.

31. W. L. Henrich, personal interview by Raymond S. Greenberg, January 17, 2019, University of Texas System, Austin.

32. Henrich, personal interview.

33. Henrich, personal interview.

34. Henrich, personal interview.

35. Henrich, personal interview.

Chapter 14: Moral Authority

1. A. N. Hornblum, "They Were Cheap and Available: Prisoners as Research Subjects in Twentieth Century America," *BMJ* (*British Medical Journal*) 315 (November 29, 1997): 1437–1441, ncbi.nlm.nih.gov/pmc/articles/PMC2127868/pdf/9418095.pdf.

2. E. Langer, "Human Experimentation: Cancer Studies at Sloan-Kettering Stir Public Debate on Medical Ethics," *Science* 143 (1964): 551–553.

3. S. Goldby, "Experiments at Willowbrook State School," *Lancet* 297 (1971): 749.

4. J. Heller, "Syphilis Victims in U.S. Study Went Untreated for 40 Years," *New York Times*, July 26, 1972, 1, 8, nytimes.com/1972/07/26/archives/syphilis-victims-in-us-study-went-untreated-for-40-years-syphilis.html.

5. US Congress, National Research Act, HR 7724, PL 93–348, 93rd Cong., 2nd Sess., July 12, 1974.

6. US Congress, National Research Act.

7. P. A. King, interview by LeRoy B. Walters on September 9, 2004, *Oral History of the Belmont Report and the National Commission for the Protection of Human Subjects of Biomedical and Behavioral Research*, Office of Human Research Protections, US Department of Health and Human Services, Rockville, MD (hereinafter "Belmont Oral History Project"), hhs.gov/ohrp/education-and-outreach/luminaries-lecture-series/belmont-report-25th-anniversary-interview-pking/index.html.

8. K. A. Lebacqz, interview by LeRoy B. Walters on October 26, 2004, for the Belmont Oral History Project, hhs.gov/ohrp/education-and-outreach/luminaries-lecture-series/belmont-report-25th-anniversary-interview-klebacqz/index.html.

9. King, interview for the Belmont Oral History Project.

10. King, interview for the Belmont Oral History Project.

11. D. I. Height, interview by Bernard A. Schwetz on June 30, 2004, for the

Belmont Oral History Project, hhs.gov/ohrp/education-and-outreach/luminaries
-lecture-series/belmont-report-25th-anniversary-interview-dheight/index.html.

12. R. E. Cooke, interview by Bernard A. Schwetz on May 15, 2004, for the Belmont Oral History Project, hhs.gov/ohrp/education-and-outreach/luminaries-lecture-series/belmont-report-25th-anniversary-interview-rcooke/index.html.

13. National Commission for the Protections of Human Subjects of Biomedical and Behavioral Research, "Transcript of Proceedings, February 11, 1977," Report Number NCPHS/M-77-07 (Washington, DC: US Department of Health, Education and Welfare).

14. A. R. Jonsen, interview by Bernard A. Schwetz on May 14, 2004, for the Belmont Oral History Project, hhs.gov/ohrp/education-and-outreach/luminaries-lecture-series/belmont-report-25th-anniversary-interview-ajonsen/index.html.

15. National Commission for the Protection of Human Subjects of Biomedical and Behavioral Research, *Research on the Fetus: Report and Recommendations*, DHEW Publication No. OS 76–127 (Washington, DC: US Department of Health, Education and Welfare, 1975).

16. National Commission, *Research on the Fetus*.

17. Lebacqz, interview for the Belmont Oral History Project.

18. National Commission, *Research on the Fetus*.

19. Lebacqz, interview for the Belmont Oral History Project.

20. US Congress, National Research Act.

21. P. C. Moss and L. Hill, eds., *Seeking Freedom: The History of the Underground Railroad in Howard County* (Columbia, MD: Howard County Center of African American Culture, 2002), 64.

22. B. Mishkin, interview by Patricia C. El-Hinnawy on June 17, 2004, for the Belmont Oral History Project, hhs.gov/ohrp/education-and-outreach/luminaries-lecture-series/belmont-report-25th-anniversary-interview-bmishkin/index.html.

23. National Commission for the Protection of Human Subjects of Biomedical and Behavioral Research, *The Belmont Report: Ethical Principles and Guidelines for the Protection of Human Subjects of Research*, DHEW Publications OS 78–0012 (Washington, DC: US Government Printing Office, 1978) (hereinafter *Belmont Report*).

24. National Commission, *Belmont Report*.

25. National Commission, *Belmont Report*.

26. T. L. Beauchamp, "The Origin, Goals, and Core Commitments of the Belmont Report and *Principles of Biomedical Ethics*," in *The Story of Bioethics: From Seminal Works to Contemporary Explorations*, ed. J. K. Walter and E. P. Klein (Washington, DC: Georgetown University Press, 2003, 17–46).

27. Beauchamp.

28. Height, interview for the Belmont Oral History Project.

29. Height, interview for the Belmont Oral History Project.

30. National Commission, *Belmont Report*.

31. National Commission, *Belmont Report*.

32. D. W. Seldin, interview by Bernard A. Schwetz on May 14, 2004, for the Belmont Oral History Project, hhs.gov/ohrp/education-and-outreach/luminaries-lecture-series/belmont-report-25th-anniversary-interview-dseldin/index.html.

33. D. W. Seldin, "Position Paper: The Establishment of a Center for Humanistic Medicine," undated internal document, University of Texas Southwestern Medical Center, Dallas, provided by F. Grinnell to Raymond S. Greenberg on May 14, 2019.

34. C. Grady, *The Search for an AIDS Vaccine: Ethical Issues in the Development and Testing of a Preventative HIV Vaccine* (Bloomington: University of Indiana Press, 1995), 42.

Chapter 15: Life Partners

1. D. W. Seldin, quoted in W. C. Roberts, "Donald Wayne Seldin, MD: A Conversation with the Editor," *Baylor University Medical Center Proceedings* 16 (2003): 193–220.

2. D. W. Seldin, quoted in Roberts.

3. D. W. Seldin, quoted in Roberts.

4. M. Emmett, telephone interview by Raymond S. Greenberg, February 7, 2019.

5. E. P. Frenkel, personal interview by Raymond S. Greenberg, February 6, 2019, University of Texas Southwestern Medical Center, Dallas.

6. M. S. Brown, personal interview by Raymond S. Greenberg, November 13, 2018, University of Texas Southwestern Medical Center, Dallas.

7. J. S. Fordtran, personal interview by Raymond S. Greenberg, December 12, 2018, University of Texas Southwestern Medical Center, Dallas.

8. Fordtran, personal interview.

9. Frenkel, personal interview.

10. R. J. Glassock, telephone interview by Raymond S. Greenberg, February 14, 2019.

11. J. H. Stein, telephone interview by Raymond S. Greenberg, January 15, 2019.

12. H. H. Hobbs, telephone interview by Raymond S. Greenberg, March 5, 2019.

13. Brown, personal interview.

14. L. D. Hillis, telephone interview by Raymond S. Greenberg, January 18, 2019.

15. N. A. Kurtzman, telephone interview by Raymond S. Greenberg, December 2, 2018.

16. J. P. Kokko, telephone interview by Raymond S. Greenberg, November 28, 2018.

17. Hobbs, telephone interview.

18. Kokko, telephone interview.

19. Hobbs, telephone interview.

20. E. T. Seldin, quoted in W. C. Roberts, "Ellen Taylor Seldin: A Conversation with the Editor," *Baylor University Medical Center Proceedings* 16 (2003): 221–229.

21. E. T. Seldin, quoted in Roberts, "Ellen Taylor Seldin: A Conversation."

22. E. T. Seldin, quoted in Roberts.

23. E. T. Seldin, quoted in Roberts.

24. E. T. Seldin, personal communication to Raymond S. Greenberg, February 24, 2019.

25. W. B. Yeats, "Politics," from *Last Poems (1938–1939)* (Dublin: Cuala Press, 1939). Copyright © 1939 by W. B. Yeats. Reprinted by permission of Scribner (Simon & Schuster, Inc.).

26. E. T. Seldin, personal communication.

27. D. W. Seldin, quoted in Roberts, "Donald Seldin: A Conversation."

28. Kokko, telephone interview.

29. B. M. Brenner, telephone interview by Raymond S. Greenberg, January 16, 2019.

30. Brenner, telephone interview.

31. Emmett, telephone interview.

32. E. T. Seldin, quoted in Roberts, "Ellen Taylor Seldin: A Conversation."

33. Brenner, telephone interview.

34. Brenner, telephone interview.

35. E. T. Seldin, personal communication.

36. E. T. Seldin, quoted in Roberts, "Ellen Taylor Seldin: A Conversation."

37. E. T. Seldin, quoted in Roberts.

38. E. T. Seldin, quoted in Roberts.

39. E. T. Seldin, personal communication.

40. E. T. Seldin, personal communication.

41. W. B. Yeats, "The Young Man's Song," in *The Green Helmet and Other Poems* (New York: The MacMillan Company, 1912), 37.

Chapter 16: Joi de Vivre

1. N. A. Kurtzman, telephone interview by Raymond S. Greenberg, December 2, 2018.

2. J. J. Warner, personal interview by Raymond S. Greenberg, December 12, 2018, University of Texas Southwestern Medical Center, Dallas.

3. Warner, personal interview.

4. Warner, personal interview.

5. Warner, personal interview.

6. Warner, personal interview.

7. D. W. Seldin, quoted in W. C. Roberts, "Donald Wayne Seldin, MD: A Conversation with the Editor," *Baylor University Medical Center Proceedings* 16 (2003): 193–220.

8. R. J. Alpern, telephone interview by Raymond S. Greenberg, November 18, 2018.

9. Warner, personal interview.

10. Warner, personal interview.

11. D. W. Seldin, quoted in Roberts, "Donald Seldin: A Conversation."

12. Alpern, telephone interview.

13. D. W. Seldin, quoted in Roberts, "Donald Seldin: A Conversation."

14. F. L. Coe, telephone interview by Raymond S. Greenberg, January 21, 2019.

15. B. M. Brenner, telephone interview by Raymond S. Greenberg, January 16, 2019.

16. Brenner, telephone interview.

17. Alpern, telephone interview.

18. Alpern, telephone interview.

19. Alpern, telephone interview.

20. Alpern, telephone interview.

21. Brenner, telephone interview.

22. Brenner, telephone interview.

23. H. H. Hobbs, interview in *Donald W. Seldin: The Lengthened Shadow of One Man*, October 10, 2013, University of Texas Southwestern Medical Center, Dallas, youtube.com/watch?v=wA74-SKeWng.

24. H. H. Hobbs, telephone interview by Raymond S. Greenberg, March 5, 2019.

25. D. W. Seldin, quoted in Roberts, "Donald Seldin: A Conversation."

26. D. W. Seldin, quoted in Roberts.

27. D. W. Seldin, quoted in Roberts.

28. D. W. Seldin, quoted in Roberts.

29. W. B. Yeats, "Under Ben Bulben," in *The Poems of W. B. Yeats: A New Edition*, ed. R. J. Finneran (New York: Macmillan Publishing Company, 1983), 328.

30. N. Kurtzman, personal communication to Raymond S. Greenberg, December 9, 2018.

31. T. F. Parker III, "Donald Seldin, MD, and His Impact on Nephrology," *Nephrology News & Issues*, August 2018.

32. W. B. Yeats, "Vacillation," in *The Collected Poems of W. B. Yeats* (New York: Macmillan Publishing Company, 1956).

33. Coe, telephone interview.

34. W. B. Yeats, "An Acre of Grass," in *The Collected Poems of W. B. Yeats* (New York: Macmillan Publishing Company, 1956).

35. Coe, telephone interview.

36. Coe, telephone interview.

37. D. W. Seldin, quoted in Roberts, "Donald Seldin: A Conversation."

38. J. H. Stein, telephone interview by Raymond S. Greenberg, January 15, 2019.

39. Stein, telephone interview.

40. D. W. Seldin, quoted in Roberts, "Donald Seldin: A Conversation."

41. D. W. Seldin, quoted in Roberts.

42. W. P. Carr, interview in *Lengthened Shadow of One Man*.

43. C. K. Wildenthal, interview in *Lengthened Shadow of One Man*.

44. N. A. Kurtzman, "Donald Seldin—An Interview," *Medicine and Opera: Comments and Reviews of Opera, Music, and Medicine*, medicine-opera.com/2012/08/donald-seldin-an-interview.

45. Kurtzman, "Donald Seldin—An Interview."

46. E. T. Seldin, telephone interview by Raymond S. Greenberg, March 1, 2019.

47. E. T. Seldin, telephone interview.

48. L. D. Hillis, telephone interview by Raymond S. Greenberg, January 18, 2019.

49. Hillis, telephone interview.

50. Hillis, telephone interview.

51. Warner, personal interview.

52. J. S. Fordtran, personal interview by Raymond S. Greenberg, December 12, 2018, University of Texas Southwestern Medical Center, Dallas.

53. Stein, telephone interview.

54. R. J. Alpern, "Presentation of the 1995 Jean Hamburger Award to Donald W. Seldin," *Kidney International* 48 (1995): 2036–2038.

55. Warner, personal interview.

56. Warner, personal interview.

57. J. L. Goldstein, remarks in *Seldin: A Celebration of Life*, June 16, 2018, University of Texas Southwestern Medical Center, Dallas, vimeo.com/275851709/56f3109c4e.

58. Coe, telephone interview.

Chapter 17: The Final Class

1. D. W. Seldin, quoted in W. C. Roberts, "Donald Wayne Seldin, MD: A Conversation with the Editor," *Baylor University Medical Center Proceedings* 16 (2003): 193–220.

2. D. W. Seldin, quoted in Roberts.

3. W. G. Reed, telephone interview by Raymond S. Greenberg, March 6, 2019.

4. E. P. Frenkel, personal interview by Raymond S. Greenberg, February 6, 2019, University of Texas Southwestern Medical Center, Dallas.

5. T. F. Parker, telephone interview by Raymond S. Greenberg, February 19, 2019.

6. W. G. Reed, remarks in *Seldin: A Celebration of Life,* June 16, 2018, University of Texas Southwestern Medical Center, Dallas, vimeo.com/275851709/56f3109c4e.

7. Reed, remarks in *Seldin: A Celebration of Life.*

8. Reed, telephone interview.

9. J. J. Warner, personal interview by Raymond S. Greenberg, December 12, 2018, University of Texas Southwestern Medical Center, Dallas.

10. Warner, personal interview.

11. Reed, telephone interview.

12. R. H. Collins, telephone interview by Raymond S. Greenberg, March 13, 2019.

13. D. W. Seldin, as dictated to E. M. Seldin, April 14, 2018, and communicated to Raymond S. Greenberg, February 13, 2019.

14. Beauchamp, personal communication to Raymond S. Greenberg, April 30, 2019.

15. Code of Federal Regulations, Part 46: Protection of Human Subjects. Subpart A—Basic HHS Policy for Protection of Human Research Subjects. 46.102. Definitions for Purposes of This Policy, (l). July 19, 2018, ecfr.gov/cgi-bin/retrieveECFR?g-p=&SID=83cd09e1c0f5c6937cd9d7513160fc3f&pitd=20180719&n=pt45.1.46&r=PART&ty=HTML#se45.1.46_1102.

16. H. H. Hobbs, remarks in *Seldin: A Celebration of Life,* June 16, 2018, University of Texas Southwestern Medical Center, Dallas, vimeo.com/275851709/56f3109c4e.

17. J. S. Fordtran, personal interview by Raymond S. Greenberg, December 12, 2018, University of Texas Southwestern Medical Center, Dallas.

18. Fordtran, personal interview.

19. Fordtran, personal interview.

20. Warner, personal interview

21. H. H. Hobbs, telephone interview by Raymond S. Greenberg, March 5, 2019.

22. Hobbs, telephone interview.

23. Hobbs, telephone interview.

24. Hobbs, telephone interview.

25. E. T. Seldin, personal communication to Raymond S. Greenberg, February 17, 2019.

26. E. T. Seldin, personal communication.

27. W. B. Yeats, "Poems by William Butler Yeats," *The Atlantic* (Boston: Atlantic Monthly Company, January 1939), 71–72.

Hamburger, Jean, 152–153, 155
Hamm, Lee, 169
Harris, Alfred W. "Al," 54–55
Harrison, Tinsley, 68, 71
Harrison's Principles of Internal Medicine (Harrison), 71
Harry's Bar, 204
Harvard Medical School, 119, 120
Harvard University, 10, 16, 20, 40, 98
Hayes, Elmer Russell "E. R.," 55
Head Start program, 176
Health System Affairs, 57
Height, Dorothy, 176–177, 181
Helsinki Declaration, 174
hematocrit, 57
Hemingway, Ernest, 204
hemodialysis, 156
Henrich, William, 79, 81–82, 94, 170–171
hepatitis, 43–44
Herrera-Acosta, Jamie, 172
HGPRT enzyme, 131
Higgins, John, 168–169
Hillis, David: on basic sciences research, 135; on faculty training, 95; and Seldin-Rector research collaboration, 114; on Seldin's loyalty to colleagues, 131; and Seldin's recruitment efforts, 73; and Seldin's social life, 188; on Seldin's teaching style, 77–78; and travels with Seldin, 204–205
Hillis, Nancy, 204
Himmler, Heinrich, 42
Hindemith, Paul, 12
Hippocratic Oath, 180. *See also* ethics of medical research
Hiroshima, Japan, 39
HMG-CoA reductase, 125–129
Hobbs, Helen: on Seldin's art collection, 199; and Seldin's declining health, 215–217; and Seldin's final days, 215; on Seldin's relationship with Muriel, 187–189; on Seldin's teaching style, 75–76, 78–79
Hoblitzelle, Karl, 7, 8
Holberg, Christer, 172

Hook, Sidney, 19
Hôpital Necker, 152
hormones, 69, 72
hospice care, 213
Houston, Texas, 2
Houston and Central Texas Railroad, 2
Howard Hughes Medical Institute, 143, 144
Hufstadter, Albert, 19
Hyde-Lees, Georgie, 218
hypothermia, 84

"Ice Bowl" (football), 206
immune tolerance, 136
immunodeficiency syndromes, 211
indigent patients, 96–97
informed consent, 45, 180. *See also* ethics of medical research
insomnia, 210
Institut de recherches cliniques de Montréal, 128–129
Institute of Human Relations, 21–22
Institute of Medicine, 72
insulin, 72
interdisciplinary education, 22, 138–139
International Congresses of Nephrology, 153–156
International Society of Nephrology (ISN), 153–156
Isselbacher, Kurt, 119

Jacobson, Harry, 168–169
James Madison High School, 15
Janis, Carroll, 148, 188
Jean Hamburger Award, 155
Jewish Chronic Disease Hospital, 174
John Punnett Peters Award, 158
Johns Hopkins Medical Hospital and Medical School, 97, 104, 175
Johns Hopkins University, 89–90, 176
Johnson, David, 75, 95, 132
Johnson, Lyndon, 135
Jonsen, Albert, 176, 178, 180
Jonsson, Anders, 172
Jonsson, Erik, 140–142
Jordan, Lee Ray, 205